COURAGE TO LOVE

COURAGE TO LOVE

LITURGIES FOR THE LESBIAN, GAY, BISEXUAL,
AND TRANSGENDER COMMUNITY

Compiled by
GEOFFREY DUNCAN

THE
PILGRIM
PRESS
Cleveland

Published in the USA, Canada, and the Republic of the Philippines by
The Pilgrim Press
700 Prospect Avenue, East
Cleveland, Ohio 44115-1100
pilgrimpress.com

Originally published in 2002 by
Darton, Longman and Todd Ltd
1 Spencer Court
140–142 Wandsworth High Street
London SW18 4JJ

© 2002 Geoffrey Duncan

ISBN 0-8298-1468-X

06 05 04 03 02   5 4 3 2 1

Designed and produced by Sandie Boccacci
using QuarkXPress on an Apple PowerMac
Set in 10/13pt Palatino

Printed and bound in Great Britain

For Pat, Jane, Ruth and Anil

*With much love for all your support and practical help.
Many, many hugs.*

I feel a rich closeness and warmth for the many friends and acquaintances who have contributed to this anthology. We are scattered all over the world in a variety of local situations. Praise and thanksgiving for the mail systems, the email technology and the many human resource networks through which we have found each other.

It is with much pleasure that the royalties from *Courage to Love* will be given to non-governmental organisations in south India with whom I have personal contact, for their work with marginalised people who are physically or mentally impaired, especially children and young people. I shall be pleased to supply information and give presentations about this necessar   . Contact may be made through Darton, Longman and Tod

'I think that we are living through a very painful period. The Church always moves forward through crisis. Crises are times when cracks appear in the Church through which the Holy Spirit pours.'

Elizabeth Stuart

Contents

Foreword

Courage to Love is a timely and moving anthology of verse, prayer and human testimony for people in or outside the Church. It will provide strength and inspiration to those who want to celebrate their God-given sexuality in the face of continuing rejection and hostility from Church leaders.

It will also help those engaged in the painful process of coming to terms with themselves and reconciling their natures with their faith and with their families and friends.

I hope this anthology will also be read by those who would like to push the issue of human sexuality under the carpet, who hope it will simply go away. It won't, and this invaluable collection of writings shows quite clearly why.

From the heartrending account by a loving mother of her anguish when her son came out to her to the joyful celebration of love, we are led through the tears and fears to the calm and the laughter that so many of us will recognise from journeys of our own.

Congratulations to those who have researched so meticulously to bring together such a comprehensive and rich collection, and one which will be appreciated by so many.

Ben Bradshaw MP

Introduction

During recent years many of us in the Church have lived through a variety of debates about human sexuality. In fact, we continue to live in the situation. We need to face the living, God-given, Spirit-filled, fact of sexuality and to feel free to speak openly about sex and sexuality, whether we are gay, straight, lesbian, bisexual or transgender. Women and men and young people who are aware of their emerging sexuality are creations of our Loving Creator. As such, we are valuable both as ourselves and for each other. Each one of us is an integrated spiritual and sexual human being. People are individual and precious. For me, Jesus Christ is made real in people.

My Creed – My Beatitude

I believe in the precious nature of each individual.
Peace to the people who respect their challenging and exciting neighbours.

I believe in Justice for all people.
Peace to the people who promote just and equal opportunities for humankind.

I believe in Human Rights for everyone.
Peace to the people who support the right for people to be accepted for who they are.

I believe in the acceptance of women and men of whatever sexual orientation and persuasion.
Peace to the people who speak out against persecution, bullying, verbal and physical abuse of individuals and groups of people.

I believe in an Inclusive Church.
Peace to the people who, with their love and desire for the wholeness of humankind, create communities and churches where we are enabled to worship in the spirit of diversity, honesty and love.

Dale Rominger has summed up my feelings in his article 'The Demands of Love and the Intimacy of Justice' on page 151. Dale says, 'For the sake of love and justice it doesn't matter if I am gay or straight. It does matter where I stand when others inflict spiritual, emotional and sometimes physical violence on God's people.' I applaud his position.

Many n. hs ago, I had a growing feeling that I should consider the compilat 1 of an anthology of worship material which would focus on um 1 sexuality. Over the years I have come to understand that if a project is to come to fruition my Loving Creator – my God – in his/her fatherly/motherly way will lead me to the point where things begin to happen. I continued to think for a long time about the possibility and shared my ideas with various people in the UK and North America. Those ideas were greeted with acclamation. Then by chance, one day, I met Katie Worrall, Commissioning Editor for Darton, Longman and Todd, and shared my thoughts with her. Katie was keen for me to submit a proposal, which I did very quickly. Within a month it was agreed that I should proceed. The response from writers has been overwhelming. My life has been enriched by an ever-increasing number of friends and acquaintances as we discover each other in various parts of the world.

I appreciate very much the thoughts and practical concerns that people have shared with me. My thanks extend far and wide but I have decided not to mention particular people or organisations because I may omit the names of deserving persons who, unknown to me, have been working hard in the background. So please will everyone known and unknown accept my sincere thanks for enabling this anthology to come to fruition. I hope this broad collection of work will help many people with their understanding and practice of sexual orientation. Be refreshed in your living, day by day, night by night, inside the walls and outside of the churches where you endeavour to worship. Use the anthology in private devotions, share it in the workplace, utilise it for open discussion in the wide variety of meetings of which you are a part – human rights organisations, peace meetings, union meetings . . . and in public worship, be encouraged.

Our daughter, Ruth, and her Indian fiancé, Anil, live and work in south India. They asked me to write the Blessing for their wedding. I believe it is relevant for a variety of wedding and blessing ceremonies.

The Blessing

Living God, Creator of Humankind,
Bless N and N as they go on their way together
in love and unity of purpose.

Loving Christ, Creator of Compassion,
Bless N and N as they develop their skills
so that their love will bring wholeness to people.

Refreshing Resilient Spirit, Creator of Vitality,
Bless and encourage them to engage in lively activity
and to seek justice throughout their lives,
to turn disappointments into challenges,
to transform darkness into light,
to root their ideals in the ground that they walk.

Go in Grace
with Confidence
and know Peace.

Amen.

Geoffrey Duncan
August 2001

WHO AM I?

God Who Meets Us

O God, whom no image can encompass,
no definition encircle
and yet
who meets us in the gentle touch of love,
the beauty of a butterfly's wing,
and the laughter of children,
help us to move beyond our attempts to limit you,
intellectualise you
or to eliminate you from all that is earthy,
sensuous or vibrant,
so that we may greet you
in every particle of this spectacular universe
which you are creating.

W. L. Wallace
Aotearoa New Zealand

Walking God

You.
You in me.
You beside me,
walking with me
on every journey:
in every prayer,
in every thought
in everything that is me,
in all that I may be,
at every turn of the road,
on every journey
walking with me.
You beside me.
You in me.
You.

Richard Watson
England

To Know Myself

Give me a way, O God, to know myself well enough not to be afraid
of what is inside me.
Help me not to watch myself, but instead to watch you and listen to you.
Then let me return to the world to love and serve others as fully as I can.

Donna E. Schaper
USA

I Am A Loveable, Creative Person

All: I am a loveable, creative person
made in the likeness of God.
I give myself permission to enjoy being myself
to love without fear of rejection,
to create with imagination,
to change without dread of the future,
to use my power responsibly,
to work for justice and peace
And live as a singer and dancer
within God's all embracing being.

W. L. Wallace
Aotearoa New Zealand

I Am

Creator God, Lord of all life,
the great 'I Am',
you know that
I am what I am.
By whatever quirk of nature,
or product of nurture,
I am what I am ... and I am loved by you.

I did not choose to be gay / lesbian
in some rebellious fit of rage.
It is not some wilful façade,
or superficial covering.
It cannot be removed by
repeated scrubbing or endless repentance,
nor erased by persistent denial.

No Lord,
you know that
I am what I am . . . and I am loved by you.

You Lord,
when you saw me in my mother's womb,
affirmed your creation.
As your child I bear the likeness of your Son.
I too feel the pain of living on the edge of acceptability.
I too bear the scars of rejection and vulnerability.
Like Him I have to count the cost,
of striving to live with integrity,
being true to my very nature.
You Lord, know that burden.
You know that
I am what I am . . . and I am loved by you.

Liz Styan
England

Coming Out (1)

I
       swirl,
                curled,
crouched
       small,
through corridors,
womb-red.

Until I am
        pushed
                        pressed out
                                exhaled
Until I am
                long-limbed
                                born
                                        bruised
and
                        wonderfully alive!

Suzi B.
England

Coming Out (2)

Come into the light
Be brave
God's light brings life
Though bright and penetrating
The energy of those laser beams
Empowers
Makes weak limbs strong
And mute tongues sing.
Stand up!
Take hold of that small pearl of faith
That God has given
You
And hold on.
So will the judging arrows of your fear-filled friends
Not harm
Though hurt and pain be real
And in bewilderment of storm
Be found rare gifts of peace
And in the wilderness
Enough bread.

Sigrid Rutishauser-James
England

A Coming-out Poem

From behind a locked door
I hear muffled sounds
of a haunting melody.

On rusty hinges
the door creaks open.

I watch
moved by your faith and courage,
as you dance out
to the sound of your own music.

Jan Berry
England

Am I Alone?

Like a little child in its mother's arms
I am cradled, nurtured, upheld:
by those who love me
by those who trust me
those, who at this point of time are all I have
those whose worth is untold,
whose value is inestimable,
those in whose beauty I see God.

Beloved, trust in the Lord, now and for ever.

Richard Watson
England

Who Am I?

Who am I? Everyone around me seems to think they know me but how
can they, I don't even know who I am. I know you know me and I ask
you to guide me as I struggle to find my own identity. Sometimes, I
want to scream. I get impatient for the journey to end. I know I will get
there eventually but sometimes eventually isn't enough. Lord, at these
times send me patience. Let me feel your love and acceptance surrounding me. Acceptance for the person I will become but most of all
for the person I am now. And if it's not too much trouble lift this fog
soon. I am desperate to know myself and in knowing myself, I will
come to know You more fully for You created me. I will try to be patient
but forgive my lapses, Lord.

Sian Wallis
England

I'm A Lesbian

When I say I'm a lesbian
you say it's not an issue.

Well, it's an issue for me.
It has changed my life.
It's made me see things
in a different light.

Not just relationships,
but the way the world works;
not in boxes, black and white,
but in diversity and possibility,
a world always changing.

And it's made me see God in a different light too –
no longer male,
maker of judgements,
giver of rules.
But compassionate,
woman
my lover.
What else?

It's not an issue, you say.
Well, it's an issue for me.
Because when I say I'm a lesbian,
it's about what I see.

Suzi B.
England

Proof

It's obvious I possess a gay gene
As I've always liked ABBA's *Dancing Queen*,
My orientation's written in blood,
I was born not made: it's been fixed for good.

I'm damaged, of course, by childhood abuse,
And when a small girl I made too much use
Of Action Man, and not Barbie and Ken,
So I was clearly a tomboy by ten.

My father was weak, my mother too strong,
I had no women there when I was young;
I watch too much *Brookside*, I ride a bike,
These are the reasons that make me a dyke.

I'm lesbian out of political choice
For this is the way I find my own voice;

I've never liked men – known that all along,
My mother was weak, my father too strong.

I'm stuck on Freud's developmental line,
And as a Christian I'm in deep decline;
Without healing your church can't let me in:
You'll love me a sinner but hate my sin

Your no-win logic does not allow me
To be able to live life happily;
You must find a preventive solution
To rid Christendom of sex pollution.

If I make love to a woman it's clear
My faith will gradually disappear,
And naturally, these questions that vex
Would go if I screwed the opposite sex.

I can't be a Christian and say I'm gay,
They don't go together, there's just no way,
But *I'm* gay, *I'm* Christian – *both* matter to me –
How dare you deny my integrity.

You'd like to be able to reduce me
To a simplistic aetiology:
There must be a reason why I am gay,
It's too unsettling any other way.

Rosie Miles
England

Force of Nature

I am a bisexual woman. I exist.
My being is a dangerous conclusion.
I am a force to be reckoned with.

My God loves upside down and sideways,
        all at once and full of mercy.
My Spirit is wide, expansive, weighted with longing,
        tipping over your box.

Truly I am seeping beyond your boundaries,
     shapeshifting texture and form,
     confounding your categories,
     eliminating your rules. This game is new.

My heart is full of buried treasure,
     memories of lovers and empty rooms.

My soul is scarred with bittersweet beauty –
     struggle to be whole, struggle to be true.

My feet are fragile from walking,
     always stranger in a strange land and walking.

Sometimes the journey comes to this:

I know the marker when I come upon it,
     point of grace in a wide open sky.
To trace desire's map I only need the clear bell of recognition,
     sounding jubilation –
You are home, you are home, come home.

Louise Green
USA

A Single Woman's Manifesto

I want to be single
and not considered sexless,
frigid from the neck downwards,
lacking in passion and sensuality.

I want to be single
and not treated as dysfunctional,
pitied as unlovable, unchoosable, unhaveable.

I want to be single
and not rendered invisible,
ignored in restaurants,
passed over in advertisements,
relegated to the small print by travel agents.

I want to be single
and not regarded as infantile, incomplete or lacking in humanity,
'still searching' for the perfect partner,
'still waiting' for life to begin.

I want to be single
and not assumed instantly available,
able to drop whatever I'm doing
to respond to others' more pressing and immediate needs.

I want to be single
and not presumed timid, unadventurous or innocent,
having my hunger for life and for fullness diminished
by society's narrowness.

I want to be single
and not have my needs considered insignificant,
assumed that I will be content with
hand-me-downs, second-hand bargains
and someone else's cast-offs.

I want to be single
and not have my friendships belittled,
considered less important than partnerships
or less committed than romantic relationships.

I want to be single
and have my capacity for parenthood recognised,
my need for nurturing and cherishing others validated,
my skills in caring and growing lives celebrated.

I want to be single
and not denied ritual, story and liturgy
to celebrate my choices and my struggles,
the milestones and the markers of my life's journey.

I want to be single
in a church and a culture
which celebrates diversity and distinctiveness,
solidarity in difference,
friendship across otherness.

I want to be single.

Nicola Slee
England

My Body

I honour what my body knows –

that women must struggle
to be themselves;

that the rhythm of my walking, moving,
can match the rhythm of my thinking,
the rhythm of my praying,
the rhythm of the Spirit;

that the manner of my swimming
reflects my moods
til I surrender all
to the encompassing water of life;

that time and effort
taken over food
reflect my being;

that quiet rest and sleep
are needful
and a gift from God;

that there are times
when sanctuary,
safe space,
is necessary
to being;

that I am a woman
with sexual needs and desires;
harbouring life's potential
periodically experienced;

that men cannot always be trusted
to keep their hands to themselves;

that flattery disguised as praise
is false;

that words can penetrate the mind
and shake the body to the soul,

with power to hurt
or to heal;

that pain is a warning,
anger an indicator,
needing to be heard;

that touch can be restorative,
respectful friendship,
gentle in its healing;

that God is shaking,
moving, stirring,
speaking, calling
me to life.

I honour what my body does not know –

the ecstatic union
of two become one flesh
in the sanctity of marriage;

the internal mystery
of a growing life within;

the labouring of love
and the nursing of a helpless babe.

God
I honour my body,
May my body honour you.

Rabeta
England

Because A Woman . . .

Because a woman took on my anger at the church
Because a woman has unshakeable faith in me
Because a woman drove all night to be with me in my pain
Because a woman cradled my head in her lap when I had no home

Because a woman gave my words back to me and said I had a voice
Because a woman has touched me like no other
Because a woman has found me new words for things
Because a woman gives me space so I can ask who I am
Because a woman fires the passion in me:

Because women work
Because women bear
Because women break bread
Because women bleed:

I am a lover of life
        a lover of others
        a lover of God
        and a lover of justice.

Rosie Miles
England

I Have Been Broken

I have been broken
in ways you won't speak of

But you are my people
so I too am silenced

Open your eyes and
cry with my cries
in my anger and pain

So we can go forward together
in justice and love.
In Jesus' name.

David Coleman and Zam Walker
Wales

With Confidence We Stand Before You

Suffering and glorified Christ
who shares with us the pain of this world:

we bring to you our weakness, our failings and vulnerability.
With confidence we stand before you
in all our brokenness,
knowing that in our midst
you yourself are broken.

Richard Watson
England

Where Do I Fit, What Is My Place?

Where do I fit, what is my place?
Amid my family and friends?
How can I keep integrity
With who I am, with what God sends?

What is my part within this frame
That holds a picture of the past:
A mother, father, sister, child,
Where can I stand, what place will last?

One in a body bound by love:
My love for them, I hope they see.
Just as I am, accept me God.
Just as I am may they love me.

Andrew Pratt
England

Wrestling the Unnamed to a Blessing

night crouches behind
the stones by the river
devours the last of
twilight's bones then
pounces
pins and drags me
to the brink
tosses and turns me
face to face with God
knows what –

a mask staring from
fathomless depths with
night-filled night-filling
eyes –
    the I that decks itself
in others' standards
to procure their blessing
    the I that grabs
what-is by the heel
to haul it to what-I-prefer
    the I that would rather
run than wrestle
whose every action
    is a reaction

I want to run but
something holds me back
some nocturnal thing
that dares not speak its name
that knows – if I could name it
I might tame it
recloset it behind the stones
    so I could run again
but something
has me pegged
knows my given name and
the one I should have had
perseveres only to bless
    me with it now

I cannot run
some nocturnal unnamed thing
lames me
blesses and
renames me
tells me
    I won.

Norm S. D. Esdon
Canada

Homosexual Declaration

I believe in God,
God created human beings in God's image.
God was pleased with what God had created,
including homosexuality and heterosexuality.
God's kindness and righteousness grant us the rights of equality –
the right to love and to be loved.

I believe in My Saviour Jesus Christ;
His sacrifice redeemed us. He came to earth
to save the ones who were being oppressed
and being discriminated against.
We deeply believe that He loves homosexuals as well.
So we can serve others who have the same needs
through His love.

I believe in the Holy Spirit;
She makes me witness to the Lord's immense love and glory.
She lives among us to prove that homosexuals
are also members of the Lord's family.
When the Day comes, we can earn the crown and glory
like other Christians.

I believe in the Church of holiness and righteousness,
The Church of reconciliation,
The Church where people love one another,
The church that accepts different sex orientations.
Amen.

10% Club
Hong Kong
(translated by Ling Ho)

As Children of God

As children of God, we celebrate the beauty and individual worth of
all creation.
We believe in God:

> who created each of us, who breathed into us our uniqueness,
> who delights in who we are and what we can still become.

We believe in the love of God:

> who laughs with us in our joy, who cries with us in our pain,
> who wants all creation to seek peace, reconciliation, and love
> for each other.

We believe in the justice of God as revealed in scripture and
through the lives of prophets of yesterday and today.

God alone created us. We are not alone. God loves us.
Nothing will separate us from the love of God.
Amen.

Reconciling Church Programme
USA

Let Me Be Me

Help me, Creator God, to resist the temptation to be what I am not. Let
me be me – as you have created me. Help me to enjoy the blessings in
my own yard, knowing that they are very good indeed.

Donna E. Schaper
USA

It Is Not a Crime

It is not a crime to love,
Only a crime not to acknowledge
Such desire.

It is not a crime to look longingly
At another's body
And want to touch and be touched.

It is not a crime to make love all night
And wake up
Sleep-scented with sex.

It is not a crime to want to make a life with someone:
To move into and alongside
The rhythms of their days.

No, this love is not a crime.
Should anyone ever say it is,
They do not know how we love.

Rosie Miles
England

To Reflect On . . .

There is no pain greater than not being able to be yourself.

True humility is not the putting down of the self
but the putting down of roots into the earth,
the cultures of the earth
and the mystery which we call God.

To enter the wilderness
is to discover one's true home.

What you are seeking lies within you.
No one can give it to you.
All you have to do is to own it.

The greatest achievement is to learn
to be
and to rest in that awareness.

Abandon yourself to the otherness
and you will find yourself in the process.

Nurture the mystic within you
for she is the guardian of the most sacred mysteries.
She alone is the 'you' that cannot be destroyed;
for her name is compassionate wisdom
and her aspect is divinity.

When you can see the divine in yourself
You will be able to see the divine everywhere.
When you reverence the divine in yourself
You will be able to reverence the divine everywhere.
When you nurture the divine in yourself
You will be able to nurture the divine everywhere.

W. L. Wallace
Aotearoa New Zealand

Silence and Reflection

Make time to sit in comfort
to breathe deeply
to relax in the presence of God
like a cat asleep on a chair
or a rabbit sunnily on a path:

> The loving one, who made you,
> who yearned over you in the womb,
> who cherished you as a baby,
> who tended you as a child,
> who gave you glimpses of glory
> from your pram;
> the One who moulded you,
> the One whose loving arm is always
> under your head,
> says:

> *'Have no fear for I have redeemed you.*
> *I call you by name and you are mine.'*

I . . . am loved by God
Keep silence in that thought.

Kate McIlhagga
England

Reflection
(John 11:1–6)

Leader: I am Lazarus. I'm the only one they talk about,
                        but do not talk to.
                I am the only one they labelled as 'ill'
                        without asking me how I feel.
                When I am labelled, people do not see me
                        for who I am.
                Christ sees me for who I am.
                I am a child of God. I am Lazarus.

People: **I am a child of God. I am Lazarus.**

Leader:	I am the homosexual person you call pervert. I am the mentally challenged person you call ignorant. I am the AIDS patient you call cursed. I am the Native woman you call squaw.
People:	**I am a child of God. I am Lazarus.**
Leader:	I am the healer you call witch. I am the child you call stupid. I am the alcoholic you call drunkard. I am the passivist you call coward.
People:	**I am a child of God. I am Lazarus.**
Leader:	I am the unemployed person you call bum. I am the poor person you call beggar. I am the single mother you call loose. I am the welfare recipient you call lazy.
People:	**I am a child of God. I am Lazarus.**

Ken DeLisle
Canada

In a World of In-Between

Like shorebirds living between sand and surf
we live in a world of in-between

between punching the clock and smelling the roses
    serving others and renewing ourselves
between hanging on and letting go
    sticking with the old and risking the new
between speaking the truth and sparing feeling
    seeking justice and avoiding division
between the economy and the environment
    the 'loonie' and the loon
between computer byte and human touch
    avoiding harassment and needing a hug
between who we are and what others may think we should be
    who we are and who we may become

We are shorebirds living
between cross and rolled-away stone
between the alpha and the omega
    the beginning and the end

And the spirit of the one
who walked the shore before us
walks with us
hallows this in-between world
as God's world –
    We are not alone
    Thanks be to God

Norm S. D. Esdon
Canada

I Thank You for Those Things which Are Yet Possible

O God of timelessness
    and time,
I thank you for my time
and for those things that are yet possible
    and precious in it:
        daybreak and beginning again,
            midnight and the touch of angels,
                the taming of demons in the dance of dreams;
a word of forgiveness,
    and sometimes a song,
for my breathing . . . my life.

Thank you
for the honesty which makes friends
    and makes laughter;
for fierce gentleness
    which dares to speak the truth in love
        and tugs me to join the long march toward peace;
for the sudden gusts of grace
    which rise unexpectedly in my wending from dawn to dawn;
for children unabashed,
    wind rippling a rain puddle,
        a mockingbird in the darkness,
            a colleague and a cup of coffee;

for all the mysteries of loving,
  of my body next to another's body;
for music and silence,
  for wrens and Orion,
    for everything that moves me to tears,
      to touching
        to dreams,
          to prayers;
for my longing . . . my life.

Janet Schaffran and Pat Kozak
USA

God Release Me By Your Power

God release me by your power
To be who I'm born to be,
From my agony, your outing
Making me alive and free.

No more subject to oppression
Of the norms that others brought;
Not deny or complying
Agonised, with tension fraught.

Let me face the world unfettered,
Knowing I am good as you,
Dancing on to greet the dawning
Of a world that's fresh and new.

Andrew Pratt
England

When Israel Camped In Sinai

When Israel camped in Sinai,
God spoke and Moses heard,
'This message tell the people.
and give them this My word:

"From Egypt I was with you,
I bore you on my wing,
the whole of your great nation,
from slavery I did bring.

"Just as a mother Eagle,
who helps her young to fly,
I am a mother to you,
your needs I will supply.
And you are as My children,
my own who hear my voice,
I am a Mother to you,
the people of my choice."'

If God is like an eagle,
who helps Her young to fly,
and God is also Father
then what of you and I?
We have no fear of labels,
we have no fear of roles,
God blends them and transcends them,
we seek the selfsame goals!

Our God is not a woman,
our God is not a man,
our God is both and neither,
our God is 'I Who Am'.
From all the roles that bind us,
our God has set us free.
What freedom does God give us?
The freedom just to be!

Larry Berthier
and the Universal Fellowship of
Metropolitan Community Churches
USA

Christianity, Love and Gay Sex: A Practitioner's View

I am a Christian and a homosexual. I was born gay but I have chosen to be a Christian. Being gay is compatible with Christian ethics and biblical teaching in two different ways.

The first, conservative position, attends literally to the word of God as revealed in the Bible. The sin of the men of Sodom is condemned and it behoves us to obey the conditions of cleanliness of living and persecution of the unclean and morally backward as set out in Leviticus.[1] This teaching condemns the man ' . . . who lieth with another man, as a woman.' I take this to mean that a man may not have penetrative intercourse with another man i.e. sodomy is proscribed. In an age of AIDS in which anal intercourse is a significant route for the HIV transmission, this is sound advice. The Levitican principle is echoed in the Pauline epistle.[2]

Men can, nay should live together in affectionate and supportive partnership in lifelong emotional and physical union without the need for anal intercourse. The Bible does not proscribe the affectionate touching of one man for another, nor does it proscribe mutual stroking and kissing, mutual masturbation and oral sexuality. True, the sin of Onan is condemned. But Onan 'spilled his seed on the ground' in an act of *coitus interruptus,* while having intercourse with his brother's wife.[3] For obscure reasons Christians have equated Onanism with masturbation but this is incorrect. Masturbation, individual or mutual is nowhere condemned.

But strictures on adultery do logically apply to homosexuals. A man should not practise sexuality with another man unless he has committed himself to faithful and lifelong partnership with that man. The biblical laws against adultery apply both to homosexual and heterosexual couples.

David and Jonathan express the highest ideal of the love of one man for another: ' . . . the soul of David was knit to the soul of Jonathan and Jonathan loved him as his own soul'.[4] The community of homosexual men is currently beset by the sin of promiscuity, behaviour which clearly transgresses the Bible's teaching on adultery. In part this status is imposed on the gay community by intolerant heterosexuals who will not admit gay couples into sanctified relationships. Christians, alas, are among the worst offenders in purveying this intolerance. Church leaders and congregations should, in a truly moral world, instruct their ministers and priests that gay marriages should be sanctified in temple and church. True, gay couples will not 'be fruitful and multiply'. But churches hardly hold this to be a principle which should inevitably guide heterosexual marriages.

The second type of theological argument relating to homosexuality and gay marriage stems from Christ's teaching. He argues against the literal interpretation of the Leviticus rules of conduct, in a notable example, which by inference may apply to all of the Levitican rules. He prevented the stoning to death of the woman taken in adultery, on the grounds that rigid application of this rule inevitably involved hypocrisy. Indeed, such stoning is still practised in some Islamic countries. One of my graduate students, who had been a member of a feminist group in Pakistan, has observed several such stonings in rural Pakistan. The woman to be killed is buried up to her neck in the village square. The Imam drops a large rock on her head and the woman is probably unconscious at this point. The villagers then stone the woman until she is dead. Islam, a religion stemming, like Christianity, from the Abramic tradition should of course stone homo-sexuals as well, although I know of no recent case. Simple beatings usually suffice.

The gospel of the love of Jesus Christ preaches against such hatred. Gay people throughout the world still suffer hatred, persecution, social exclusion, beatings and murder. Christians, unfortunately, both express and support such hatred. Many gay people in despair consider suicide and do engage in serious self-harm.[5] In a world full of love all kinds of sexuality that does not offend biblical principles should be tolerated and gay men and women should be joyfully accepted into the life of the church. Some gay men will of course not wish to be Christians, will not adopt safe sex practices and will con-tinue to be promiscuous – but of course the number of heterosexuals who are equally sinful is likely to be much greater. For them we pray.

We pray also that Christians will come to believe that a gospel of love should incorporate and accept into the institutions of the church, men and women whose only crime is love.

[1] Leviticus 20:13

[2] 1 Corinthians 6:9–10

[3] Genesis 38:6–10

[4] 1 Samuel 18:1

[5] Bagley, C. and D'Augelli, A., 'Gay, Lesbian and Bisexual Youth Have Elevated Rates of Suicidal Behaviour: an international problem associated with homophobic legislation', *British Medical Journal*, 320 (2000), 1617–18

Christopher Bagley
England

We Are . . .

We are The United Church of Christ Coalition for Lesbian, Gay, Bisexual and Transgender Concerns.

We are fabulous and we are you. We are ten per cent and we are everywhere. Some of us are same-gender loving people. Others of us love either gender. Some of us are women in men's bodies, or men in women's bodies.

We are black and white, yellow, brown and red. We are tall and short, blue-eyed, blonde, brown-eyed and brunette. We are able-bodied or not. We walk and run, we have wheelchairs and read Braille. We play football and dance in ballets. We ride horses and drive motor-cycles. We study algebra and physics and build things from wood. Sometimes we are invisible for you cannot always see who we are.

But we are fabulous and we are you. We are your brother, your sister, your parent, your cousin and your neighbour. We are the bag boy at your grocery store and we deliver your newspapers. We take your orders at McDonald's and sell you shoes at the mall. We dance and sing in the youth group talent show. Sometimes we are invisible for you cannot always see who we are.

But we are fabulous and we are you. We read the Bible. We pray to God. We go to church and sing in the choir. We pitch in at the clothing drive and are counsellors at camp. Sometimes we are invisible for you cannot always see who we are.

But we are fabulous and we are you.

*The United Church of Christ Coalition for
Lesbian, Gay, Bisexual and Transgender Concerns
USA*

Life from Your Love

Dear Lord
When you lived on this earth
You were marginalised, oppressed, loved and misunderstood.
May we who are marginalised, oppressed, loved and misunderstood

Derive courage from your strength
Hope from your life
and life from your love.

*Michael Reiss
England*

Thanks for Gay Men

Creator of all the varied wonder
    of the universe, we praise you
    for likeness and difference,
    for what unites and makes unique.
We give thanks and special praise
    for learning from gay men:
for all that gay men can teach
    straight men of tenderness, love
    and affection;
for all that gay men teach other men
    of grace and courage under great
    pressure;
for all gay men teach us of the will
    and strength to be unique and
    openly caring toward our brothers;
for all that gay men teach me
    of honesty and passion.

We give thanks that gay men have been
    and are so very much
    pioneers in exploring the fullness
    of what it means to be men.
But most of all we thank you
    for their reaching out
as Jesus, our brother, reached out,
    for community and trust,
    honour and respect among all humans.

Teach us, Jesus, we who are straight
    and so often afraid,
    teach us through our gay brothers,
that our differences and likenesses
    are gifts for the common weal,
and our unity lies in your love
    for us all.

George M. Wilson
USA

The Body Meets . . .

Creator God, you made us all different
and we rejoice in those differences.
Companion Christ, you called each person into your body,
and we welcome each others' contribution.
Renewing Spirit, you encourage us to explore new ways
and we are excited by new opportunities.

Living God,
as this body lives
so you live in us.
We acknowledge your life in us.
We are sorry when we have failed you.
Once again we are ready to
be your body here and now.

Janet Lees
England

The Woman Caught in Sexuality
(John 8:1–11)

Jesus, you talked about
liberating the captives,
letting the blind see,
raising up the lowly.

But you didn't say
anything about
gay men and lesbian women,
so what are we to think?

There are those who say
we're perverse.
We can't be spiritual
because we're not natural.

There are those who say
it's a choice,
a choice about being sinful.

But my experience is of
loving and being loved,
of nurturing and being nurtured,
of holding and being held.

And so I can't believe that you would say
Go, and sin no more,
because I don't see it as sin,
I see it as gift.

A gift that liberates me to love,
opens my eyes to being loveable,
raises my expectations of what life holds.

Should I really spend my life writing in the sand?

Suzi B.
England

Leah's Story
(Genesis 29:1–35; 30:1–21)

Leah – invisible,
    Trapped,
        Surviving,
            Released . . .

Invisible, overlooked in favour of catwalk obsession,
hesitant beauty buried beneath veiled eyes.
Weaving God, open our eyes to see the beauty
hidden deep within our brokenness.

Trapped, owned by another's love-less possessiveness,
abusive traditions re-enacted by successive generations.
Spinning God, grant us the courage to break free,
journeying towards the dawn of new beginnings.

Surviving, enduring, digging deep and holding on,
nurturing the seeds of life springing from a barren relationship.
Mending God, give us the inner resources
to face the future with courage and strength.

Released, oppressive cycle broken by a daughter's birth,
the persistent pulse of life weaving Leah's story to new horizons of
hope.
Celebrating God, release in us the wisdom and power
to proclaim our own stories.

Jill Thornton and Clare McBeath
England

Blessing the Thorn in the Flesh

Bless you Wise and Holy One
    for your Word made
    thorn in the flesh
for answering No when I prayed
    to have my thorn removed

Bless you
for the thorn of alienation that
drives me deep into inner desert
    to face my need to please –
the desert where you recreate me
    deeper than popularity
    wider than the majority
    truer than hypocrisy

Bless you
for the thorn of hardship that
helps me get the point –
    that my thorn can serve
    as another's therapy
    that the best healer
    is a wounded healer
    that the hardship I cannot change
    and that threatens to embitter me
    can change me – for the better

Bless you Wise and Holy One
for this epiphany –
    that praying away Good Friday
    prays away Easter too

Bless you,
for answering No when I pray
    to have a thorn removed
Bless you Wise and Holy One
    for your Word made
    thorn in the flesh

Norm S. D. Esdon
Canada

Solo Voice
(Inspired by the third movement of Shostakovich's Violin Concerto No. 1)

Solo voice,
emerging out of deep desolation,
are you the only voice to be heard,
rising sweetly out of the pain,
born out of the creator's agony and oppression?

Solo voice,
created by the ground-bass of being,
bring together beauty and tension,
        dissonance and harmony,
thank you for sweetening the bitter herb of my suffering.

May you be blessed, solo voice,
way, truth and life,
redeemer and life giver.
You tell me that there is life amidst death;
        hope amidst desolation;
And I am saved, solo voice,
by your tender, life-giving melody.

Peter Colwell
England

Jesus Rose and Went Out to a Lonely Place
(Mark 1:35)

Dear Jesus,
the closet is already a lonely place,
but the point is well taken.

Those of us in closets
may use our wilderness experience
as an opportunity for prayer.

Those of us out of closets
may escape the pressure – and share the glory –
such freedom brings
by taking time to be with you.

In prayer, the closet doors open
between the human and the divine,
between the gay and the non-gay,
between the closeted and the uncloseted.

Thank you, God, for opening doors
in the midst of dividing walls,
making us one in the Body of Christ
as we pray together.

Thank you, God, for opening doors
to the glory of Jesus Christ
and the glory we share in Christ
illumining our darkest closet,
casting in shadow our brightest revelations.

Thank you, God, for opening doors
among disparate geographical locales
as we pray as one community,
transcending our present diaspora.

In Jesus Christ,
you have made all the distance between us
holy ground.

Chris Glaser
USA

CREATING LOVE:
SUSTAINING LOVE

Our Families:
To Be Pro-Active People

Discernment

Discernment is knowing
> when to speak and when to remain silent,
> when to move and when to be still,
> when to consume and when to abstain,
> when to include and when to leave out,
> when to hold and when to let go.

W. L. Wallace
Aotearoa New Zealand

The Love of Family and Friends

My husband, Neville, and I attend Emmanuel Church, Holcombe, Greater Manchester, England. We have a son, Adrian and a daughter, Sarah. When he was thirty-one, Adrian told us that he is gay. We were shocked to realise that he had kept this from us for almost twenty years. His difficulty in accepting his sexuality and the awareness that society is largely anti-gay had kept him firmly closeted. It was hard for him to tell us – he did not want to cause us disappointment and unhappiness. He did not wish to risk rejection.

Our relationship with Adrian has always been close and we felt guilty that we had not sensed any underlying tension. We grieved that he would lack much in his life that we have taken for granted in ours. We felt as confused and isolated as Adrian must have done when he was in the closet. It was difficult to accept that our son could experience prejudice, inequality, and injustice, not for anything that he had chosen or done but because society disapproves of homosexuality.

It was more than two years before we felt confident enough to tell anyone and yet we wanted and needed to talk as others do about their families and their relationships. We questioned God. We worked through the seven or so texts in Scripture quoted as proof that God too disapproves of homosexuality. They did not support our belief in a God of Love. But in the gospels we found no mention of homosexuality, only Christ's command that we love one another and His warning that we are not to judge.

The paradox of our experience is that it has strengthened us as a family. It has increased our belief in the power of love – God's love, family love, the love of friends, Christian and non-Christian to whom we have come out as parents of a gay son. Amongst such family and friends Adrian has found love and acceptance as a gay person in ways that he never thought possible, nor would have known if he had not been given the courage and the strength to face the risks involved and leave the closet.

It is four years since we learned that we have a gay son. By God's grace our family has survived. Others are less fortunate.

Christine Holt
England

Family Prayer During Coming Out Process

We cry today, God
    and feel very real pain
    but we ask you to forgive our selfishness as we dwell only on
    our grief.
We cry for our dreams that we now see as lost,
    and lose sight of the miracle in our midst.
We cry out of fear for what our loved one may now face in an
    intolerant world,
    and forget that you are our God and care more deeply than we
    ever can.
We cry for the hurt that we have ignorantly caused,
    and neglect to work for justice here and now.
We perpetuate our sadness,
    and forget all our reasons to celebrate.
Oh God, have mercy.
Oh God, hear our hurts.
In your power and love, God, please make us whole.
Amen.

Jennifer Pope
USA

New People Came This Time

New people came this time, and we shared
our stories, the familiar truths, about
shock and healing and being glad that at last
our children can say who they are,
and we know them now, love them more.

Funny stories and good news rippled around,
and smiles about lesbigay ways, and jokes
against ourselves, taking the masks off
to show the same donkey faces underneath.
A communion of laughter.

And several dawns once more lit up among us,
the sharpness of beginning sight,
a slower sunrise over the years,
other eye-openings – painful or proud – all good.
A communion of wisdom.

But this time –

we nearly all wept:
wept with the blinding new hurts,
winced with what we thought
had been healed – old wounds, waiting.
We put the tissue box in the middle
and passed it round.
A communion of tears.

Geoffrey Herbert
England

He Was Waited On By Angels
(Mark 1:12)

No cop-out.
No cheat.
In the wilderness
beyond his strength.
Humility kept him alive.

Don't
YOU
be afraid
To seek the help you need.

If you find it
angels fed you.

David Coleman
Wales

A Father's Prayer of Thanks

O God, thank you for the example of love and the gifts of grace which gay men and lesbians continue to bring to the community of faith.
They know your acceptance even though they have been denied acceptance from family, friends and community; they have that sense of wholeness which can come only from putting one's being in your hands; they cope with misunderstanding, fear and hatred because they know that you love them; they joyfully realise their sexuality is a gift from you and part of your creation; they experience humility learned from adversity, know compassion rising out of suffering, give unconditional love through your example; they understand the value of each day's life even though they face death from persecution and disease; and they rejoice in the conviction of the reality of life beyond death because of Jesus Christ. Thank you, God, for our daughters and sons!

Merrill M. Follansbee
USA

True Parent

God of our likeness,
a father you are, in fighting our darkness;
but like a mother you bring us to light.
As a father should be, you care and protect;
but like a mother you comfort and hold.
Hear us today.
Soothe our wounds, dry our tears.

Be the one we strive to follow,
whether we be mother or father,
sister or brother,
free or committed,
sibling or friend.
And forgive the example we show
to those who seek you,
the true parent,
in us.

Duncan L. Tuck
England

Flowers for My Wife
(when we received a letter from our son)

White daffodils will say it,
honest and joyful,
open wide to celebrate.

And yellow daffodils in bud,
closed up and waiting
as he has been.

And freesias, our flower,
your bridal flower,
fragile and half open,
half knowing as we have been.

White daffodils will say it,
and we shall hear it,
but they will not bear it;
that is for the freesias
when they unfurl their faces
and smile the truth,
written this Annunciation Day,
that our son is gay.

Geoffrey Herbert
England

'Not Freak You Out . . .'

A political science professor was marking final exams for his class of some 200 students. The first question focused on the Canadian Charter of Rights and Freedoms. After accurately describing the history and intent of the Charter, one of the students added: 'I am an in-the-closet gay teenage male. In a home that is openly prejudiced about gay relations, I find it hard to accept who I am and I also live in fear of being "discovered".' The student recognized how the Charter is trying to protect people from violence based on sexual orientation and to ensure that gays and lesbians have the freedom and opportunities taken for granted so long by heterosexuals. He admitted the Charter challenges him to be brave enough to live out this freedom because legislation alone does not influence the opinions of all citizens. The student concluded that the Charter was 'an incredible beacon of hope . . . with possibilities that are endless'. However, at the very end of the examination answer booklet, he added one final note: he hoped his answer to the first question did not freak out the professor.

Betty Lynn Schwab
Canada

The Family of God

As the family of God,
we affirm that this is the place where we have no prejudice.
Under God, here we may be mothers, fathers and children,
beyond the limits of genes and blood.
Here we are the children
called to love as God loves:
as mothers would care for their own;
as fathers would protect their own.
Here, it is not our blood which holds us apart,
but the blood of Jesus which draws us together.
Here is our fulfilment, as we follow the one
who has mothered and fathered us.

Duncan L. Tuck
England

Yours, with Pride

Here follow extracts from Yours, with Pride, a book written by a mother and composed of letters written by herself and her gay son.

Thank You for Telling Me . . .

Dear John

I remember so clearly that winter afternoon, ten years ago, when you told me you were gay.

You looked so pale and anxious as you came into my bedroom and said, 'Mum, can I talk to you for a minute?' I could tell from your face and the tone of your voice that it was serious. My throat went dry. Did you want to leave university? Had you got a girl pregnant? Then you said, 'Mum, I want to tell you something. Mum, I'm gay.' It was an absolute bombshell, something I had never suspected at all. I had no idea. As I put my arms round you, I remember offering up a pleading arrow prayer, 'Dear God, please not this.' I think it was one of the biggest shocks I had had in my 48 years.

I froze; I suppose someone else might have screamed and shouted or perhaps even been dismissive but I went all still inside, like ice. The panic welled up. I just couldn't believe it. I couldn't seem to take it in. I was sure you were telling the truth as you saw it but I so wanted you to be mistaken.

I put my arms around you. You whispered, 'Mum, I thought you might reject me.' Reject you? Did you really believe I would do that? I realised then just how desperately frightened and vulnerable you were feeling, how much courage it must have taken to tell me. We cried, and held each other tight. I remember thinking, 'I can't believe that anything else that happens to me will ever be more difficult to manage than this.'

As we talked I gradually became aware of your real need to explore and find yourself. I was so frightened of the implications of what you were saying, for you, for me, for Dad and for all of us. I wanted to reassure you that it would be all right, that I would support you in your searching, that I would cope but it all felt so unreal and difficult. I suppose it was the shock. Suddenly my world seemed to have turned upside down. Things were going on as normal – I could hear a radio, people talking in the street and the cars going by – but I felt isolated and detached from it all. My heart was pounding, I couldn't think straight and I didn't know what to do. I couldn't believe that things were still the same as before when I felt so gripped by panic and confusion. Everything seemed to have gone topsy-turvy and I didn't know how I was going to cope. Here you were telling me something that made you seem so different, yet it was still *you* and you were just the same!

I remember the enormous sense of relief that flooded your face when the telling was done. You were so kind and thoughtful, realising the shock it had been for me. Do you remember saying to me how many young gay people never risk telling their parents about their sexuality because they are, quite genuinely, frightened of ridicule or rejection? I've often thought about that and wondered why a mother, in particular, who has given birth and nurtured a child over many years, would suddenly reject him or her. Hopefully, it would only be temporary – perhaps words spoken in the heat of the moment when distress and panic took over. Surely the whole family would get torn apart.

I know, for myself, that news shook me to the core. It took many months really to come to terms with it, and this came as I gradually learnt more. I suppose for many of us homosexuality is something quite outside our experience and understanding and most of us fear the unknown. I know I also had the awful feeling that it was something dirty, abnormal, even deviant but I just couldn't equate such things with you so I knew that somehow I had to question my assumptions. I remember I was forever asking you to explain things to me. Thank you for being so patient.

Yours, with Pride

Continuing the Story with the Family

We both knew the telling had only just started; yes, the ice had been broken, the crucial words spoken but we were a family and your father, sister and twin brother were downstairs. You knew that fathers often found the news much more difficult to manage than mothers. I wonder if this is because, on top of everything else, men feel some rejection of their own masculinity, perhaps that their sons aren't quite men, which makes them, as parents, feel awkward and vulnerable. Maybe mothers have more difficulty over lesbian daughters, with a sense that the maternal function of child-bearing has been denied. Then your twin brother Richard: you must have had many an anxious moment as to how he would react. You'd been together so much, had he really not guessed? Or might he now find the close bond embarrassing? Your sister, Alison, was probably the least worrying for you with her broad-based social work background and an already established rapport with people with all sorts of personal difficulties.

I'm sure you remember that you didn't feel able to face them all with the news, so you asked me to do it. I felt very nervous. Dad was in the lounge reading the paper. I felt it hard to know what to say. I think he realised something was up as you and I had been 'missing' for some time! Rightly or wrongly I plunged straight in. He was totally taken aback as you would imagine; he wasn't one to show much emotion and he withdrew into himself and was silent. I wasn't sure what to do next, so I just stayed with him sharing what you had told me. After about half an hour I asked him if he would come and talk to you. He looked rather panic-stricken but agreed to do so. Only you are aware of what was said during your time together but from then on I know he supported you in any way he could. Throughout the months ahead he and I shared and learnt a lot together. He was challenged, too, but he was much more prosaic, much less emotional, than I was. He was always ready to listen or talk. I was very fortunate and so were you. Until Dad died I reckon he was your number one fan!

So how did I tell Richard and Alison? Well, I plunged straight in again! They were both very surprised as neither had had any idea at all. This was followed immediately by tears and dismay. It wasn't so much shock as an enormous sadness that you had had to manage this all on your own for several years. They knew how really frightened you must have been not even to have dared to mention it to either of them. Alison said, 'If only I had known I could have been there for him and shared it with him.' And Richard, 'I can't believe I didn't realise. He must have been so isolated and frightened.' I don't think either of them has ever wavered in their care and support of you. I know you were all away at different universities for some time, so there wasn't day to day contact but they were both always concerned as to how you were managing and always ready to meet and welcome your friends. Perhaps homosexuality is nothing like the same challenge for brothers and sisters as it is for parents. I suppose, by and large, young people today are freer and less conventional and may well not have the same sexual hang-ups as those of us in middle years.

As we faced the situation then, the family was for both of us a safe place where we could sort out all that this meant. At this point and as you well know, we took a trusted friend into our confidence and then battened down the hatches. Thank you for not pressurising me and for giving me that space and time to find my way as I could. Someone told me recently that it can take parents as long to find acceptance of the situation as it took their son or daughter to 'come out'. I think it took you about six years. It seemed to take me about four.

Yours, with Pride

John's Story

I feel convinced that nothing, or nothing that I'm aware of, happened in early years that had any effect on sexuality. I just knew, by about 13, quite instinctively and quite differently from the 'crush on the prefect' syndrome, that I was basically attracted to other males; that somehow I was different.

I didn't dare say anything at home or at school. I so wanted to be like everyone else and couldn't bear the thought that I might be rejected, teased, made fun of. The fear of ridicule and worse puts enormous pressure on you to conform. Why was I like this? Was there anyone else in the class who felt as I did? I didn't know. I didn't dare ask. I was frightened, confused and isolated. I was easily embarrassed, shy and awkward. My friends didn't really know ME. So I tried very hard to go with the herd, to have girl-friends, to say the 'right things' so that no one guessed and I wasn't in any way singled out. I reckon I managed quite well, very well even! No one suspected as I reached the sixth form and became a prefect and then Head Boy at a large comprehensive all-boys' school. It took its toll, though. I felt alone with my secret, so lonely inside.

There was no mention in human biology classes that perhaps one person in ten was homosexual: no guidelines, no information, no acknowledgement. These classes were the only times of formal sex instruction that we were given at school and probably for many children the only instruction at all. So this further reinforced the sense that how I felt was wrong. I really don't think Mum had any idea. Although undoubtedly my personality was affected, this was the John she knew. Increasingly I felt marginalised, with all sense of creativity and self-expression denied behind my sense of lack of self-worth.

For many gay people I know and certainly for myself, the process of trying to come to terms with being gay was a real burden on young shoulders. There seems to be so much pressure to conform – both parental and peer-group – and so many negatives. Some of my friends found it easy and even said that, from an early age, they were happy and comfortable with it but not me. How often I longed to be 'normal' like the majority – no more hiding or pretence.

It did undoubtedly affect my happiness during the teenage years. I did feel very isolated and alone. I had friends but this didn't help me to feel at ease with myself deep down. My insides were so often in turmoil. I felt alone even when I was with my friends. I was sometimes referred to as a 'loner'. This only played into my isolation and made me feel angry too. I'm really not a loner at all.

As my teenage years progressed the pressure simply built up.

Friends were having girl-friends, leaving me feeling jealous and inadequate. I tried to conform and did have a girl-friend for a while but overall I just don't think I gave off the right vibes! So, increasingly there was a feeling of missing out and living rather on the sidelines of life.

Then there was increasing pressure within me to tell someone how I felt. Even so, I said nothing until I was 19 and then I told my family. I had wanted to tell for so long but it seemed to me as though the act of telling would be the final trapping of my self in something I didn't want. How could I ever go back? I so wanted to be like everyone else – to get married and have children – above all else the thought of not having children was crushing! Also, I didn't know any gay people. What were they like? I felt sure they wouldn't be like me. I was also scared. Gay also seemed to mean AIDS – I didn't want to die of AIDS.

All of these worries had held me back for years but in the final analysis I just had to move on. I knew I had to face my parents but it's so difficult to find the words to tell this to people you've known all your life.

John

The Church

Perhaps 'the Church', in particular, tends to see issues in the traditional light in which it has always seen them. Doesn't there have to be an element of pre-judgement if understanding is based solely on a literal interpretation of Scripture, without much modern, considered opinion being taken into account? Surely it isn't an intrinsic fault in the divine plan that people are both heterosexual and homosexual? I can't believe that – not one in ten or twenty people, throughout the ages. It surely can't be just a chance phenomenon. Doesn't it, in some way, have to be part of the overall pattern, part of the wonder of creation?

Much of the Christian church still tends to see the issue in the traditional light of sin and perversion but people don't stand at a crossroads, do they, and make choices about their sexuality? A person can't be *required* to be celibate; that surely, can only be chosen. So there has to be room for acceptance of sexual expression. It isn't moral or immoral to be homosexual. Morality, I feel sure you'll agree, has to lie within our God-given identity, in how we choose to behave towards and relate to other people.

Personally, John, I don't think that I can accept that the Bible has the whole picture. Current knowledge and understanding must surely hold sway. Even if I really felt, though, that the literal rather than a more liberal interpretation seemed right, I would want to look at the whole pattern of your life. I'm sure I would still have to believe the evidence I have seen and learnt from you, rather than what I have read. I just cannot accept that you are living an immoral life.

So I have to ask myself how I feel about belonging to a hierarchical church from which many people, gay and straight, feel left out! Often our churches must seem like exclusive clubs for middle-class, married, white, heterosexual people. I don't think anyone means this to happen but moral judgements surely have just that result. They separate people and leave some outside.

Progress and understanding will surely only happen if committed, church-going, Christian people allow it to, if we can in some way mirror Christ's affirming unconditional love. What does exclusion do to the sense of worth of young gay Christian people and their own faith pattern? It may surely lead to deep feelings of guilt, to a lonely searching or to feeling that religion has no relevance in their lives and simply walking away. The message coming across, John, must seem to be that the only way to be acceptable is to keep silent and pretend to be 'normal' – more pretence, more hypocrisy. Is it surprising that you are not in one of our mainstream churches?

Bishop Spong helped me to realise that as responsible Christian people we can't hide behind Biblical quotations and say they are the 'word of the Lord'. We must open our minds to the 'knowledge explosion in the field of human sexuality'.

I wonder just how long it will be before the churches feel able to bless, affirm and accept committed lesbian and gay couples as part of the wonderful panoply of our humanity, as something to be treasured within the total complexity of human relationships. Not yet awhile, I feel sure!

Yours, with Pride

Discrimination

The pattern of discrimination starts early. As you have told me, John, homosexuality was never spoken about at school helpfully or seriously. You've mentioned how you longed for a teacher to voice something that allowed you to say, if only to yourself, 'Yes, I feel like that'. But there was nothing, only a wall of silence. The law leaves the one in ten or twenty who aren't heterosexual floundering and lost. It negates any sense of self worth. It doesn't allow for guidelines or role models. Schools are not allowed to portray a positive image of homosexuality, so there's moral judgement, an implicit denial that it's OK to be gay. How often you must have clammed up through fear, kept very quiet, hidden behind a mask or listened to camp jokes and laughed along with everyone else, hoping no one would guess. Discrimination simply hurts those who are most vulnerable. Do you remember I once mentioned a teacher who was lesbian? It must be so difficult for her in this position to broach the subject: laying yourself open to 'suspicion', reprimand, possible loss of job, yet seeing and knowing that some young people are struggling to find their way through the sexual maze and may be feeling quite desperate. Do you think that gradually, with a broader understanding of homosexuality, there will be a relaxation of such rigid policy in schools? I can only hope so – not that you can legislate against prejudice only against the effects of it, the discrimination. To eradicate prejudice is surely going to be like the drip of water on a stone.

Yours, with Pride

Thelma Gabriel
England

The All-Loving God
(Luke 1:46–9)

My soul magnifies the all loving God and my spirit rejoices in God my saviour, who esteems, honours and loves my gayness. Behold all my family and friends shall recognise my blessedness, for the one who is mighty has done great things for me by creating me in that sacred aspect of the Divine Essence which is gay. Holy is God's name. I praise God and give thanks for being so honoured and so blest. Through my gayness, God's strength is shown: the proud and the privileged are put down from their thrones; their prerogative is shattered. Through my gayness, God exalts the sensitive, the expansive, the inclusive. God fills my hunger with overwhelming love, while the rich and greedy are sent away in the lonely isolation of their loveless power. Through my gayness, God will heal the human race in remembrance of God's mercy and covenant, as God spoke to Abraham and Sarah, to Noah, to Mary, the Mother of Jesus and to their posterity forever. Amen.

Tony Gryzmala
USA

For a Young Man and His Mothers

In the crowded room he found me.
'Good evening, Mrs Schwab. How are you tonight? Your son performed well in the play, didn't he?'
Relaxed. Well groomed. Confident. Polite.
Thus you stand before me. I am impressed.
'Yes, my son did well tonight. I am well also. Thank you. And you? How is it going?'
I want to add 'really' but the word sticks in my throat.
I dare not.
We are not yet friends. Some kids know and speak so openly about it.
While they have one mother and one father or perhaps one mother alone, you, you alone have two mothers.
While some are kind, do you hear the others mock and jeer?
Born of a mother and a father yet raised by two women who love deeply, who are committed.
What to a one and three year old seems so natural because it simply is, to a seven and ten year old is obviously different and to an older teen demands an explanation.
How did you handle it?
With what sharp pain did that first vicious cut thrust deep into your heart and soul?
How do you speak of it now in your own most inner self?
With your friends? With your too often cruel peers? Taunting, bullying, has it ever ceased?
Was either mother a ghost parent because you just preferred she not come? Or that they not come together? 'This is my preferred Mom. This is my Mom.'
Lesbigay youth – fourteen times more likely to commit suicide, thirty per cent of high school dropouts; forty per cent of kids selling their bodies on our streets; kicked out of their homes; discrimination; put downs; homophobic slurs and lies. How does one unsure youth ever answer them all other than with death?
Was that their life and struggle, your mothers?
How can those youth find safe people like your mothers?
What stories could they tell each other if truth were their focus and sharing their gentle means?
And you tonight, before me now, talking with a teacher not far from my quiet gaze.
You already so manly, so ready to begin your path through university and a job. What do you hear? What do you see?
What will you hear? What will you see?

The law givers rule your mothers have rights – just like me.
But churches rally as to a battle cry and tell the government 'Legislate
not on their behalf! We don't want them.'
The Hatred. The Mockery. The Jeers. The Slurs. And the deaths of so
many gentle, honest, gifted people.
Will you weep alone? Or with a loving wife/partner somewhere?
Will you live to see acceptance one day the norm?
Long after I'm gone, I fear.
How deeply I admire you.
You stir nobility in me I never knew I had.
You evoke courage in me I never knew I had.
You awaken Christ in me.
Love not hate!
Your will be done, O Lord.

Betty Lynn Schwab
Canada

His Deepest Nature

God, you know I have loved hymns,
and when I sang, I meant them.

Open my eyes, that I may see,
Visions of truth thou hast for me.

You opened mine!
And I learned my husband is Gay –
    that he struggled alone for years
    before he could accept this truth.
I learned that being Gay
    had something to do with his
        deepest nature,
    and that, while Gay,
        he loved me in a special way.

Open my mouth and let me bear,
Gladly the warm truth everywhere

This is so much harder, God.
There is so much hate around.

So many want to stop up their ears,
        bind up their minds,
                and close their hearts
    to more light and truth and justice.
    How can we bear the warm truth to others?

    Oh God, teach us 'patient endurance'!
    Give us faith, that, in your time,
            Your love and justice
                will fill the earth with peace.

Sarah, wife of a gay man
USA

After a While You Learn

After a while you learn
The subtle difference
Between holding a hand
And chaining a soul
And you learn
That love doesn't mean leaning
And company doesn't mean security
And you begin to learn
That kisses aren't compromises
And presents aren't promises.
And you begin to accept your defeats
With your head up and your eyes ahead
With the grace of a woman or man
Not the grief of a child.
And you learn to build all your loads on today
Because tomorrow's ground is too uncertain for plans
And futures have a way of falling down in mid flight.
After a while you learn
That even the sunshine burns if you ask too much
So you plant your own garden
And decorate your own soul
Instead of waiting for someone to bring you flowers
And you learn
That you really can endure
That you really are strong

And you really do have worth
And you learn
And you learn
With every failure you learn.

Source unknown

I Will Not Leave You

I will not leave you.

But I will not leave
Or forsake you.
You are mine and I love you.

In whatever I ask of you
I will provide for
Even if you cannot see
The gifts I have set out for you.

In your time of joy
I will rejoice with you,
In your times of sorrow
I will share your tears.

Wherever you find yourself
Remember this
Do not be afraid for I am with you always.

Debbie Hodge
England

A Hamilton Conversation

In Hamilton, Aotearoa New Zealand, one Sunday afternoon, a mature aged man stopped me in the street and asked, 'Is your name George Bourne?'
    'Yes.'
    'And you organise the Gay Welfare Group?'
    'Yes.'
    'Can I talk with you?'
So we sat on a seat in the sun and this is the story that he told me.

He was brought up in Hamilton, though he then worked in Wellington in a government related job.

His elderly mother still lived in Hamilton and he visited her from time to time. Some time previously he had answered his door in Wellington one evening to find a young lad of about fourteen or fifteen years of age standing there. He knew the boy and discovered that his parents had made things so difficult for him because he was gay that he had left home. Now, because of his age, and in any case, it was illegal in those days whatever his age had been, to be gay, there was no way that the guy, who was talking to me, could have let him live there with him which is what the boy wanted. He kept him there that night, gave him the fare back to Hamilton and sent him back next morning, with, no doubt, the best advice he could offer, to his parents who were staunch Christians.

He never heard any more of the boy. And so when he next visited Hamilton to see his mother he made enquiries.

The boy had gone into a field and shot himself.

The parents' reaction?

They had been telling people that he had gone to Australia.

George Bourne
Aotearoa New Zealand

I Thought of You

The heading in the newspaper of the man opposite in the train read

'Vanessa's Guide to Finding True Love'

And I thought of you
And how I nearly never knew about love
What I know now.
I would probably have been satisfied,
if nagged by an unacknowledged apprehension of faint boredom,
and an increasing realisation of inappropriateness,
But now I look upon those years
Not as a waste or even an unnecessary delay
But more as a time that simply was before what now is as you are and
I am.

Michael Reiss
England

Just Now and Then

We need to hold each other
in silence now and then;
language can be misleading
and two-edged words cause wounds
even though used in jesting,
jousting thrust and parry.

But I would wrap you round
with tenderness,
lay aside swords and arrows
Raise the visor, drop the shield,
hold and be held and let
the gift and need of love
encircle us in silence –
now and then.

Helene McLeod
England

A Housewarming

Everyone gathers outside the home. The occupants place a pink triangle, gay flag or other lesbian or gay symbols on the door of the home and say:

Just as the ancient Israelites marked their door lintels with blood as a sign that they were blessed and chosen by God, so we mark our door with a sign of blessedness as lesbian women/gay men. The people of Israel marked their doors on the eve of their exodus from slavery into freedom. By marking this house/flat we identify with them on their journey, for gay and lesbian people are also in the process of coming out of oppression. May everything that happens in this home and all who come into it take us further in our journey towards liberation.

Everyone goes into the main room

God of all creation look down in love on your friends gathered here in N and N's new home. We pray that this home may become the tent of your presence. May it radiate your wholeness, love and peace, your shalom. May hatred, evil, apathy, narrow-mindedness and destruction

find no sanctuary here. Bless and preserve all who live in this
house/flat and all who come in and go out of its doors.

Elizabeth Stuart
England

Ros and Liz Housewarming Celebration

Music: Bach: Jesu Joy of Man's Desiring

Everyone gathers in the hall.

Welcome

Liz and Ros: We welcome you – our friends –
to warm our home with your presence
in celebration of our life together.
You have been our companions
in the journey we have made
to bring us to this day.
As you have crossed the threshold of this home
we ask that you will stand with us
at this, the threshold of our future together,
to be our witnesses
as we celebrate the goodness of what we share
and commit ourselves to seek together
to grow in love.

All: **How good it is when friends live together as one.**
(Psalm 33)

Celebration of Friendship

Liz: You our friends have helped us weave our lives.
Weaving with us in times of joy and sadness, confusion
and clarity, anger and peace. We ask you now to join in
creating a sign of what you have given us to celebrate
our friendship and to remain as a symbol of community
in this place.

Music: Pachelbel: Canon

> *Each person weaves their ribbon into the web, saying their name.*

Liz: We leave our work unfinished for friends yet to join us ...

All: **This is a symbol of our interwoven journeys which have brought us here to celebrate this day. May it be in this home a source of encouragement to Ros and Liz and all who come and go here, that they may delight in diversity and choose solidarity and so be builders of community.**

Readings

Voice One: Your house shall not be an anchor but a mast ...

Voice Two: To say I love you is to say that you are not mine ...

A Sign of Union

> *Liz and Ros kindle oils.*

Voice: Keep your passion alive ...

A friend: O Holy Spirit who is known to us as love, we pray that Ros and Liz may continue in the journey they have begun to share. May they find much happiness and fulfilment in their lives together, marked by a sense of personal freedom as well as mutual responsibility. May they find in each other companionship as well as love, understanding as well as compassion, challenge as well as agreement. May they have courage when the road is rough and humility when fortune favours them. Shall we spend a few moments in quietness together each with our own thoughts and wishes ... it is our great adventure in faith, our giving and receiving of the gifts of life.

> *We move now from the hall to gather around the table.*

> *We continue when all have found their place and are seated.*

Ros: We gather round this table to celebrate with food and drink but first we share a sign of communion. It represents connections of the past with the present and the present with the future. Please all share in it.

Lighting of the Candles

Voice One: We live in many darknesses. We are often uncertain. We are sometimes afraid. In the darkness we light a candle of hope.

A candle is lit.

Voice Two: We all have sorrows. We have known pain. Each of us carries special regrets. In our pain we light a candle of forgiveness.

A candle is lit.

Voice Three: We are sometimes lonely, and the world seems cold and hard. In our loneliness, we light a candle of warmth.

A candle is lit.

Voice Four: We have our joys, our times of happiness. Each of us receives gifts. In our gratification we light a candle of thanks.

A candle is lit.

Voice Five: We have known awe, wonder, mystery, glimmerings of perfection in our imperfect world. In our wonder we light a candle of praise.

A candle is lit.

All: **We bring together many uncertainties, many sorrows, many joys, much wonder. We bring together many candles, many lights. May our separate lights become one flame that together we may be nourished by its glow.**

The Threshold Meal

> *Bread*

Liz: Here is bread –
                Grain of the earth. Labour of body. Leaven of our
                sharing.
                It reminds us of our daily needs and of our need of each
                other to help us to grow.

> *Bread is passed around and shared but not yet eaten.*

> *Salt*

                Here is salt –
                A reminder of our tears in times of struggles to be our-
                selves but through which we discover our distinctive
                gifts. It signifies our empowerment to use our gifts to
                inspire each other.

> *Salt is passed and each sprinkles some on their bread.*

                Let us live in peace together.

> *We eat the bread and salt.*

> *Champagne*

Ros: And now . . . Champagne . . .
                For times of joy and plenty. To celebrate the delight of
                this day and all that gives us pleasure.

> *Champagne is opened and poured.*

Proposers: **The Toast**

Music: Handel: Arrival of the Queen of Sheba

Lunch

> *Ros and Liz*
> *England*

We Praise You God For You Have Made

We praise you God for you have made
A world of such variety;
A world of colour, light and shade,
Of varied sexuality.

We come as ones who love you, God,
In many different frames and ways.
Indulge us, help us find a place
To share your loving, daring days.

We hold each other, hold us now
And never, ever let us go
God, give us generosity
That we may share the love we know.

Andrew Pratt
England

Our Communities:
To Be Inter-Active People

Tread Lightly

Tread lightly on the earth, my friend,
It's there for everyone
Who turns the soil and tends the seed
And works in rain and sun:
Who marvels at the season's change
And braves each unknown way
And recognises God's sure touch
In every new-born day.

Tread lightly with each other, friend,
Step softly side by side,
In difference and acceptance
True love and trust abide.
So can we see in all around
Reflections of His face,
And recognise our Saviour's touch
In every warm embrace.

Tread lightly on my dreams, my friend,
For they are your dreams too,
Of people in community
Of visions born anew:
Of love and hope and sharing
Of dangers safely past,
Of praise and jubilation,
His kingdom comes at last!

Alix Brown
England

An Inclusive Community

Jesus calls us to an inclusive community.
Yet he promises no greatness and no soft beds.

He calls us only to follow,
and walks, himself, the way of pain and conflict.
Today, in our ignorance and weakness,
we commit ourselves to follow;
to build a community where all may find rest
without prejudice or favour.
We recognise that Jesus
      – was not tempted to see the Kingdom
          in power and glory;
      – was not discouraged by what seemed
          to be death, or failure;
      – was prepared for pain and conflict
          in reaching out to others;
      – and was always ready
          to leave the result to God.
Jesus calls us to follow.

Duncan L. Tuck
England

So Many Kinds of Awesome Love

There are so many kinds of awesome love,
I bless them all:

Love of kindred for their kin
Love of lover for their mate
Love of country for the native
Love of land for the explorer

Love of the labourer for his work
Love of the scholar for her truth
Love of the artist for the muse
Love of the preacher for the word
Love of the disciple for the way
Love of the mystic for their God

There are so many kinds of awesome love,
We need them all:

Love of brother, sister, father, mother
Love of parent, grandparent, uncle, aunt

Love of the beloved, love of the friend,
Love of the stranger, love of the needy

Love of the woman for the man
Love of the man for the woman
Love of woman for her woman
Love of the man for his man

There are so many kinds of awesome love,
Why must we set one above the other,
Say some are worthy and others base?
Why must we choose one love
When we need all the kinds we can get?

There are so many kinds of awesome love:
The love that knocks you off your feet
        and sets you to desperate things
The love that is gentle and kind
        and swells the compassionate heart
The love that is joyous and life-giving
        and keeps you singing for days
The love that is steadfast and loyal
        and sits out long nights of pain

Young, jocular love
Old, wise love
Rich, extravagant love
Poor, pitiful love
Strong, encouraging love
Vulnerable, wounded love
Passionate, sensual love
Free, philial love
Fiery, prophetic love
Self-emptied, contemplative love

There are so many kinds of awesome love,
I bless them all.

Nicola Slee
England

The Blessing of Diversity
(Genesis 9:16)

Gracious and merciful God,
      Creator and Author of Life:
            You see people as persons,
            beautiful in their diversity
            whether it be cultural, age, gender,
            sexuality, nationality, race, creed, or other.

We pray that these realities may be lifted up
            and made holy
      that they will become channels of blessing
            peace and understanding.

A positive spirit to respect others for who they are
            and to be forbearing towards others
            and their self-expressions
      will bring us closer to the dawning
            of the new covenant symbolised
      by God's setting a rainbow in the heavens
            After the flood.

We pray this in the name of Jesus the Christ.
Amen.

Paul Louie
Asian American USA

To Seek with Open Minds

God of the sun
and the moon
and the stars
bless those who seek illumination
in matters
of sexuality
and inclusivity
that they may be
'like trees planted by streams of water

which yield their fruit in its season
and their leaves do not wither'.

May they prosper in all that they do.[1]

[1] Psalm 1:3

Chris Glaser
USA

Celebrate Values

God of all colours:
The one who made me want
To speak and to write
With quiet, eloquent significance,
Was black.
Yet, though principal of my high school,
His family was not allowed
To buy a home in our neighbourhood.

God, forgive us.
God, deliver us.
For we have accepted the gifts of many
While rejecting their body-selves
Because of colour, gender, age,
Disability, sexual orientation, appearance.

Help us to realise
If the gifts are beautiful, so are they.
Help us to celebrate others' value
By their fruits
Not the shape of the trees.

Chris Glaser
USA

Lover of Us All

Holy Trinity,
divine and blessed relationship,
bless the ecstasy of these lovers
as their faces kiss,

as their bodies touch,
as in their love making
they overcome the fear and the hatred
and the garbage heaped upon them
by the church and the society.

Holy Trinity,
bless their adoration of one another
as they worship the holy
of your divine imprint
and celebrate the communion
of a loving covenant.
May such sacrament
bring them ever closer to you
Lover of us all.

Chris Glaser
USA

Consider your Call
(1 Corinthians 1:26a, 27b)

We pray for the especially vulnerable, God.
We pray for lesbians and gays already marginalised
by colour of skin, gender,
economic or educational poverty,
age.

We pray for Black, Latino and Asian gays and lesbians
who sometimes face homophobic constituencies,
who often face a homophobic and racist church.

We pray for lesbians, particularly those in the church,
whose vulnerability and resulting fear
even gay males cannot comprehend.
We pray for lesbians and gays who are poor,
economically or educationally,
whose financial insecurity
or lack of information
limit their ability to assert or articulate
their needs
let alone establish ties with gay communities.

We pray for lesbians and gays
who are very young or very old,
who live at home with families,
or in homes with strangers,
both limiting access to gay family,
both expected to be asexual.

O God,
may the church consider its call
as a community of the vulnerable,
welcoming further self-disclosure,
offering affirmation to all your children
through Jesus Christ
in the unity of the Holy Spirit.

Chris Glaser
USA

Strengthen Me To Act

Help me to find a place where I can be alone with you, O God.
There let me notice what is going on through your eyes.
When I return to my community, strengthen me to act in your name
To make this world a better place.

Donna E. Schaper
USA

Alien Messiah

But then, of course, Jesus was a foreigner.
It's true!
He lived under a hot sun
and would have had a darker complexion
than we like to admit.
Perhaps he had a hooked nose –
        terrible,
        but there it is.
And his eyes would not have been blue,
        but black or brown.

His hair, most likely, was dark,
      maybe curly,
      a little shaggy, unkempt,
      wild, even –
      what a thought!
And, as for his fingernails –
      what do you expect from someone
      who lived on the road?
(Would you want him to touch you
with hands like that?)
Perhaps, just perhaps,
his breath smelt of olive oil
      and figs.
Perhaps there was an odour
of sweat and garlic –
      hard work and little hygiene.
Does this shock you?
Are you happy with an alien,
      foreign,
      dark-skinned,
      unwashed,
      disreputable
      Messiah?
Or have you made him
      in the image of
      suburbia?

Duncan L. Tuck
England

Marriage

Everyone enjoys the gathering in the local square.
Today is the day.
Two lines for the dance.
Young girls are dressed up to meet the men of their future.
The boys are ready to be engaged.
I must choose
like the others.

The time goes by.
Everybody has favoured somebody.

I am staying on the wrong line!
I do not want to play the same game.
I can't take it any more.

For me there is nothing to do in this village.
I want to go
far away,
where the most beautiful men are
waiting for me!
In a line
for a dance.

Omar Nahas
The Netherlands

Prayer of Confession

God who is Love,
Loving God,
God our lover,

Since the first giddy days
of our meeting,
you have beckoned us,
desperately longing
for us to share
intimacy with you.

You desire
to share power, identity
and excitement.
We respond
with nervousness
and misunderstanding.

You make
yourself vulnerable
to our rejection.
We hurt,
tease,
and mock you.

Sometimes
you respond as only
a jealous lover can.
Will you hold us
to yourself
once more?

Gary Gotham and Clare McBeath
England

Coming For Many

In coming as a man,
Christ sanctified both sexes.
In holding little children,
Christ freed adults into play.
In speaking to women,
Christ unblocked the ears of all creation.
In touching the leper,
Christ blessed everyone,
no matter how unworthy they felt,
and opened a holy artery,
from heart to heart,
and hand to hand.
Praise God.

Duncan L. Tuck
England

You and Me

Being in love is higher than
you and me.
It is our way
to be.
It is a key
to our hearts,
yours and mine.

You say:
'he will always be
my reason to live,
my wine.'

I say:
'his face is the creation
that makes the wonders of the creator
rise
in my eyes.'

We are in love
with the same man
who 'deserves to be loved',
says your heart.
'The same,' says mine.

We walk, we talk
we can't deny
what we believe in and why.

At the end of the story
we will listen to him.
This is you
and this is me.

Omar Nahas
The Netherlands

The Wife of My Lover

In the presence of God
shall she defend us both:
me
and
her husband.

Rivers of joy
will be the rewards
for her patience
and the love
she gave us both:
me
and
her husband.

With angels
she shall dance
in circles
around us both:
me
and
her husband.

May God please her
for what she has to miss
here on earth:
her husband.

Omar Nahas
The Netherlands

Regarding Making a Public Witness on Behalf of Lesbian, Gay, Bisexual and Transgender Persons

Gracious God,
We give thanks for your presence in all of life and for your presence with us now as we seek to discern your will and your wisdom for this community. Remind us, Divine Spirit, that you seek to fill us with your life-giving power. Encourage us, Eternal Wisdom, to loosen our grip on our individual assumptions so that we might hear your voice speaking through our community. Disturb us, Holy Advocate, that we might be unsettled from our complacency in order to become agents of your grace to a world in need. As we gather as your people, called forth to proclaim your Word and to transform hearts turned cold, give us a clearer sense of what we are to say and do. Lead us back to our ancestors of the faith who sought your guidance when fear, confusion and despair seemed to rule the day.

Fill us with the Spirit of Moses, Aaron and Miriam as they led the Hebrew people from slavery to freedom;

Fill us with the spirit of Queen Esther as she defied conventional wisdom to save her people from sure destruction;

Fill us with the spirit of the disciples, bereft from the departure of their friend and saviour Jesus, yet able to organise a new community founded on compassion, courage and shared resources;

Fill us with the spirit of Stephen, Lydia, Paul, Timothy and Dorcas and other early Christians who risked living a minority faith in an empire of oppression and enforced conformity.

O God, hear the prayers of this community as we seek to make a public witness on behalf of our Lesbian, Gay, Bisexual and Transgender sisters and brothers.

Help us to honour the voices of those who have personally known exclusion, heartache, fear, uncertainty and even violence. Broaden our awareness of the movement of your Holy Spirit in our world, so that we might know once again that your ways are not always our ways. Call us to more fully respect the blessed worth of all your beloved children. Guide us to new ways of being church for a new age.

In passionate, eager and joyful expectation we pray. Amen.

Allen V. Harris
USA

Aspects of Our Worship

Opening Sentences

Sisters and brothers, open your hearts,
for faith has come,
and in faith you are set free.
Free, not to mind your words,
but to speak the truth in love.
Free, not to look up at some,
and down at others,
but to look kindly eye-to-eye.
Free, not to close your senses,
but to feel clearly the pain of others,
and to take it to yourself.
So clothe yourself in Christ –
the fashion of the heirs
of promise.
And praise God.

Duncan L. Tuck
England

Hymn: Toast Our God

Within the shade of love's spreading tree,
we find a place where the streams may flow.
And there we lay the dreams of this hour,
and there we dance the Christ we know.
Come, will you tread the hope and the pain?
Trace, with faith, drops of blood in the rain.

Within the arms of love's open heart,
we find the nails that built our glee.
Clasp hand to hand. Play merry and sing.
And feel the scars that have set us free.
Come join the body of dead now alive.
By his touch, quicken, waken, revive.

Within the field of love's swelling grain,
we find the grace mature and full.
Collect the vine's profuse offering,
and welcome those who have hoped it all.
Come, join the feast where the downtrodden dine.
Share the bread. Toast our God with the wine.

Tune: Sussex Carol

Duncan L. Tuck
England

Closing Prayer

Leader: Jesus says, Come to me,
            and I will give you rest.
            A rest that is not passive,
                    but is having the weight and concern
                    of this life taken from you.
            A rest that is not the hurry of the world,
                    but is growing at the proper pace.
            A rest that is not the closing of your eyes,
                    but is opening them at last.
            Come to my rest, he says.
            To where you belong.

All: Lord, give us your rest
and take us up
into your striving for this world.

Duncan L. Tuck
England

Our Churches:
To Be Inclusively Active People

Prayer Round the Tree
(At a baptism)

Holding up the baby or standing with the child held by another, the Priest says:

N, we pray for you the blessing of God the Creator –
may you grow well in His/Her creation.

As you discover little stones and the earth,
may you enjoy and love them.

As you explore what you can and can't do with plants and animals,
may you enjoy them and learn they have needs as well as you.

As you climb your first hill,
may you find the struggle is worth it.

As you discover enormous seas and skies,
may you know God gives us space in which to grow.

May the Sun and the stars delight and touch your heart with fire
and so may you find passion to be creative.

As this tree shades us from heat in summer and shelters us from wind
in winter,
may you learn to trust the goodness of creation –
and may you in turn discover you are called to be a co-creator with
Creator God.

St James's Church, Piccadilly
London, England

Let Me Be
(A homosexual's plea to parts of the church)

I have no evil demons
for you to exorcise.
I am who I am.
Don't label me with lies.

Don't rant and rave of choices
not on offer to me.
I am who I am.
Why can't you let me be?

Don't condemn me as sinful.
Don't say I am depraved.
I am who I am.
I refuse to be 'saved'.

Don't abuse your religion
to load guilt onto me.
I am who I am,
with the right to be free.

Blind guides, why must you persist
In this hypocrisy?
I am who I am,
as God created me.

My Prayer

Living God, Essence of Being,
Great, 'I AM.'
Do not let my difference
be a stumbling block
to those who fear it;
do not let their fear
be unjustly focused on me.
Open their eyes,
That they may see
not our points of difference,
but our shared humanity.
Amen.

Jean Mortimer – for Matthew and many of his friends
England

Easter Liberation
(A prayer for gay men and lesbians in the church)
(John 20:19–23)

Liberating Christ
come into our locked rooms
and speak your word of peace.
Set us free to rejoice in our bodies,
     the reality of our loving
      the integrity of our passion.

Forgiving Christ
speak your word of peace
that sees and forgives
our silent lies and unspoken denials
     of all that you have made us
      and all that we have chosen to be.

Healing Christ
speak your word of judgement
that gives us voices to name the sins of others
holding them accountable
     for the rejection sparked by fear
      and the distancing disguised as tolerance.

Breathe into us
your spirit of forgiveness
so that
     loved and loving
      forgiven and forgiving
we may be free to speak peace in your name.

Jan Berry
England

So Here We Are

So here we are
Dancing on the edge,
The dangerous and delightful edge.

So here we'll be
The irritant in the eye
Of the church:
The cracked lens through which it needs to see.

So here we'll not be silent, or invisible,
But we'll say our names
And show our colours
And others will know
Who we are.

So here we'll laugh and love and dance
And sing and play and drink and
Whose edge is it anyway?

This edge, we say,
Is ours; and we will
Fill that edge
To overflowing:
Loving it with passion,
Embracing it with desire,
And flirting unashamedly with the centre.

This dangerous and delightful edge
Is the edge where we are dancing,
So, here we are.

Rosie Miles
England

Women and Men

We have met tonight
As women and men:
Sexual and whole,
Human and flawed;

We are Church.

In our humanity
We bring our desire:
For relationship with God,
For relationship with others;

We are Church.

We bring our differences and diversity
And celebrate them;

We are Church.

Rosie Miles
England

Gay Christians and the Church

George Hopper is a Local Preacher and his wife, Carol, is a Circuit Steward in the Methodist Church.

For a long time, like many Christians who have not knowingly met anyone of homosexual orientation, George wanted nothing to do with such people; he had always assumed that they had deliberately chosen a way of life that was both unnatural and offensive to God. But what he glimpsed of the lives of some homosexual people through the media – and later through the testimony of one gay man – caused him to question his long-held assumptions. The result was a pilgrimage of faith. George and Carol realised that they knew little about the matter and set out to learn directly by meeting and sharing with homosexual Christians in worship and fellowship. This led to a thorough and prayerful re-examination of the Bible. In his book *Reluctant Journey: a pilgrimage of faith from homophobia to Christian love*, George relates the story.

There are some amazing stories in the New Testament about the early church and the Apostles. There is the remarkable conversion of Saul – a Rabbi and an important Pharisee, taught by Gamaliel himself – a Jew of the Jews, with utmost respect for the Law and separation from the Gentiles. He was to become Paul, the apostle, the apostle *to* the Gentiles. You will no doubt be very familiar with his story.

In Acts 10 we find a story that is no less amazing. It is about a man called Peter – a fisherman, a pillar of the Church. He, like Paul, was fastidious in keeping the Law. As regards the Gentiles, he didn't eat with them and he would only associate with them when absolutely necessary. That was the Law and that was how he played it.

Then he had this vision about unclean foods:

'Rise, Peter. Kill and eat!'

'Not so Lord. I have never eaten anything common or unclean.'

Three times the voice challenged:

'What God has cleansed, call not that unclean.'

Peter responded amazingly well when he understood what God was saying to him. For it was new truth – difficult new truth. Such truth was to throw to the wind many of the things he considered precious and holy.

But not only did he go to Gentiles to proclaim the gospel; those Gentiles were the hated Roman conquerors. His obedience opened the gate for the Gentile Pentecost!

Yet there is sadness in what I have to say here. For Peter saw no further than the immediate challenge. It was a big challenge but he interpreted it only in the sense of what he was called immediately to do. It was a staggering new truth, the breadth of which he did not seem to appreciate fully.

And not only Peter but the Church has interpreted that vision in too narrow a sense. The Church continually has to learn afresh the lesson of Peter's vision. A big struggle is needed to persuade the Church to appreciate how broad the interpretation of this vision could and should be!

The struggle for women in the ministry is still going on, 2,000 years after this magnificent vision that speaks to us. Traditionalists are still fighting the battle against that great truth.

And the struggle goes on to persuade Christians to welcome homosexual people – men and women – into the full fellowship and ministry of the Church. We are still not listening to that voice which says:

'What God has cleansed, call not that unclean.'

I have come to the conclusion that much of the intolerance in the Church – and it is not universal, thank God – is due to ignorance about the sexuality we call 'homosexuality' and lack of experience of meeting homosexual people while being aware of their sexuality.

This is one of the reasons my wife Carol and I have arranged occasional get-togethers over a buffet meal for homosexual Christian friends from the area Lesbian and Gay Christian Movement and heterosexual Christian friends who are people who have previously been to a Bible study and discussion group where the issue has been properly addressed.

It takes some courage for homosexual Christians to 'come out' to people they have not previously met, as well as for those who meet them. People come apprehensively but the ice is soon broken and they go away saying how good it was to meet each other and have the opportunity to talk.

We all know homosexual people because there are so many of them. But so often we just don't *know* we know them! If we did, many of the false images we had of them would evaporate. We would find we are just like each other! We would find that they fill many of the posts in our churches, at all levels. They are to be found in all walks of life. There would be so many astonished people if homosexuals, especially those who are Christians, all declared themselves.

The sad thing is that many homosexual people have been hurt so often that they cannot trust us with their truth. This is our problem and we need to address it. All that most of us know of lesbians and gay men is when one of them fails and we see it in the television and newspaper headlines.

The good news is that lesbian and gay Christians have so much to offer the Church. Apart from being loving, faithful people, they include many very gifted people among their number.

And they have much to teach us of Christ, who was himself despised and rejected. We need to think how we can work together for the Kingdom of God.

We Need Each Other

From what I have learned, one of the problems homosexual people, especially Christians, struggle with when they enter a loving relationship is the lack of role models. There is no knowledge of homosexuality as we understand it today in the Bible, so there is neither specific guidance nor a 'role model' for those who live in a committed, loving, faithful relationship with a partner of the same sex. The only guidance that the Church offers at present is nearly all negative.

There are, of course, some general guidelines, such as faithfulness, love and commitment in relationships – values that enrich our most important relationships and give them stability.

And Christian scholars like Jeffrey John are working at developing role models. His book *Permanent, Faithful, Stable* says a good deal about the direction this is taking.

Obviously there is a problem about children: homosexual people are denied so much and I know for some this is a great loss. It is easy for those of us who don't understand to say they should therefore get married. But pressures on marriage have never been so great and to add the pressures of a homosexual wife or husband is to place any marriage under almost intolerable strain.

While some survive, almost inevitably many such marriages fail. There is so much for us to think about here – so much to understand. Much compassion is needed. Such issues represent the difficult side of the equation.

But there is another side of the equation too – the fact that homosexual Christians are as faithful as, if not more faithful than, most heterosexual Christians.

They have had to struggle with their faith as few other Christians have and to work through that barrier of tension that has traditionally equated homosexuality with evil. But they know the Lord has called them, though many of them are mystified and mortified at his people's response to them.

I know their love is genuine Christian love and I know they need to be affirmed – not only to be accepted but to be loved with Christian love. And as Carol and I know from experience this love is something which will be returned with good measure.

We have shared worship and fellowship with lesbian and gay Christians for a few years now. We have found great understanding for those who have hurt them. And never has there been anything said or any suggestions made that made us feel uncomfortable, or question whether we are doing the right thing. Rather, have they gone out of their way to welcome us, despite our representing those who cause them problems. We are shown love and respect even though in our ignorance we have doubtless sometimes said things that have caused some pain or hurt.

Our experience leads us to hold a high opinion of them as Christian people – as faithful, God-loving, Bible-respecting Christians. But they are not to be intimidated. They know who they are. They know they cannot change that part of them that has caused them such problems. In faith they have come to terms with it and know that they are a precious part of God's Kingdom people.

They are not going to go away – or rather I hope they are not going to go away! We need them for without them we are incomplete.

We in the Church are called by Christ to love them and part of loving is seeking to understand. We should welcome them as Christians into every part of the Church. We should work with them to provide a basis and proper recognition of their 'covenant' relationships. If we do not do these things we will have failed to obey the command of Christ to 'love one another as I have loved you.'

Carol and I attended a weekend conference of Christian fellowship and worship with about thirty lesbian and gay evangelical Christian people. It was a time of Christian love, healing and joy. I affirmed them in the love of God. Carol and I received as we shared with them in all the things they had planned – prayer times, worship and sacraments, meals, conversation and laughter.

Just before the conference, Carol and I had been through emotional turmoil on account of an experience that had befallen one of our family. I was left with deep anger inside. That anger was healed as the agape love of our friends surrounded us. I was renewed by the love of Christ within them.

Isn't this how it's meant to be? Loving, sharing, supporting one another in the love of Christ.

George S. E. Hopper
England

Prayer for Women
(Written for and said at the 20th Anniversary Service of the Lesbian and Gay Christian Movement, Southwark Cathedral, London, 16 November 1996)

God who celebrates and affirms women,
We who are lesbian and bisexual name ourselves as part of your
    church;
We rejoice in the gifts, energies and passion of women in LGCM;

You invite us to befriend our sexuality:
You are able to accept in us what we cannot even acknowledge;
You are able to name in us what we cannot bear to speak of;
Out of our deepest hidden places you call us to join in the dance of the
    gospel;

We remember with pain the times when we feel afraid,
And when our lives are rendered invisible;
We remember with joy the people who are important to us,
Who accompany us on our spiritual journey:
Our friends, our partners, our families, our children;
And we give thanks for the love, support and friendship that women
    give each other.
Through Jesus Christ
Amen.

Rosie Miles
England

To See Christ

We pray, O God,
for all who are imprisoned
and for those who bring them good news.

We pray for gay and lesbian prisoners,
some of whom are innocent of all but loving,
since half the states[1] still have laws
which make our love a crime.

We pray for ministers in prison chaplaincies
who caringly and carefully counsel
gay prisoners in secure facilities.

Bless all who visit you in prison, Jesus.
May prisoners see the Christ in us
as we see the Christ in them.

[1] in the USA

Chris Glaser
USA

An Inclusive Church
(Acts 10:47)

God, who revealed to Peter
        both the circumcised and the uncircumcised
                are welcome into your kingdom;
God, who promised your spirit
        will be an advisor to the faithful,
                and a comforter to the hurting;
We pray your spirit will lead the church
        toward insights on how all your people
                can experience the welcome
                        that Peter, in your Name,
                                offered to the uncircumcised Gentiles,
        especially those whom the church rejects
                due to race, sex and sexual orientation.

God, whose grace knows no boundaries,
      teach us to avoid erecting barriers
            to human experiences
                  that cannot be found in your kingdom.

Eugene G. Turner
USA

Silence in the Suburbs

I have come to Christmas Eve Communion
in an unfamiliar, suburban church.
Midnight strikes.
The minister invites us to share the peace
and offer Christmas greetings
to our neighbours in the pew.
Handshakes are exchanged.
In response to polite enquiries I say,
'I'm visiting my son who is ill.'
No one encourages me to say more.
They do not even ask my name.
I sink into silence relieved that he is not here.
The bread and wine are served.
I wonder if they will suffice
to feed my hunger for comfort and support,
to slake my spiritual thirst.
Am I the only needy stranger in their midst tonight?
What other unspoken pain stays unreleased?
I introduce myself to the minister at the door.
I say where I have come from.
I try again to say why I am here.
But his cursory handshake
does not invite deeper conversation
so I leave as I came, hungry and thirsty,
lost and alone,
ashamed of my silence,
ashamed of my church,
struggling to hold on to my faith
battling to believe
that beyond this empty celebration,
the God whose love became flesh and blood
has heard my silent cries and understood.

Jean Mortimer
England

The Alternative
(A Gift from the Church)

You would have us walk alone,
With no one to walk with us.

You would have us wake alone
With no one to wake beside us.

You would have us end the day alone,
With no one to share the day or night.

You would have us bear life alone
With only those you prescribe to help –
From their comfortable and safe distance.

You would have us give all
And receive little to help us to grow and to give.

You would give us lonely nights and empty, endless days –
For your name's sake.

And all this, because God in his infinite wisdom
Gave us a handful of genes here
And gave you a handful of genes there.

Thank you for your gift –
But we prefer not to receive it and return it to the sender.

R. S.
England

Here's a Church

Here's a church that's ceased to be
A church that lives no more
A place where folks weren't welcome
Selective entry on the door.

Helen Garton
England

Number the Stars
(Genesis 15:5)

God said this to Abram, whose faith is 'reckoned to him as righteousness', one verse later.

Our descendants will also be innumerable, those whose lives we
will make a little easier by modelling to them and to an unfriendly
church and culture what it means to be lesbian, gay, bisexual and
transgendered.

Abraham and Sarah's descendants, however, have never had an
easy time of it. Neither will ours. In many ways it's just as difficult to
come out as a youth today as it was twenty years ago. That's why
programmes are needed for our young people.

Homes are also needed for them – our homes, places of occasional
retreat from pressure: emotional, spiritual, sexual. The more we can
open our homes and our hearts without expectations to lesbian, gay,
bisexual and transgendered youth and young adults, the more blessed
our future generations will be.

Chris Glaser
USA

Love One Another
(John 13:34–5)

If only Christians *did* love one another, the whole world would be
saved. If only Christians and Jews and Muslims and Hindus and Sikhs
and Buddhists and New Agers and New Thought Practitioners and
agnostics and atheists *did* love one another, the whole world would be
at peace.

We all forget that we are all beloved by God, that we are all thus
empowered to love others.

Ironic that some heterosexual Christians want to muzzle homosexual and bisexual love. Seems like we need all the love we can get, in
the church and world. Why betray or deny or crucify that love? Why
not serve one another as Jesus did, humbling ourselves to wash one
another's feet, bringing cooling, refreshing waters to those feet, hot
and tired and blistered from life's pilgrimage?

If you think about it, Jesus was rejected for his *spiritual* orientation
of love.

Chris Glaser
USA

Deliverance
(Ephesians 3:1–12)

May the church receive insight
        into the mystery of Christ
which was not made known to the
        human race
        in other generations
as it has now been revealed
        to Christ's holy apostles and prophets
        by the Spirit;
that is how lesbians and gays are joint heirs
        members of the same body,
        and partakers of the promise in Christ Jesus
through the gospel.

Chris Glaser
USA

A Prayer for the Church's Children
Coming Into an Awareness of their Sexuality
(Mark 10:15–16)

Holy God – Father, Mother, Child:
We pray for children and youth,
That our church's sexual immaturity does not taint their appreciation of
your sacred gift of sexuality,
nor associate for them sexual differences with hatred and prejudice,
bashing and name-calling,
suicide and suicidal behaviour.
Bless their sexuality
that it may bring them fulfilling relationships,
faithful love
and spiritual and sensual pleasures.

Chris Glaser
USA

You Are My Beloved Child;
With You I Am Well Pleased
(Mark 1:10–11)

How gay and lesbian youth
would love to hear these words, O God!
From you,
from their earthly mothers and fathers,
from their spiritual fathers and mothers
in the church:
'You are our beloved children;
with you we are well pleased.'

We pray for them in their struggle,
identifying themselves,
identifying their community,
finding significant others
     in a world now infected with AIDS,
     in a society still sick with homophobia.

Dear God,
people wonder why youth run away or are cast away,
why there are so many teen suicides,
why drugs and alcohol cloud so many young minds,
why apparently happy, successful youth
     choose death in its many forms rather than life.

Help us to remember that society's homophobia
is the cause of too much death.
Deliver us from homophobia.
And deliver us from closets created by homophobia,
which hide us as role models for lonely gay youth.

Lead us to say with you, O God,
'You are our beloved children;
with you we are well pleased.'

Chris Glaser
USA

Poisoned Chalice

Here take this chalice,
drink it up!
Drain the dregs and let it settle on your stomach.
Bitter, eh?
Well, it's a poisoned cup you've taken,
and in the time that's left, let me explain.

We're the church,
pure and holy,
and we intend to stay that way.
So we'll poison you all off,
in the name of faith and love.

You can't complain,
you took it freely,
and suffering is what we're all about.
We know you thought different,
had ideas about new life.

But we're the church,
pure and holy,
and we know what was intended.
As for living,
we can't let that happen,
after all
we've been dead for centuries.

**Life Giver,
we take the broken bread
and drink the wine
believing
that in remembering you
and not the death dealers
who pass poisoned chalices
we will rise again.**

Janet Lees
England

Jesus Said

Jesus said
Everyone is welcome into my kingdom, especially those on the margins.
We say
Everyone is welcome into the kingdom, except those on the margins.

Jesus said
Everyone is equal in the eyes of God.
We say
We have made a nice, hierarchical Church where men hold most of the power.

Jesus said
Everyone is made in the image of God.
We say
God is male, white, Western and definitely heterosexual.

Jesus said
Nothing is impossible to God.
We say
We would rather stick to the things we know are possible.

Jesus said
Love your neighbour as yourself.
We say
I'll love my neighbour as long as they are the same as me.

Jesus said
Sell all you have and follow me.
We say
I would rather leave Jesus and his challenging statements at the Church's door.

Jesus said
Feed the hungry.
We say
I think that means feed myself first.

Jesus said
I have come to turn the world and its values upside down.

We say
We have turned the world back up the right way.

Suzi B.
England

A New Piece of Wood

My husband and I, a clergy couple, were on summer vacation when our denomination (the United Church of Canada) wrestled officially with the question of church membership and, therefore, with the ordination of gay and lesbian people.

We were driving home in a remote part of our country, wondering if the decision had been made. Eagerly we listened for any news on the radio but had caught no announcement so far. Our two pre-schoolers, our camping routine and getting in enough miles each day occupied our minds most of the time. But, as we passed through yet one more small town, we noticed their United Church located right on the highway. We glanced over at the board on the front lawn of the church. 'Welcome to . . .' it read but on the second line of the sign, instead of 'Anywhere United Church' the sign read 'Anywhere . . . Church'. Someone had already nailed a small, unfinished piece of wood over the word 'United'. My partner turned to me and said quietly, 'We've got serious problems.'

Betty Lynn Schwab
Canada

The Tauranga Story

I was having a discussion with some psychology students on the subject of Transcendental Meditation, which was all the rage at the time. I wanted to know what the difference was between that and Christian Meditation. They tried to tell me that the latter involved consciously thinking about a subject whereas the former did not. Years before, in the days when I preached sermons I used to practise Christian meditation to help me with subjects to preach about. That evening, even though I had not done anything of the sort for several years, I involved myself in an exercise of Christian meditation. Lo and behold, I found myself in possession of a sermon. That, I found rather amusing: since I had absolutely nothing to do with churches there was not the slightest chance that anybody was going to ask me to preach anywhere at any time. It did, however, prove that the system worked. I remained and still remain, unconvinced that Transcendental Meditation does anything much at all.

A short time after that I was driving from Hamilton to Mount Maunganui with the idea of spending a day on the sands. When I reached the top of the Kaimai saddle, a range of low mountains between the centre of North Island and the east coast, I could see that it was raining hard down there so the idea was washed out. I decided to go into the port of Tauranga instead, look around the shops and have lunch at a restaurant I knew of. But the restaurant was closed for redecoration. So I walked into the next street and found a vegetarian café. Sitting at the next table was a most gorgeous hunk. I suppose he would have been about twenty, young farmer written all over him. I think I must have looked at him harder than I intended because before long he got up from his table and came over to me. I did not feel I was likely to get beaten up. He didn't look the type for that and certainly not in a well patronised café. But I expected to receive advice as to my future behaviour if I wasn't able to talk my way out of it.

He asked, 'May I bring my coffee over to your table?'

Of course he might.

After some small talk he started to talk about my personal salvation. Here was a young guy in his twenties, at the most, talking to someone in his late fifties, about something that the fifty-year-old had been steeped in from his earliest years. I knew exactly where he was leading. I could almost have predicted what he was going to say next. I was wearing round my neck a lambda on a chain. After some minutes of listening to him, I stopped him, and pulling up the chain so that he could see it clearly, I asked him if he knew what it represented. Yes, he knew that I was wearing it as a sign that I was gay. It appeared that he had been heading in that direction until under pressure from his church he 'took Jesus into his heart'. At that point I became quite certain who the sermon which I had received (if that is the right word) was meant for. It was meant for him. So I started doing the talking. The details of the address don't matter, the gist was to the effect that the god of the people who had been teaching him was much too small a god. God was far bigger than they ever knew.

In the end I had to go with him to the bus station otherwise he would have missed his bus for Wellington. He was fascinated by meeting someone of my age and obvious experience of being gay who could say that there need be no conflict with godliness and gayness.

I was in a town I didn't want to be in; in a café I didn't plan to be in; with a sermon I didn't know what to do with because there was a young guy there whose church had let him down.

I sometimes tell people I don't think I believe in God but I think she must have angels and watch their faces while they work it out!

George Bourne
Aotearoa New Zealand

A Meditation on the Stories of David and Jonathan, and Ruth and Naomi
(Readings from 1 and 2 Samuel and Ruth)

Reader One: When David had finished speaking, the soul of Jonathan was bound to the soul of David, and Jonathan loved him as his own soul. Jonathan made a covenant with David, because he loved him as his own soul. Jonathan stripped himself of the robe that he was wearing, and gave it to David, and his armour, and even his sword and his bow and his belt. And Jonathan said to David, 'Whatever you say, I will do for you.'

Reader Two: And after Naomi's husband died, followed by the deaths of her two sons, she said to her daughters-in-law, 'Go back each of you to your mother's house. May God deal kindly with you, as you have dealt with the dead and with me. God grant that you may find security, each of you in the house of your husband.' Then she kissed them and they wept aloud. But to Ruth, who continued to cling to her, she said: 'See, your sister-in-law has gone back to her people and to her gods; return after your sister-in-law.' But Ruth said, 'Do not press me to leave you or to turn back from following you!'

Reader One: Jonathan said to David, 'May God be with you. If I am still alive, show me the faithful love of God; but if I die, never cut off your faithful love from my house, even if God were to cut off every one of your enemies from the face of the earth.' Thus Jonathan made a covenant with David, saying, 'May God seek out the enemies of David.' Jonathan made David swear again by his love for him; for he loved him as he loved his own life. Jonathan said to him, 'Tomorrow is the new moon; you will be missed because your place will be empty.'

Reader Two: Where you go, I will go; where you lodge, I will lodge.

Reader One: David rose from beside the stone heap and prostrated himself with his face to the ground. He bowed three times, and they kissed each other, and wept with each other; David wept the more. Then Jonathan said to David, 'Go in peace, since both of us have sworn in the name of God, saying, "God shall be between me and you, and between my descendants and your descendants, forever."'

Reader Two: Your people shall be my people, and your God my God.

Reader One: On the third day, a man came from Saul's camp, with his clothes torn and dirt on his head. When he came to David, he fell to the ground and did obeisance. David said to him, 'Where have you come from?' He said to him, 'I have escaped from the camp of Israel.' David said to him, 'How did things go? Tell me!' He answered, 'The army fled from the battle, but also many of the army fell and died; Jonathan also died.' Then David took hold of his clothes and tore them; and all the men who were with him did the same. They mourned and wept the death of Jonathan, and fasted until evening.

Reader Two: Where you die, I will die – there will I be buried.

Reader One: David's lamentation over Jonathan's death was taught to the people of Judah: 'Jonathan lies slain upon your high places. I am distressed for you, my brother Jonathan; greatly beloved were you to me; your love to me was wonderful, passing the love of women.'

Reader Two: 'May God do thus and so to me, and more, as well, if even death parts me from you!'

Joe McMurray and Eric Cole
USA

Reflection on Thomas

Once again the truth is denied. We are not believed. The wounded Body of Christ is revealed but there are those who refuse to see it.

Like Thomas, they believe that only they have the truth. They call their friends, their colleagues, liars. They need personal proof.

We tell them of our lives, our pains, our struggles. They tell us we're exaggerating. It isn't true. They don't know any gays or lesbians or bisexuals and therefore we don't exist.

So some of us risk. We stand up. We come out. We stand before them. Still they deny. They haven't seen us suffer so we haven't lost jobs, families, friends.

So some of us risk some more. We show our personal scars, the ones we had hoped we could hide. We show our wounded body. Still it is not enough.

Not until they push their sharp fingernails into the scars; not until their fists cover our bruises; not until they open our unhealed wounds do they begin to believe that perhaps, perhaps, there is some truth.

They open the wounds of the Body of Christ. They break open our scabs and we bleed for them. Our blood is on their hands.

I could understand our enemies denying our stories; calling us names and wanting us to bleed but those are our companions, our friends. We played together; we worshipped together but there is malice in their heart.

Blessed are they who believe without our having to bleed.

Ken DeLisle
Canada

Courage to Love

Prayer

Let us remember that we meet in the presence of God who loves us:
who knows us better than we know ourselves,
(better than we want to know ourselves sometimes)
who knows our needs before we ask;
and who, knowing us, loves us
with a love that is rich and warm, intimate and detailed,
and yet more vast than we can begin to imagine.
God who knows us, loves us:
and so here in God's presence we do not need to pretend
to be other than who we are, or how we are;
we do not need to be anxious, whether for ourselves,
or for others;
here, above all, we do not need to be afraid.

O God our Creator, your love is our home and our refuge,
a sure defence against the storm,
a strong tower where we can take shelter
from the overwhelming wave of pain and hunger,
stress and toil.
We adore you.

O God our Saviour, your love is our guardian and our guide;
a staff on which we can lean
in times of anxiety and over-work,
a support when we are burdened by the weight
of others' need.
We honour you.

O God our Life, your love is the energy
which takes us into each new day,
the faith which gives us courage to love,
the joy which renews us in hope.
We adore you.

O God our Creator, Saviour, Life,
your love is the refuge which holds us,
the fire which warms us,
the light we keep for the sake of travellers in a wild land.
You are steadfast as rock beneath our feet,
and your word is the secure foundation
of our service and our prayer.
In you, we may be assailed,
but we need never be undermined.
We give you thanks and praise.

Philippians 4:4–13

The Refuge

God's love for us is our refuge and our strength

A refuge is the place where we feel secure, loved, cherished – where
we can hide when we feel threatened or in danger – where we can
receive healing – where we can keep the world at bay when we need
to do this.

The refuge is the safe place where we can truly be ourselves – where
we can let down our guard and leave off our protective masks – where

we can expose our wounds and acknowledge ourselves to be weak, flawed, vulnerable – where we can make deep relationships with those who are willing to accept us as we are.

The refuge is the place where we keep our store cupboard of resources – where we place our most precious belongings for protection. It guards the vital resources which support our life. The better resourced our refuge, the firmer our foundation, both in terms of security and in terms of venturing beyond the stronghold.

The refuge is the place where we stand, which we can defend, but from which we must move out if we are to avoid becoming trapped in our own security.

The Border

*God's love for us gives us the courage
to engage with others on the border*

The border is the meeting-place, the crossing where our territory runs up against, or overlaps with, the territory of others. It is the place of trade, sharing, learning, excitement, romance, diplomacy, intrigue. It is the place where we move away from what we know and all that is familiar, trusted, understood, and must engage with that which is unfamiliar, strange, even alien to us. Here we must meet, work with, relate to, those who make us feel uncomfortable because their appearance, ideas, ways are not immediately accessible.

Increasing knowledge may help us to feel more comfortable in these relationships – or it may not. The Other who comes to meet us at the border may continue to be strange, may even turn out to be offensive, awkward, unwilling to co-operate, hostile.

The border is a complex place because we retain the memories of past encounters here. These encounters shape the attitudes and assumptions with which we approach the border. Those we meet there may act in ways which reinforce our prejudices. We must make repeated, persistent efforts to keep the border open as a means of communication.

The open border is a sign of good relationships, equality of power, confidence, peace. The closed border is a sign of suspicion, a power struggle, lack of confidence, the threat of violence. Where those on each side of the border are at war with each other, there might be a buffer zone along the border, a 'no-man's land' where nothing can flourish or even survive for very long.

The Wild Land

God's love for us gives us the courage
to venture out into the wild land

The wild land is not our territory. Nor is it our neighbour's territory. We may claim a piece of it; our neighbour may declare that he or she has rights to it; many people might put their names to pieces of it. But in fact, the wild land cannot be owned by anyone, for it is beyond anyone's control.

The forces which are at work in the wild land are far too powerful for human beings to master, so the land cannot be managed or tamed or exploited for very long. Only with very great care can these things even be attempted and only by those who are prepared to work with the forces, ride them, flow with them, rather than seeking to master them. These forces are impersonal – they have no friends, no enemies – but those who believe that they control their power, or, even worse, become complacent in that belief – soon discover their mistake. Eventually, the wild land will always revert to wildness as the forces break free from any constraint.

And yet, for those who are prepared to approach the wild land as pilgrims respecting its forces and willing to learn the disciplines that they impose, the wild land is a place of breathtaking beauty, of wonderful surprise, of infinite variety, of wealth beyond imagining. For the wild land is fertile, creative, vivid. Because it has no borders, it is unlimited possibility. Because it is available to everyone, but owned by no one, it is unlimited potential. Because it acknowledges no human sovereignty, and its forces treat all human beings alike, it is a place of unrestricted freedom. The wild land is the place of uncertainty and faith, of death and new life, of destruction and renewal. The wild land is the place where the scapegoat is sent out to die and where the prophet receives a word from the lord.

Matthew 7:21–9

Meditation

Let us be built on the rock,
dug down deep into the core,
clawed to the heart of stone,
our buried foundations held fast,
clamped sure, steadied and solid,
adamant.

Let us draw strength from the rock
stand tall, stand straight, course upon course:
chiselled by rain-winds, carved by frost-barbs,
we may flinch but not fail,
and if we are battered, we are not allowed to fall.
Let us draw others to the rock,
shoulder burdens, bear weight,
strengthen limbs about to break,
lift hearts, encourage souls,
speak the word which makes the torn one
smile, and take their first steps whole.

Prayer of Response

Let us draw strength from God who loves us
through our obedience:
our willingness to let God's word be laid down
in our minds – as the foundation of our thoughts,
our imaginings, our creativity,
in our hearts – as the rule of our emotions,
and the guide to our relationships
in our souls – as the ground of our purpose and our hope.
Fill us with your love, that we might be glad.
Rejoice in our hearts, that we might give praise.

Let us draw strength for today from God who loves us,
trusting that our needs are known
and that provision has been made and given,
perhaps where we had not looked to find it;
that tomorrow's need is also known,
and provision is already set aside.
Fill us with your love, that we might be glad
Rejoice in our hearts, that we might give praise.

Let us draw strength for the journey from God who loves us,
feeding each other with encouragement,
and letting our own hearts be nourished by the bread of life;
holding the concerns of friend and stranger,
and receiving the service of our companions on the road.
Fill us with your love, that we might be glad
Rejoice in our hearts, that we might give praise.

Julie M. Hulme
England

A Samaritan
(The story of Glenaven Methodist Church, Dunedin, Aotearoa New Zealand)

Once a certain church fell on hard times. Long had it been a loyal witness in its valley but modern life-styles had stripped it of its Bible Class, Sunday School, Boys' Brigade, study groups and tennis club. Only the Women's Fellowship survived. The Valley Church was near death with no more than ten regular members.

It so happened the National Church, after due consideration, decided it could not provide pastoral care; indeed some murmured among themselves that the valley church had outlived its usefulness and was a financial burden they could well do without.

Now a certain young man, an ex-Baptist minister, happened to be completing a doctorate at the nearby university. He offered part-time ministry for the Valley Church. He proved to be a presbyter of exceptional talents in all areas of ministry –

preaching
        teaching
                pastoral care
                        music and administration.

The young man preached 'unconditional love' and meant it. The marginalised heard of his teaching and came to sample it for themselves.

The alienated found succour and the 'different' a home. Those whose marital status was unconventional discovered a warm welcome. Women who had experienced church as second class citizens were liberated from patriarchal attitudes. Maori found equal partner status in the bicultural journey. Students discovered a depth in his words that met their needs.

The building was altered to provide easy access for the disabled. An attractive lounge was added as a gathering place. The pulpit was lowered and the communion rail removed. The barrier-free sanctuary encompassed the nave prompting dialogue during services – sermons were debated, stories shared and lives changed.

The original elderly congregation was delighted. They loved the young man and the people he attracted. The time came when the congregation saw fit to declare itself *A Reconciling Congregation* meaning they truly welcomed all people, regardless of gender, race, denomination, disability or sexual orientation. An inclusive congregation was born.

In your opinion, who served the valley church best – the National Church, the parish or the homosexual minister?

What is the legacy of this story? Certainly joy, but also heartache, struggle and division. Unconditional love is costly. The young man gave three years of service but the Methodist Conference could not agree to accept an openly homosexual presbyter in full connexion. He resigned.

The story didn't end. The parish has changed forever. The Valley Church remains *A Reconciling Congregation*. Others have joined its stance. The gay presbyter's input is reflected parish-wide through a policy of inclusive hymns and liturgies and a continuing adult education programme. Women are taken seriously, the marginalised valued. Gays hold office from organist to steward. The parish promotes a slogan – Finding Good in Everyone – Finding God in Everyone.

And now years later that minister is fully accepted and serves in one of New Zealand's largest Methodist churches.

Rosalie Sugrue
Aotearoa New Zealand

He Went On His Way
(Luke 4:14–30)

I suppose if Jesus Christ belonged anywhere he belonged in Nazareth.

Most scholars now think he was born there and not in Bethlehem as the Christmas carols would have us believe. His dad was a craftsman in Nazareth making a living from working in wood and stone. The family home was in Nazareth, so Jesus grew up there along with his brothers and sisters.

He probably received some kind of religious education in the local synagogue, and it seems likely that he worked in the family business until, around the age of thirty, he left for good.

He joined the movement of John the Baptist for a while before striking out on his own. In next to no time he built quite a reputation as a teacher and as a healer. People began to follow him as he walked around the Palestinian countryside. From Cana to Capernaum, from Jerusalem to Jacob's Well, people turned out to hear him, see him, be healed by him. After about a year of this something prompted Jesus to head back home to the little hillside village of Nazareth in Galilee.

It must have seemed that a happy homecoming would be assured. Even allowing for a bit of poetic licence on Luke's part, Jesus appears to have been riding the crest of a popularity wave as he arrived at the outskirts of his hometown. The scene is set for him to play the role of the local boy made good; but that is not the way it works out at all. It's interesting that everything begins to turn sour the minute he takes part in worship. Presumably it's in the same synagogue in which he was educated as a child and where he's surrounded by people who knew him then and have heard bits and pieces about what he's been up to since.

Jesus reads some beautiful and treasured words from Isaiah; words that had always held a strong sense of belonging for the Jewish people, because they allowed them to hope for the day when God would act and restore justice to their land. But Jesus changes their meaning. He tells them that he is fulfilling these ancient words in the present, right here and now. Prove it, they respond. But Jesus says, No.

Then he rubs salt into the wound by telling them that because of their parochial pride the so-called chosen people have missed out on God's blessing in the past and are all set to miss out again. He implies that their vision of God is too narrow, too limited, too restricting. That God does not in fact belong to them at all. Not surprisingly this doesn't go down too well with the congregation. So they try un-successfully to kill the man who is foolish enough to point out that nobody owns God. It's a powerful story and every time I read it I am reminded of some similarly powerful events in my own story.

Whilst studying in Germany I attended a weekend workshop to discuss gay and lesbian relationships in the church.

Having spent three years as an ordinand at Knox Theological Hall (Aotearoa New Zealand) following four years working in the com-mercial world and four previous years of tertiary study I considered myself to be an enlightened, modern person.

I was open to all sorts of insights about God, from all sorts of people.

But preferably not gay or lesbian people.

In the course of that weekend workshop I began to realise that in taking refuge in a supposedly impregnable 'biblical' position I was behaving a lot like Jesus' small town compatriots in the gospel story.

I was confronted with fear and even anger in myself at the prospect of giving up parts of my belief system – things I thought were essential for a right relationship with God.

I would have liked God miraculously to reveal to me before attending the workshop that I was right. That 'they' were wrong.

But like the angry and fearful people in Luke's story, I did not get the miracle I wanted.

Like them, I got another quite different miracle instead.

I spent an exhausting but immensely rewarding weekend talking with gay and lesbian people about their faith, their sexuality and their experiences of the Christian Church.

Many of the people with whom I spoke were risking their positions within the Church by attending the workshop and declaring their identity in this way.

And I was humbled by stories that told of people whose faith in Christ had been tested in ways my faith never has and probably never will.

To find Christ in the lives of these people was highly inconvenient for my theology.

It irritated me; made me feel fearful and angry.

But like the crowd from the synagogue in Luke's story, I found I could not hurl an inconvenient Christ from the cliff-top of my prejudices.

Instead, he passed through the midst of my anger and fear.

Turned my neatly ordered theological world upside down.

And went on his way.

Geoff King
Aotearoa New Zealand

Mamzer Jesus
A Meditation

In Luke's story, 4:14–30, about Jesus speaking in his hometown synagogue at Nazareth, he is suddenly and violently rejected by the people who want to hurl him headfirst from the top of the hill on which the town was built. On previous occasions they had welcomed this ordinary hometown boy whose family they all knew and were even amazed at his gracious words about the prophet Isaiah. But something was different this time. This time he changed the words and applied them to himself. This time Jesus openly told them something he felt and believed about himself that they did not want to hear. He told them who he thought he was and what his mission was. He said he was a God-anointed prophet like Elijah and Elisha. He said he was sent to declare that the traditionally accepted labels of *outcast, sinner, toll collector, law-breaker, unclean, enemy, prostitute, impure* put on certain individuals and even entire classes of people were, in fact, in God's eyes also able to be whole and acceptable to God. Such a claim flew right in the face of the label they had already given him from birth. Who was he to step outside that label and role?

In his book, *Rabbi Jesus*, Bruce Chilton advances the theory that because of the suspicions about the religious legitimacy of his paternity, Jesus was classified in Israelite society as a *mamzer*. A *mamzer* was not a person of illegitimate birth but a child born from a prohibited sexual union such as incest or sex with the wrong person like a man outside the woman's own community. If Joseph lived in Bethlehem and Mary in Nazareth, suggests Chilton, then it was impossible to prove he was the father. Opponents of the Jesus movement later slandered Jesus by saying his birth came about from an illegal union of Mary and a soldier of the occupying Roman army which was Israel's sworn enemy.

Another meaning of *mamzer* was a 'silenced one', a person without a voice in the public groups that regulated and controlled the social, political and religious life of the Israelite community. They lived as a caste apart, unable to marry according to the religious traditions and were often excluded from the religious life of the community. They were in truth ostracised from their own religious family. The book of Deuteronomy says, 'No *mamzer* shall enter the congregation of the Lord.' That statute continued for ten generations.

He was a circumcised Son of the Covenant and permitted to speak in synagogues outside his hometown where the circumstances of his birth might not have been known publicly. But the fact of his doubtful fatherhood must have played some part in how he viewed himself early on in relation to his neighbours, the village, the clan, his place in the synagogue and his mission and ministry. Throughout his life Jesus lived and worked in that ambiguous state of belonging to God's chosen people and being an outcast in his own society. This status helps us understand some of the reactions to his deeds and words among various groups like the Pharisees and Scribes, the Essenes, the Levites, the Sadducees, the Chief Priests and the Elders; even some of those ordinary people of the land who came to believe in him: 'We are not illegitimate,' they retort in John's gospel (8:41) suggesting that Jesus might be: 'We have one Father, God.'

Could this explain his strong predilection for the other voiceless people in his world – the sinners, the lepers, the unclean, the prostitutes, the toll collectors, the possessed and those on the religious, political and social margins of his day? And yet he ate with the leading religious leaders, spoke in the synagogues outside Nazareth and observed the annual feasts in Jerusalem's temple as an observant Jew.

Jesus was a lay person, not an anointed member of the priesthood or even one of the Temple assistants. He was a simple rabbi with a few followers and a very new message. But he was also, in turn, a prophet, an exorcist of impure spirits and a holy man who could heal. His status as *mamzer* did not stop him from speaking when and where he thought necessary. Nor did he decline to remain silent when he knew his words would have no effect, as when he stood in total silence before Pilate refusing to engage in a dialogue with him.

Like people in our congregations, churches and religious groups today, he called the religious leadership to open their eyes and minds and hearts to new things that the God of Israel was doing. Quietly and simply he restored a person's health and human dignity with a few words of hope for some; words of forgiveness and encouragement for others; with a simple gesture of touch, holding or embracing. If impurity through sickness, blood, death and body fluids made one unclean and therefore an outcast, Jesus restored them to wholeness of body and also to the body of the community to witness to his power and to bring others to faith in him. If impurity was contagious and people had to be segregated, Jesus said purity was contagious also. All were fit for his kingdom. Purity came from within a person and when that person experienced that kind of purity of heart, wholeness and belonging, then no one could be labelled *mamzer*. All had voices. All had dignity. All had responsibilities for their gifts. All had the mission to build the community of God's family. All were welcomed to dine with Jesus and that was the sign of their acceptance and dignity in God's eyes. The table fellowship of Jesus with the rich and the poor, with saints and sinners, with outcasts and Jewish religious leaders replaced the cleansing water by John the Immerser. Table fellowship was the new sign of the outpouring of God's cleansing Spirit bringing purity and wholeness and acceptance in Jesus, calling each to life and growth in the reign of God.

There are *mamzers* of many kinds in our churches and congregations today who quietly and silently accept their status because they fear rejection by the community if they speak or identify themselves in certain ways. They choose silence because in the wisdom of their lives there is 'a time to reap and a time to sow; a time to be silent and a time to speak' and only they can discern when to sow and speak. There are others who decide to speak and act only in limited circumstances where there are no threats to the comfort level of their personal status before God. And there are still other *mamzers* who feel empowered by a spirit or a Spirit to speak openly and honestly about their relationship with the God they love and worship and the impact of that relationship on their life in the community. They choose to sow the seeds of justice and truth and to reap a harvest of understanding and affirmation. Jesus' status as *mamzer* was perhaps in God's mysterious plan a way to remind us all that God chooses the simple to confound the wise, that power is shown in weakness, that grace was sufficient for Paul's struggle with the sting of the flesh, that in God's eyes we are all *mamzers*. It is only God's love shown in Jesus' death and rising lived in our bodies and souls that makes us beloved, whole, pure and daughters and sons, brothers and sisters in the human family.

Robert Nugent
USA

A Song of Welcome

It doesn't matter who you are or where you're coming from,
This place has got an open door to make you feel at home.
And if you will come in and join us, you will soon perceive
That though we might all have our doubts,
    there's something we believe:

The shape and form of every person comes from God's own hand;
And though you might not recognise it, or yet understand,
To all who see your deepest nature there's a sign that shows
You share a likeness with the One
    from whom all life arose.

This world may soil you or contort you, robbing you of pride,
And people leave you feeling small, with words aimed to deride,
Still nothing can defeat the truth that you derive from One
Who counts your worth today as much
    as when you first were born.

So join your hands with ours and let us grow in self-respect,
And hear the story of a Friend who calls us to connect
Around this table where we share the bread and wine that give
A healthy new-found confidence,
    and let your spirit live.

Stephen Jay
England

BREAKING THE BARRIERS

The Vast Varieties of Humankind

O God, of all the vast varieties of humankind, help us to move beyond the exclusiveness of an 'either/or' mentality to the inclusiveness of a 'both/and' way of thinking which moves behind the definitions to the mystery, beyond over-simplifications to the complexity of your all-embracing reality.

W. L. Wallace
Aotearoa New Zealand

The Disturbing Comforter

O God, who comes as the disturbing comforter,
shattering the rigid preconceptions of our minds and hearts,
give us the grace to welcome your coming,
>to trust beyond where we can see,
>to have hope in the midst of chaos,
>to learn from our mistakes,
>to accept your forgiveness
and to walk steadfastly in the way of Gospel gladness.

W. L. Wallace
Aotearoa New Zealand

Prayer for the Spirit
(John 14:17, 26; 16:13)

God, source of all life, we pray:
>Fulfil your promise and bless us with your presence.
>Without you we cannot live as a new creation.
>Only you lead us into the truth.
>Only you broaden our horizon and our heart
>>so that we can accept each other
>>with empathy and without prejudice –
>>whatever our culture and tradition,
>>our gender or sexual orientation,
>>or our age and education may be.
Each day transform us so that we may become more human,
>more friendly towards our neighbour
>>and all your creation.

Make us co-workers and partners
        in your work of love and liberation.
May evil be overcome with good in us and around us.
        May your will prevail.
                For your endless mercy hear our prayers
                        and accept the grateful praise of your name.
                Amen

Jana Opocenska
Switzerland

A Form Of Confession

You reveal the depth of compassion,
as we shelter in our own preoccupation.
Lord, have mercy.
Lord, have mercy.

You challenge the narrowness of our vision,
as we underestimate the bounds of grace.
Christ, have mercy.
Christ, have mercy.

You offer life in all its fullness,
as we build the walls of self security.
Lord, have mercy.
Lord, have mercy.

Richard Watson
England

Prayer of Confession

Leader: O Christ, you open up the close-minded,
                    you soften the hard-hearted,
                    you lift up the downtrodden.

A moment for sitting with Christ

Leader: We confess

People on the sides: We have been close-minded and hard-hearted.

People in the centre: It freezes us.
Soon we are too numb to care –
about ourselves or for others.

A moment for private confession

Leader: We confess

People on the sides: We have experienced the pain of being shut out,
downtrodden, excluded, unwanted.

People in the centre: It freezes us.
Soon we are too numb to care –
about ourselves or for others.

A moment for private confession

Leader: O Christ,

All: forgive us.
Warm our spirit
until with your grace
we, too, open up the close-minded,
soften the hard-hearted,
and lift up those who are downtrodden.

Betty Lynn Schwab
Canada

Life From Your Love

Dear Lord
When you lived on this earth
You were marginalised, oppressed, loved and misunderstood.
May we who are marginalised, oppressed, loved and misunderstood
Derive courage from your strength,
Hope from your life
And life from your love.

Michael Reiss
England

Glad to be Gay

When I can . . .
shout my sexuality
from the rooftops,
dance cheek to cheek
with my partner
in any party, disco or club
without being cat-called,
stared at or asked to leave

then
I'll be glad to be gay.

When I can . . .
embrace my partner in the street
and walk hand in hand in the park
without being the butt
of dirty jokes,
snide innuendo,
physical or verbal attacks

then
I'll be glad to be gay.

When I can . . .
walk my way,
talk my way,
dress my way,
nail my true colours to the mast,
put prejudice and bigotry back into the closet,
where they, not I belong;
when 'Gay Pride' marches and demonstrations
are no longer needed

then
I'll be glad to be gay.

When homosexual marriage is legal,
homosexual couples deemed fit to foster or adopt,
homosexual partners counted as next of kin,
homosexual clergy not required to pretend to be celibate

then
I'll be glad to be gay.

In the meantime . . .
sometimes I will be glad,
sometimes angry or sad
as I wait and work
for a more just, accepting,
tolerant and unhypocritical world.

A Prayer

Patient and persistent God,
listen to my pleading
hear my cries
help me to believe
that my suffering will be seen,
my protest heard,
even when everyone seems
to pass by on the other side
or turn a deaf ear.
Show me how to work for change,
and when to wait for change to take effect.
But do not let the waiting be too long.
Amen.

Jean Mortimer – for Matthew and many of his friends
England

Rights of Passage

At my birth
I was wrapped in my parents' love
and cradled in their care.

At my baptism
I was blessed and named,
received into the church
and welcomed as a child of God.

At my coming of age
there was a family party
and I received the key of the door.

My coming out was different . . .
without ceremony or celebration;
an awkward, inarticulate struggle
to find the right moment,
the most acceptable words
to explain and justify myself
to family, friends and the
world at large.
This most meaningful rite of passage
remains a milestone unmarked.

I love babies and children,
but I will never know the joy
of cradling and caring for my own.
I love God and I still want to believe
that God loves and welcomes me,
but I cannot belong to a church
where some count me abnormal,
sinful or cursed.

I love my partner.
Our commitment to each other
is as strong and true
as any marriage 'made in heaven',
blessed by the church
and recognised by law,
but our loving union must remain
unorthodox, unofficial.

Though I grieve for all that is denied me,
I will not let my life be marked by loss.
I will celebrate my right of passage
from struggle to acceptance,
through the power of resurrection,
through the pain of the cross.

Jean Mortimer – for Matthew and many of his friends
England

Shame

Our hearts cry out to our God,
we plead with our Creator.

Day and night your church brings shame to your holy name.
They claim to follow your love,
to uphold justice and peace.

Yet, they have forgotten your love.

We hang our heads in shame by our association.
Give us courage to speak up for our brothers and sisters
that your love may rule once more.

Shame on you church leaders,
who feel constrained to reject and denounce,
whilst the glimmers of private compassion
are masked behind a cold public face.

Shame on you people,
you congregations of comfortable silence.
By your inactivity
you sanction exclusion and prejudice.

You have forgotten God's love.

We hang our heads in shame by our association.
Give us courage to speak up for our brothers and sisters
that your love may rule once more.

Shame on you politicians,
who hope that by gagging and suppression,
you can quell the very life force
of your 'problem' constituents.

Shame on you teachers and educators,
you parents and guardians.
You keep us in ignorance,
while your sexual double standards
fan the flames of mis-information.

You have forgotten God's love.

We hang our heads in shame by our association.
Give us courage to speak up for our brothers and sisters
that your love may rule once more.

Liz Styan
England

Wise and Loving God

Wise and loving God –
where prejudice makes cruel conduct blind – open hooded eyes to
your truth.
Where condemnation is deaf to alternatives – make your inner voice
heard.
Where bigotry shuns contact – show the power of your loving touch.
And wherever people are hurting – make them aware of the depth of
your compassion –
and of your ability to transform broken lives,
for your understanding love is often their only hope in an unfeeling
world.

Marjorie Dobson
England

Keep Our Minds Open

Creator God,
the world you gave us is so diverse
that its complexities may never be unravelled,
so extravagant that its riches may never be spent,
and so extraordinary that we find it a constant source of amazement.

Yet, when we come to people, we expect it all to be so simple.
As if everyone made in your image should look and act the same.

God of many faces,
help us to rejoice in our diversity,
to be prepared to be understanding about other people's complexities,
to be generous in our dealings with others
and to be amazed at the new revelations you give to us each day.

We cannot all agree about everything –
that would be unrealistic –
but we can follow the pattern set by Jesus,
who accepted all who were prepared to take up his cross
and be obedient to your will.

Understanding and all knowing God,
as we travel the road of faith together,

keep our minds open and our hearts united,
so that barriers fall and images fade
as we join in the worship and work of your kingdom.

Marjorie Dobson
England

A Matter of Human Rights

I have no human rights.

I'm different
therefore I have no human rights.

I look different
therefore I have no human rights.

I look and act differently
and people say that won't do
therefore I have no human rights.

I am different
and people say that won't do
because I won't fit into one of their boxes
don't conform to their stereotype
therefore I have no human rights.

A society has its rules and codes – all unspoken, all unwritten, all
unknown by everyone. A society has a place for everyone and they
have to stay in it. A society frowns on anything that is 'different'.

I don't conform
Like the single mother – she brought it on herself
Like the black family living in a white area – asking for trouble.
Like the lesbian lovers living openly as a gay couple –
    it's such a disgrace
    flaunting it like that
    that kind of thing should be kept in private.
Like the homeless person begging for change on the street –
    that kind of thing
    shouldn't be out in the open
    shouldn't be encouraged.

Like the bisexual woman – well she's only playing games.
Like the gay man wanting to be a Christian –
      he's been told that kind of thing
      won't be tolerated.
Like the man with long hair – really he should tidy himself up.
Like the child who asks
why . . . ?

I am different
I don't conform
therefore I ask for all I get.

If people look down their noses at me in the street,
if people call me cruel names
      laugh mercilessly at me and ignore my feelings,
if people look at me and tell me I'm not wanted,
if people gossip behind my back and slander my name,
if people deny me employment and have me forced out of my house,
If people attack me,
      raining violence down upon me
      because I don't fit in,
if people cut me out,
      reject me,
      because I'm not 'socially acceptable'
if people hate me because of who I am
What should I expect – it's all my fault, isn't it?

I have no human rights.

I am different
therefore I have no human rights.

Drew Payne
England

Outsiders

The Relatives and Carers Support group has been cancelled
but I have not been informed.
I stand alone in the alleyway outside the locked security door,
waiting in vain for someone to let me in.
I rattle the metal grille on the window

but there is no one there.
Saturday afternoon shoppers hurry by, trying not to look me in the
    eye.
It is cold and windy and it starts to rain.
Lunchtime drinkers exchange knowing looks
as they pass by me on their way out of the pub.
I want to scream and shout at them.
What can they know of my son's plight and pain?
but the anger and hurt remain locked inside.
I give up and go home.
Did I get the day and time wrong?
I discover later that it was not my fault.
I am the victim of circumstances beyond my control . . .
The stress-related illness of a support worker . . .
Administrative changes . . . funding cuts . . .
Office chaos . . . an incomplete address list . . .
Too many demands on too few people with too little time.
Apologies are offered and accepted but my anger and sense
of isolation remain.

We are outsiders, my son and I.
We have to find the courage to stand alone,
knocking on doors that remain bolted against us
even in the places set up for our support and care.
There are too many like us.
Resources are limited.
Public opinion is apathetic and hostile
and private compassion will never be enough.

Christ the outsider,
lover of the outcast and oppressed,
give me the courage to risk rejection and hostility,
run rings around bureaucracy and red tape,
run the gauntlet of wagging fingers and tongues
in the fight for justice and acceptance,
the battle for realistic funding, benefits and support.
Give to me and my son the courage of your convictions.
Give to me and my son the courage and strength of your love.

Jean Mortimer – for Matthew and many of his friends
England

Dancing on the Edge

You take one step forward and three steps back,
you're not sure of the rhythm and it's confidence you lack
for you fear that on this journey you will leave the beaten track
but you're dancing, you're dancing on the edge.

Your family have abused you so from now you're all alone;
the doorways of the city are the place you call your home
and you really do not know if you can make it on your own,
so you're dancing, you're dancing on the edge.

The baby wakes you screaming and you don't know what to do;
the giro's almost finished but all the bills are due
and there's no one that you trust, no one you can turn to
as you're dancing, you're dancing on the edge.

You've fled from persecution and you want to find some peace;
but they've put you in a prison and you can't get your release
and you know they'll send you back to face the secret police,
for you're dancing, you're dancing on the edge.

The pain you feel inside is too much for you to bear,
so you turn to drink and drugs to find some comfort there
and the only human contact is the needle that you share
as you're dancing, you're dancing on the edge.

When the church will not accept you because they know you're gay
and the righteous congregation all turn their face away
and you wonder who their God is when they're kneeling down to pray
as you're dancing, you're dancing on the edge.

When they've pushed you to the limit and you feel you can't go on;
rejected and reviled and your hope has almost gone:
in Jerusalem, this happened to God's only precious Son
as he was dancing, dancing on the edge.

Sometimes together, sometimes far apart;
to love song or martial tune, we each must make a start;
sometimes, quite simply, to the rhythm of His heart,
we're dancing, we're dancing on the edge.

Alix Brown
England

A Prayer for Lesbians and Gay Men in Latin America

(Psalm 103:6–7)

Dear God,
   this fundamental portion of a favourite psalm
         is commonly omitted in our comfortable liturgies
            and hymnic paraphrases.

         No wonder, God!

It's easier to domesticate you
      for idolatrous incantation
than to worship in Spirit and Truth –
      and pay the 'cost of discipleship'.
Authentic Lesbian and Gay Liberation
      is but the most recent chapter in the story
            of your historical project
            of cosmic liberation.

We pray for the forty million
      Gay men and Lesbians in Latin America,
            for the handful of national pastors
            and missionaries who seek to minister to them,
and for the struggle for all human rights and dignity
      on a continent long dominated
            by violence, oppression and poverty.

Tom Hanks
USA/Argentina

A Prayer for Straight Men Who Are in the Closet

God of creation,
you made all people sexual.
We straight men confess we spend
      a lot of time in the closet
      anxious about our sexual nature.
We are often afraid and pre-occupied
      with potency –
      how we compare with others,
      our 'performance,'
and closet these fears with macho,
      inflated and sexist behaviours.

Teach us through our gay brothers
      that our sexual nature is a gift
      for community, not competition,
      to be honoured in ourselves
      and in others.
We need the company, trust and
      affection of other men,
      but closet these needs
      in stereotypical banter, jokes,
      and calculating behaviour
      to avoid being thought gay.

Teach us through the example
      of our gay brothers
      that in risk and honesty
      with other men, we will find
      the company of your Spirit,
      and a deeper, truer understanding
      of what it means to be male.
We long for acceptance of who we are
      and what we are,
but too often we closet that longing
      in either fear or rejection
      of gays and others.

Teach us through your son Jesus
      and through your gay servants
      that we cannot find acceptance
      of ourselves
      through rejection of those
      you have made in your image.

Through Jesus who did not hide
      but shared his life with all,
      help us straight men
      to leave our closets.

George M. Wilson
USA

I Have Heard Your Cries
A Litany of Affirmation
for homosexual men and women

Insert the names of the people concerned and encourage them to prepare their own stanzas appropriate to their experiences.

The Loving, Liberating God,
who holds a rainbow arch
of acceptance and hope
over your downcast head,
Says to you . . .

I have heard your cries;

When you longed to be able to tell someone
yet dared not name a love like yours.

> When the one you loved has left you
> to look for comfort in another's embrace.

> > When believers have berated you
> > as blasphemous and bent

I have heard your cries;

When thugs have bashed and beaten you
or trampled you with hobnailed words.

> When you have wept by an isolated bedside
> and been the only one to hold death's hand

I have heard your cries;

When your longing to parent children
Has been dismissed as antisocial or unnatural.

> When you have lost your job
> your dignity or your self-respect,
> because of other people's bigotry or fear

The Loving, Suffering God,
who was hammered to a cross
Says to you . . .

I will stretch out my arms to defend you;

> When the fist of fear is screwed up in a rage against you;
> When the finger of suspicion is pointed in scorn

I will reach out my arms to support you;

> When it seems like all the world is against you;
> When you long to be accepted for what you are

I will hold out my arms to welcome and embrace you;

> When you are sick of being shunned
> or told to stick together with your kind

The Loving, Suffering, Liberating God
Says to you . . .

I will bring you through this sea of trials,
I will hold you in the hollow of my hand.
For you belong with all my people.
I have called you . . .
And my promise stands.

Jean Mortimer
England

Openness and Sharing

An officially endorsed liturgy of blessing, as well as affirming God's
love for the couple themselves, would help immeasurably towards
creating in society the same acceptance and support for gay partnerships that any marriage needs to flourish. Among the sadnesses
frequently imposed on gay people are the inability to celebrate their
relationship publicly and the need to keep their love secret from
family or colleagues or friends. As Sanderson notes in *Making Gay
Relationships Work*, this enforced secrecy robs the relationship of
dignity, denies it space to grow, and deprives it of the kind of support
network that we recognise is essential to marriage. Maximising the
possibility of openness and sharing is as vital to the health of a gay
relationship as to any other. Heterosexual Christians of goodwill need
to recognise the heroic level of courage and the cost which may be
involved in overcoming the fear of 'coming out'. If they are in a

position to help, there is plenty of help they can give. For homosexual partnerships, simple things that married couples take for granted – joint invitations, anniversary cards, inquiries about one's partner – become immensely important signs of affirmation. The whole point is that, whatever one calls it, the relationship is analogous to a marriage and should be reacted to in the same way.

Jeffrey John
England

To Mercy, Dead of AIDS at Twenty-One

It was my job to take your details down.
I sat beside you, pen poised and I asked
name, age, status, weight and occupation.

You told me none of these: progressing AIDS
had robbed you of your speech; your smile
sought mine and told me all that I could know

henceforth, of you. Then trembling, you drew
an orange from your pocket. Colour glowed
against your long, dark fingers and you peeled

the pitted strips back, slowly, one by one,
until the sweetest centre was revealed.
You opened up the ripened segments carefully

and placed two pieces gently in my palm.
I put my papers down, still blank and useless,
and we ate the orange globe together.

Mercy, you shared with me all you had left:
your eyes half shut, your movements shaky, slow.
Mercy you were, where no mercy was shown,

while you held my hand fast as doctors came
and helped you walk away. Later a nurse,
unthinking said, 'I wouldn't have touched that fruit.'

Mercy, today I still revere our meal. I long
to touch once more your hand, see you again.
You did not show up at your next appointment:

they said you'd died. And all the powers-that-be
lamented my sad lack of information.
– It was my job to write your details down.

Anne Richards
England

Litany of Healing
(from the liturgy 'Drops for Water')

Leader: In the beginning . . .
All: **In the beginning . . .**
Leader: There was only pain and anger.
All: **In the beginning . . .**
Leader: There was only denial and humiliation.
All: **In the beginning . . .**
Leader: There was only frustration and fury.
All: **In the beginning . . .**
Leader: There was only loneliness and destruction.
All: **In the beginning . . .**
Leader: What else was there. Tell us and we will listen.
All: **In the beginning . . .**

Leader: Gracious God of Justice, Loving Goddess of Restoration, in the beginning there was all of this and more. You know our hearts and our minds, our feelings and our thoughts. Be with us as we mourn the pain of individuals and the entire community in the face of betrayal and abuse. Strengthen us as we break silence and confront evil, as we support one another and cry out for justice. We ask this in the name of all women and children. Amen. Blessed Be. Let it be so.

The Stone Ritual

(The leader picks up a rock and shows it to those gathered.)

The stone ritual symbolises a release from pain and a renewal of loving, healing energy. As we sit in this circle together, let us relax and focus on the stone. (*Pause.*) Let us pass the stone around the circle. As you receive the stone, hold it, imagine that you are pouring your pain into it, and then pass the stone to the next person.

When each one has filled the stone with her or his pain, the leader puts the stone in a bowl of water, washes it, and dries it with a towel.)

Let us pass the stone around the circle again. This time when you receive it, hold it and fill it with loving energy.

(When each person has filled the stone with loving energy, place it in the centre of the circle.)

Let us reflect on the stone, the drops of water, released from pain and filled with loving energy. Please share what you would like to about this experience.

Litany of Healing

All: **In the beginning . . .**
Leader: there is the support of community.
All: **In the beginning . . .**
Leader: there is courage to speak truth to power.
All: **In the beginning . . .**
Leader: there is the compassion of friendship.
All: **In the beginning . . .**
Leader: there is the wisdom of love.
All: **In the beginning . . .**
Leader: what else is there? Tell us and we will support you.
All: **In the beginning . . .**

Sending Forth

Let us go forth from this safe place filled with support for one another. When times are tough – and they will be – let us remember that this time we are not alone.

Let us go forth from this safe place committed to working to create a world where abuse is non-existent.

Let us go forth from this safe place remembering we are like drops of water . . . and the water comes again.

Diann Neu
USA

We Patiently Wait

In her poem, 'The Final Solution',[1] Pamela Sneed speaks about how lesbianism is described as a disease by parents and the 'moral majority' and that if our perversion is not cured there will be a 'final solution'. I like to think these things are not that bad and most days they are not. Then, I remember that we were made to wear pink triangles in the concentration camps, that thousands were killed and no one ever talks about that. I remember that even people I love think homosexuality is a disease that can be cured. I remember that I cannot kiss my lover in the street, that I cannot tell anyone she is my lover, that I cannot take her home, that I cannot take her out with me to certain events. I remember until recently I would never have told any-one who I really was, that I cannot have my union recognised by the church, though it has already been recognised by God for more than a decade, that I cannot adopt children, that when I die my loved one will probably inherit nothing. I remember that my church and most other churches do not accept me fully as I am, though they could not function without us. I remember and I get angry.

'Love your neighbour as you love yourself' (Luke 10:25) is the greatest commandment. It doesn't say only your straight neighbours.

'There is no longer Jew or Greek, there is no longer slave or free, there is no longer male and female; for all of you are one in Christ Jesus' (Galatians 3:28). Therefore, though straight, gay or bisexual, we are all the same and equal in the eyes of God.

'After Moses and Aaron went to Pharaoh and said, "Thus says the Lord, God of Israel, Let my people go ... "' (Exodus 5:1). In his book *The Word is Out*,[2] Chris Glaser tells how lesbians and gay men can readily identify with such liberation. We have suffered the confine-ment and prejudice, discrimination and abuse of the closet, the closet both self-imposed and forced upon us by many 'pharaohs' ranging from parents to ministers of local congregations. And still it continues. Many of the mainline churches are now legislating against homo-sexuality, it not being enough to just ignore the issue. Jesus took the outcasts to himself, the sinners, the tax collectors, the 'gays' of his era. He sat down and ate with them and washed their feet. Isn't the role of the church to be like Jesus?

[1] *Imagine Being More Afraid of Freedom than Slavery*, Pamela Sneed, Henry Holt & Company, 1998
[2] *The Word is Out*, Chris Glaser, HarperSanFrancisco, 1994

You Can't Criminalise Love

A teenager can buy a gun and kill thirteen classmates,
but two people in love can't get married.
Four white policemen can kill a black immigrant,
shoot him forty-one times
and suffer no punishment,
but two people in love can't adopt children.
Distant relatives can keep a father from his son,
because he's 'Castro's puppet', but in many places
two people in love can't legally make love.

You can't criminalise love
no matter how hard you try.

We're your son, brother, father, friend,
your daughter, sister, mother, friend.
We're good enough to die in your army,
as long as you don't know who we are.
We're good enough to teach your children,
as long as you don't know who we are.
We're the best church leaders,
until you know who we are.

You can't criminalise love
no matter how hard you try.

Someday, we will ban all guns
and make same sex marriages a legal right.
All people will believe racism is a crime
and families come in all shapes and sizes
and sometimes with two mommies.
We will treat all immigrants the same,
not just those fleeing communism
and the next Pope will be young, coloured and gay.

'When you tell the truth, justice is done, but lies lead to injustice'
(Proverbs 12:17).

Lies and silence lead to injustice. 'Silence Kills' was a catch phrase
for the AIDS awareness campaign and so it did and continues to do,
not just literally but spiritually. Silence is eating people alive. We have
ministers who cannot be and say what God created them to be and
say, we deny people their rights, we exclude them from everything

from family picnics to staffroom chitchat, because they cannot say something as simple as we went out to dinner, or we went to the pictures, for fear of what the question 'with whom?' might lead to.

'We hope for something we have not yet seen and we patiently wait for it' (Romans 8:25). Who waits more patiently than us? Now for seven years [since 2000] the United Reformed Church has declared a moratorium on resolutions about the human sexuality issue. 'Six years you shall sow your field and six years you shall prune your vineyard and gather in their yield; but in the seventh year there shall be a Sabbath of complete rest for the land, a Sabbath for the Lord . . . The land will yield its fruit and you will eat your fill and live on it securely' (Leviticus 25:3, 19).

Naomi Young
England/USA

Waiting for Full Acceptance by the Church

Colour the sky blue: dark blue, deep blue, cloudless blue;
Paint the garden with butterflies: hedge brown, meadow brown, tor-
    toiseshell,
Fill the trees with singing birds with gaily tinted feathers;
Make the grass green, lush green, with the occasional clover for a
    warm honey bee.
Laden the boughs with ripening fruit, the beds with bright flower
    heads;
Glory in the richness of creation.
Look and see that the harvest is coming.
Taste not, for it is bitter yet to savour.

Sarah Ingle
England

I Am Swinging at the End of My Tether

Help me, my God, my support,
    for I am swinging at the end of my tether.
For days I have been barely enduring.
I don't know how much longer I can last.
I arise most mornings discouraged,
    my head heavy, my body slow.

I return many nights crying,
   wetting my pillow with shame.
Your people ought to cope better,
   not toss themselves hither and yon.
I have lost most of my courage.
Every little thing gets me down.
Once I enjoyed fine prospects.
Like a meadow my life opened out.
Now my ways are dull and laboured.
You have clouded my soul,
   ripped my fine dreams away.
What good does this do you, O God?
How can our misfortune redound to your praise?
Into your hands I commit my spirit
   but my bones give me little joy.
I do not ask for money or status.
I have no desire for worldly fame.
It would be enough
   to feel your peace in my soul.

John Carmody
USA

God of Night

'A light shining in the darkness' is how you are described
But we know you to be God in the pitch black of night.
You are Emmanuel, God with us.

When we are rejected by our friends on coming out;
When we are sneered at by the stranger in the street;
When we are attacked for simply being who we are;
When our local church community tells us to go away;
When we are alone, bereft, for no one really cares;

Help us to turn to you in trust in the hours of dark,
Knowing that you shared with us the agony of being on a cross.

Sarah Ingle
England

Open the Box!

Dear Enemy, why do you hate me so?
Is it that I as lesbian challenge you,
Made as I am, imagined after God?

And is God set free from the 'Father' box
Too much for you,
Too wild to comprehend,
Too fearful to be true?

But this God is not new,
Depicted in the Rublev icon:
God of strength in relationship;
Bond of love round symbols of sacrifice;
Of no particular gender;
Empowering through mutuality.
Dare to seek the door for we may humbly enter
to find ourselves renewed.

Dear Enemy, I care for you.
Can you find it in your heart to have compassion too?

Sarah Ingle
England

Confusion

Black and white,
once innocent,
now politically correct.
Male and female,
clear-cut
no longer.
Right and wrong,
edges blurred
by genetics, environment,
psychology.
Values and norms,
absorbed in childhood,
fuelled by faith,
overturned by change.

Help me, Lord,
blundering through
new moral mazes,
to tread lightly
in areas strange to me
and to speak softly
in unfamiliar surroundings.

Keep my mind open, Lord,
to possibilities
not yet considered
and, when acceptance is difficult,
keep me loving
beyond my reason.

Marjorie Dobson
England

What's In a Word?

What's in a word?
think carefully.

God – Father
Did your father beat you?

God – Justice
Did you get a fair trial?

God – Nature
Did the earthquake kill your family?

God – Love
Did love hurt you?

God All
All Beauty
All love – pure love
Sensual
Touching
Feeling

A candle flickering
A stream flowing
The feeling of floating, flying

Think carefully
of your words.

Naomi Young
England/USA

Them
(Matthew 25; John 21)

So you love me, do you?
but who are you?

do you want me
to put up with you?

or love you?

Problem.
Not mine.
Problem.
Yours.
Them.

So you love me, do you?
and you want to share it?

So do I.
So do They.
With you
with me
with us
No buts.

You love me, do you?
I'm one of Them
Is that a problem?

Because so are you.

Not quite nice
Not quite nice.
My God wouldn't like it.
He'd better not, anyway
or I'll get a better one
more tasteful
that won't complain.

David Coleman
Wales

Words With Mother

Dear Mother,

Thanks for making me a
heterosexual, so that I will
not be identified as 'pagan'
and suffer discrimination as
well as humiliation from the
majority of people.

Thanks for giving me a
church where I can obtain
sisters' and brothers'
support. Unlike homosexuals
who are expelled from the
Church, I can enjoy the
Church's fellowship. They
must wander outside.

Thanks for giving me faithful
pastors. My spiritual life
grows under their pastoral
care. Unlike those
homosexual Christians who
are being neglected as lost
sheep, I do not have to search
for a way of life on my own.

My dear daughter,

How can you have forgotten
love makes no difference,
between rich and poor,
between different sexual
orientations?

How can you have forgotten
when I was in the world, I
struggled with the sinners,
prostitutes, those who were
oppressed and discriminated
against?

How can you have forgotten
I left the other ninety-nine
sheep and went looking for
the one that got lost until I
found it?

How can you have forgotten
I asked you to go to the
disregarded Samaritan?

Thanks for making me holy,
for accepting me as righteous
and for allowing me to
worship you and praise you
in the Church of high
prestige, unlike those
homosexual Christians who
worship you secretly and
walk near you suffering
others' blame.

Thanks for bestowing me
with wisdom to differentiate
between the sinful and the
innocent. Unlike those stupid
Christians who are willing to
walk with homosexuals,
worship you with them, feast
in their house, infringe upon
your name.

My daughter, now you view
the Church as your own
property and reject the ones I
love. Now you view your
sisters and brothers as
sinners. You see the speck in
their eyes but pay no
attention to the log in your
own eye.

My daughter, the one who
hurts me is not them but you.

Winnie Ma
Hong Kong
(translated by Ling Ho)

Captivity

I saw a film once,
foreign with subtitles,
about a man who was kidnapped.
Kidnapped for many months,
maybe years.
Blindfolded
he never knew where he was,
only saw the faces of his captors
and four brick walls.
Then they released him
and he spent the rest of his life
looking for them.
He couldn't be free.
He missed captivity.
They say the truth will set you free,
but is freedom what we want?

Can we live without the four walls,
without the silence,
can we live if we tell those things
that never see the light of day?
We can't take it back once it's said.
Can you imagine being more
scared of freedom than of captivity?
I think I can.

Naomi Young
England/USA

What Would Happen?

What would happen
to me
if I abandoned
the idea
that my way of thinking
           living
           being
is the one way to
fullness of life?

Would I drop
into an abyss
of anonymity
      uncertainty
      non-being
or is there something
      deeper
      fuller
space where disparate parts
reside in complex unity
place of non-threatening connection
      divine diversity
      integrated complexity
      infinite variety
Like the bifurcation
of stream and vein
      root and branch

part of the
      laughing
      dancing
      flow
of the River of Life
beside which grow
the trees
for the healing
of the nations

W. L. Wallace
Aotearoa New Zealand

The Time To Speak

Simon Peter answered, 'You are the Messiah, the son of the living God.'

(Matthew 16:16 REB)

Jesus then gave his disciples strict orders not to tell anyone that he was the Messiah

(Matthew 16:20 REB)

Son of the living God – Yes
but you give strict orders
not to tell anyone.

Why?
Why hide who you are?
Why closet yourself?

Aren't you being dishonest
presenting yourself as one of them –
just the carpenter's son from Nazareth?
Aren't you being hypocritical
like the Pharisees and the scribes
    you severely criticise?

No . . . you love who you are
You choose not to declare it
You live what
in your heart you know

is good and acceptable
in God's eyes,
what would be blasphemy
    only in others' ears.

Is it fear that keeps you quiet –
fear of sticks and stones
and broken bones?
    Self-declared Sons of the living God
    are a thorny issue –
    are met with stony silence
    from Temple and Capitol
Is it fear?

No – Fear would never risk
a Judas' betrayal, a Peter's denial
a Pharisee's revenge, a Pilate's contempt.
Fear would never wear
its crown of thorns
    with the dignity you do.

It must be a matter of timing, then
    a time for every season under heaven
    a time to keep silence
    and a time to speak
    a time to plant
    and a time to pluck what is planted
a time to plant
your down-to-earth human side
in the hearts and minds of the people,
that the time to keep silence might bear
as its fruit of the vine
    the time to speak.

Norm S. D. Esdon
Canada

De Profundis
(Written on 30 April 1999 following a bomb attack on the gay pub, the
Admiral Duncan, in Soho, London, England)

A time there was –
when no one knew.
When we were not seen,
save a 'crime' or scandal.

A time there was –
when we were hated.
When a pink triangle marked us,
and the unmarked grave in Auschwitz beckoned.

A time there is –
when we are attacked:
When nails pierce our flesh,
and bibles are used as baseball bats.

A time there is –
when we are ignored:
when we are asked to wait
and we are less important than others who are despised and rejected:

How long, how long,
O God.

Peter Colwell
England
(with apologies to Thomas Hardy)

The Silence of Jesus

**Jesus himself, the founder of Christianity, made no criticism at all,
at any time, of homosexuality or same-sex sexual behaviour.**

For the followers of Jesus, this silence has weight. It was not due to
ignorance. Same-sex sexual behaviour was familiar to the Jews.
Amongst the Romans, the rulers of Judaea at the time, it was regarded
as a natural option within a normal sex-life, so long as it was con-
sensual. (They gave same-sex marriages the same status as heterosexual marriages but they had strict laws to punish rape and
child-abuse.)

Jesus spoke freely about his contemporaries' moral and social behaviour but never mentioned this. If he had wished to criticise any aspect of same-sex love or sexuality, let alone to forbid same-sex sex to his followers, three years of teaching gave him ample opportunity. **But He did not.**

Michael Halls
England

A Litany of Compassion and Consolation in Times of Particular Difficulty
(Written for a house of gay people being verbally and physically abused by a local Church group.)

The words are to be said slowly, without emotion, but with feeling. There should be a pause between each phrase and response.

When they raise their voices against us and denounce us
May We Hear The Still Small Voice Of Your Love

When they bash us with their Bibles
Help Us To Hear Your Word

When they lift their voices in righteous indignation
Help Us To Hear The Song Of The Angels

When they spit upon us
Help Us To Remember The Waters Of Baptism

When their queer bashers pounce on us
Help Us To Remember The Passion Of Jesus

When they discriminate against us
Help Us Not To Harden Our Hearts

When their Church slams its door in our faces
Help Us To Remember Jesus As The Sheepfold Gate

When they see us as an issue and not as your children
Help Us To Bring Life To Your Word

When they reject and disown us
Help Us Not To Turn Our Back On You

But for all those who reach to embrace us
Help Us To See In Them God's Love

And for all who make us welcome
Let Us Give Thanks

For every blessing that we receive
May We See Them As Flowers In The Desert

When we see those who would be against us
Let Us Forgive Them, For They Know Not What They Do

When the hatred would grind us down
Let Us Give Thanks For God's Gifts And For Each Other.

Christopher Wardale
England

The Stranger within Thy Gates: Otherness and Hospitality

Exclusivity is about fear. Inclusivity (I prefer the time-honoured word hospitality) is about love . . . about having big hearts. A church that excludes people is a church with heart-trouble. A church that values, honours and loves people – regardless of their race, colour, class, gender, sexual orientation, weight, glamour-rating, or whatever – is a church whose arteries are full of good, healthy, well-oxygenated (Spirit-ed) blood.

Hospitality is a great deal more than cups of tea and sympathy. It is more than being welcoming to those who venture on to 'our' territory. It is a non-defensive openness to life and life-forms . . . an openness that seeks to listen, learn and understand, to walk in the other's moccasins, to see with the other's eyes . . . Hospitality is an active reaching out to the stranger, so that the *hostis*, the enemy (which is how we so often view the unfamiliar), becomes the *hospes*, the honoured guest.

Hospitality is not an easy option these days. The risks of venturing outside one's own snail-shell seem very great in an everyone-for-her/himself society. An intrusive media, the spirit of the market (everything is for sale), an ethos in which competition is prized more highly than co-operation . . . such societal norms encourage us rather to batten down our hatches than to be more open. Life is a fear-full business.

And yet we who worship an hospitable God feel bound to go on trying to be hospitable to others. We feel bound to attempt to make the kind of space in our lives in which others are invited to sit and be utterly themselves in our presence. Hospitality is not preaching at people, setting conditions for acceptance and love, or hoping that our kindness will oblige them to change and be more like us. If people offend us, then hospitality means taking a long hard look at ourselves and getting to the root of our own hostilities; after that, it's learning how to forgive ourselves and put ourselves up for conversion. In Acts 10, Peter is called upon to go and convert Cornelius to Christianity. Before he can do that, he has to be converted himself – to see that what he has judged profane, unclean, and altogether 'other', is not so in God's eyes. God's hospitality is broader than this . . . 'wide as the wind and an eternal home.'

A second and more particular point about hospitality is this: if, instead of thinking and expecting the worst from the strangers at our gate, we open ourselves out in welcome, they frequently offer life-changing gifts. Not that we should be hospitable because of what we might gain thereby (indeed, to look for reward is completely against the spirit of hospitality) – but because God often comes in the guise of the stranger to offer us new growth and enrichment and a deeper humanity. Think about the encounters between Abraham and the three strangers at Mamre (Gen. 18:1–15) or between the widow of Zerephath and the prophet Elijah (1 Kings 17:9–24), or between two grieving travellers on the road to Emmaus and a mysterious stranger (Luke 24:13–35). In each case, hospitality is offered and a priceless gift is given in return. *And* there is a sudden creative confusion about who is the host and who is the guest; who the provider and who the recipient. Mutuality melts the distinction.

It is my experience that those who have opened their minds and hearts and been hospitable to explorations of, for instance, feminist thinking (instead of closing ranks, ridiculing or attacking it), have found themselves enriched. Men asked to look for the feminine within God or within themselves have found their experience and appreciation of life expanding. One male friend wrote to me, after he'd come into contact with some feminist thinkers and writers: 'I am discovering a huge area of my being that I'd always denied and shut off before. It's such a revelation. And such a freedom to enjoy and celebrate this "lost" part of myself.' Similarly there are cultures and sub-cultures which – in actively welcoming and affirming homosexuals in leadership roles – have discovered themselves in receipt of rich new gifts of the spirit. There are tribes of American Indians who, as a matter of course, appoint homosexuals to be spiritual counsellors to the chiefs: their wisdom is prized.

We both long for and dread radical personal change. We need to acknowledge this tension inside us before we can put ourselves in the place where angels might tread. The way we come to know and accept this tension is by appreciating that the stranger is already very intimately within our own gates. What I mean is this: that *within our own person* there is a stranger, an 'other', a shadow, a part of ourselves we don't immediately recognise, and usually wish to deny, whom we most commonly deal with by expulsion. We expel by foisting the characteristics of this stranger-other-shadow on to people 'out there' who – by being different in some immediately obvious way – conveniently offer us a peg on which to hang those unwelcome characteristics: they have a different colour skin . . . gender . . . value system . . . sexual orientation . . . This is called 'projection' – and we all do it. We all project outwards the split-off, unwelcome parts of ourselves. It is an unconscious process when we do it, although those who are very much aware of their inner workings may only take a second of reflection to bring it to consciousness and to check its recurrence in future.

Projection is at the root of all prejudice, hostility and fear. In condemning, hating or fearing the stranger 'out there', what we are actually doing is refusing to give house-room to the stranger within ourselves. Inwardly (emotionally) – and quite often biologically too – we are none of us straightforwardly and unambiguously this or that ... for instance, male or female, heterosexual or homosexual. We exist on a continuum. But this reality often discomforts us: we would rather be straightforwardly X or Y. So we push out whichever aspect we find least desirable.

If I can take courage and start to accept and welcome those apparently unpalatable parts of myself that I so readily project into others, I find that – far from being weakened, or wallowing in my own mire – I am in a stronger position than before (I'm less often taken unawares by 'rogue' attitudes or behaviours), and am even strangely enriched. Why enriched? Contrary to popular belief, the shadow part of oneself is not all negative and murky. There is – as Jung pointed out – often a seam of 'pure gold' to be mined from these shunned dimensions of the self. A mysterious alchemy transforms 'base metal' once it is owned and re-claimed – so that I find pockets of energy, creativity and compassion which were not available to me before. The stranger within myself also brings gifts. In taking the risk of accepting and loving the inner stranger, the shadow, we are rarely courting demons – but very often entertaining angels. Hospitable to the shunned within ourselves, we can then begin, like Christ, to open our hearts and arms to the shunned within our society.

Kate Compston
England

The Newspapers Say It All . . .

'Churches send delegation to seek exemption from human rights legislation.'

God said, 'Let us make human beings in our own image after our likeness.'

Men and women.
Able and disabled.
Black and white.
Young and old.
Gay and straight – the wonderful variegated image of God.

But No.

> No gays here. No women bishops.
> No blacks we might say but we dare not.
> No children to interrupt our holy meditation.
> No human rights here.
> After all we are the Church!
>
> The Church – the body of Christ.
> Christ who dined with tax gatherers and prostitutes.
> Christ who affirmed women and respected them.
> Christ who praised the Samaritan and the Roman.
> Christ who stretched out his hand to the lame.
>
> Two thousand years later, when we will we learn?

Jean Mayland
England

God, You Are the God of Huldah

God,
  You are the God of Huldah,
  of Miriam and Deborah.
      You are speaking still
      through prophets in our midst.
          You whisper an idea in our ear:
          we say, 'What's she up to?'

You rise in joy or outrage offering a vision:
we say, 'Whoa, she is out of control!'
We should cover our mouths with our hands,
amazed that you still love us.

You are our God. Forgive us.

Dumbarton U. M. C.
USA

A Call To Justice

The congregation reads the ALL and is divided into Left and Right. The read-
ers should also read the ALL to encourage the congregation. The ONE voices
should be located around the room so that the statements come from the peo-
ple. The same person should read 'When one part of the body hurts' each time.
They should be positioned in front of the congregation.

One: When one part of the body hurts,
All: **We all hurt.**
One: Sunday is the most segregated hour on the face of the earth.
When shall God's people truly worship together in spirit and
in truth?
Left: Arise and let your light shine!
Right: The fire of justice burns within us.

One: When one part of the body hurts,
All: **We all hurt.**
One: HIV / AIDS medications continue to be unavailable to most of
those with HIV on our planet, because of the high cost of
these drugs. When will meds that can save lives or improve
living be available to all of God's children?
Right: Arise and let your light shine!
Left: The fire of justice burns within us!

One: When one part of the body hurts,
All: **We all hurt.**
One: Not only are medications expensive, but many, many women
and children and men do not have access to even basic health
care. When will we treat all people as people of value and
worth care?
Left: Arise and let your light shine!
Right: The fire of justice burns within us!

One: When one part of the body hurts,
All: **We all hurt.**
One: Despite the 'war to end all wars' our world continues to be war-torn. Not only countries but also neighbourhoods are shattered by guns. For many children, killing is a way of life. When will our world discover the peace that passes understanding?
Right: Arise and let your light shine!
Left: The fire of justice burns within us!

One: When one part of the body hurts,
All: **We all hurt.**
One: Rape, abuse, and domestic violence continue to be perpetrated around the world. When will we discover that ALL people are created in the image of the Creator and that the body and our sexuality are sacred gifts?
Left: Arise and let your light shine!
Right: The fire of justice burns within us!

One: When one part of the body hurts,
All: **We all hurt.**
One: God's gay, lesbian, bisexual and transgender children around the world continue to be denied so many basic human rights, employment, and protection under the law, respect and dignity. When will ALL people enjoy human rights and be treated equally?
Right: Arise and let your light shine!
Left: The fire of justice burns within us!

One: When one part of the body hurts,
All: **We all hurt.**
One: So many of our world's children are suffering. They are hungry, ill, malnourished, homeless, alone, subjected to violence in the home and on the streets, with no or limited access to education. Too many have looked for hope to drugs, gangs, violence and children having children. When will we 'suffer the little children' to come unto us?
Left: Arise and let your light shine!
Right: The fire of justice burns within us!

One: When one part of the body hurts,
All: **We all hurt.**
One: Silence equals death. We know it. We say it. Yet silence on

issues, too many to list, persists. When will we break the
silence, our silence, and speak the truth in love?

Right: Arise and let your light shine!
Left: The fire of justice burns within us!

All: **Arise and let your light shine!**
        The fire of justice burns within us!
        We shall overcome.
        The fire of justice burns within us!
        We shall overcome!

*Repeat last line growing louder and more emphatic, with a type of walking
beat – see emphasis below – until music of 'We Shall Overcome' takes over.*

The fire of justice burns within us! We shall overcome!

Colleen Darraugh
USA

Meditations for Starters

To see the differences is to view the surface –
To see the similarities is to encounter the depth –
To hold both together is to find healing and life.

Do not search for the gate of knowledge; only stop believing in walls
and their security.

W. L. Wallace
Aotearoa, New Zealand

Someone's Sexual Orientation

. . . someone's sexual orientation or choice of sexual practices, as long
as it occurs between consenting adults, should not be a ground for discrimination and persecution . . .

Alina Rastam
Malaysia

The Demands of Love and the Intimacy of Justice

Many people are very supportive of gay men and lesbians but, and perhaps this is more true of men than women, they are also clear in establishing that they themselves are not gay. Many are willing to accept the risk of association, but not the risk of mistaken identity.

A friend, who happens also to be gay, claims my heart in unusual and profound ways. We met years ago in California, in the United Church of Christ. Walker was a student training for the ministry and I was assigned as his pastoral advisor for the duration of his training. A committee told me he was openly gay and handed me his file. I was flattered. You see, it polished my liberal inclusive identity. It rewarded my advocacy. It sanctified my struggle for justice. It redeemed my risking professional advancement and personal attack.

Our first encounter was in a Berkeley café. He was wonderfully crazy and creative and I felt ponderously conventional and established. In time mutual caution became mutual respect. Respect became friendship. Friendship became love. In time Walker was ordained and called to the only ministry the church could, at that time, tolerate. He became the AIDS minister. And all this time he was the gay friend and I was the straight friend. That is until he kissed me, on the lips.

The kiss was not an advance. It was not an invitation. It was simply a spontaneous gesture of loving friendship. The kiss was not sexually threatening, exploitive or manipulative. And yet, all my self-defined noble deeds, all my self-exaggerated risks, all my self-conceived bold public statements, all my self-important theological and biblical arguments were exposed as painfully bounded in one moment of lips touching lips. The unease I felt became articulated in a question: did I truly love this man, or was my love actually checked by the fact that he was gay?

As it turned out, others saw the kiss, the result of which was the quasi-public questioning of my sexual identity and another question for my soul to ponder. The question was this: was my commitment to justice constrained by my unwillingness to be identified, not with, but as one of those treated unjustly? The issue of sexual identity has been made profoundly complex and important due to an equally profound and complex history of homophobia in our church and society. However, if I truly believed that a gay person had as much ethical, theological, or anthropological integrity as any straight person, then why would I care if others thought I was gay or bisexual? It was not a matter of guaranteeing a correct identity. It went deeper. It went to my integrity of being. I made it clear to everybody and anybody who would listen that, while I supported gay rights and had gay friends, I was straight. Justice was one thing, my identity was another.

Until that kiss my love for gay men and lesbians was conditional and my support of gay people was qualified. In a church and society that metaphorically stitches pink patches on our clothing in the attempt to identify those who must be rejected, conditional love and qualified justice is not good enough. For the sake of love and justice it doesn't matter if I am gay or straight. It does matter where I stand when others inflict spiritual, emotional and sometimes physical violence on God's people.

Dale Rominger
USA/England

Breaking the Barriers of Prejudice Against Lesbian and Gay People

The old lines of demarcation are becoming blurred – in politics between conservative and socialist, and in religion between Christian and non-Christian. This is because issues are becoming increasingly complex. So people look for matters that do appear to fit their loyalties, and sexuality fits the bill. Pro-gay tends to imply socialist and non-Christian, and anti-gay denotes conservative and Christian. People adopt the ready-made polarisation, with all its barriers, to define their identity.

The political divide focuses at present on Section 28 of the Local Government Act 1988. This forbids the promotion of homosexuality by Local Authorities in England and Wales. In practice this often means that teachers will not even discuss sexuality with their pupils. Education is not the same as promotion, but this is a fine point and teachers are understandably not willing to risk being accused of breaking the law. So young people remain uninformed in school, and probably misinformed outside school, about this important aspect of their development and their lives.

From the religious aspect, there is the small number of anti-homosexual texts in the Bible. Jesus himself said nothing that is recorded on the subject, though St Paul refers to it. Bible scholars now say that these Pauline references are likely to be mistranslations. In recent translations such as the Revised English Bible the word homosexual has been omitted from Paul's letters. This leaves us, in the Old Testament, with the story of Sodom, which is about the violent actions of criminal men trying to discredit Lot by abusing the guests in his house. And in the arcane laws of Leviticus, homosexuality is criticised along with the shaving of beards, eating of shellfish and the wearing of garments made with mixed yarn. On this tenuous basis the Churches of England and of Rome continue their institutional discrimination, officially forbidding practising lesbian or gay people from being priests.

Sexuality should not be a political or religious issue. It is primarily a scientific and sociological matter. Scientifically, it is known that a small proportion of people, about 5%, are born with a sexual orientation primarily to the same sex. Experience has shown that this orientation cannot be changed. But there is discordance between this psychological information and the common negative social attitudes to gay and lesbian people. Given the unsympathetic cultural climate, attracting friends or choosing long-term partners is more difficult for lesbian and gay people than it is for heterosexual people. Lesbian and gay people do not have the same support and approval in their friendships, nor the help of the structure of a marriage ceremony and the married status.

Sociology is not an easy discipline and this applies also to the sociology of sexuality. Even the prevalence of gay and lesbian people is in doubt in spite of painstaking surveys involving tens of thousands of people. And all studies of perceived groups of people are subject to the iceberg phenomenon; the part that is visible is a very small part of the whole and is not necessarily characteristic of it. So we have studies of convicted paedophiles which show a higher than expected proportion of gay men. The assumption from this that gay men are more likely to be paedophiles is false, because the abuse of children by married people is more frequent and less often suspected and reported than abuse in a single or same-sex household. Similarly, the deaths of gay people in obituaries in gay newspapers have shown that they have a low average age at death. But the likelihood of a young gay person's death being reported in a gay newspaper is greater than that of an older person, because an older person's sexuality is less of a defining characteristic. So the younger ages at death as observed are to be expected. But we are repeatedly told, sometimes even in reputable sources such as letters published in the *British Medical Journal*, that these studies indicate that gay men die young.

It is the case that in some urban areas of Britain and America there has been a higher incidence of HIV infection in gay men. But this has reduced greatly since the early 1980s, showing that most gay men have responded very responsibly to this new and tragic disease. And it remains true that worldwide, HIV infection is primarily a heterosexual disease. In any case, the implication that disease is some kind of divine punishment is primitive in the extreme.

All this sophistry fuels the antipathy towards lesbian and gay people. It is not rational. It is based on historical attitudes and a strong and deep-rooted prejudice. This prejudice is based on two factors; firstly the self-evident fact that if everyone were gay the human race would die out. The philosopher Kant famously said that it was axiomatic that if something could not be appropriate to all people then it was wrong. This has been quietly forgotten in the world of philosophy but, incredibly, the Bishop of Liverpool has quoted Kant's axiom as a criticism of homosexual behaviour. Secondly, many people are uncomfortable with their own sexuality because, consciously or not, they suspect that they may be bisexual. They externalise their resultant insecurity much as the priests in ancient times transferred the 'sins' of the people on to goats which were then driven out. Scapegoating continues today in a form hardly more sophisticated.

All of this shows up the threadbare nature of the arguments against lesbian and gay people. Prejudice against people who are perceived as being different and powerless is all too frequent. We have seen it in the oppression of black people and of women. It is time to take sexuality out of politics and religion and remove the barriers against lesbian and gay people, because the barriers are based on false reasoning and are no more substantial than cobwebs.

Let us hope and pray that people come to a more accurate under-standing and sympathetic acceptance of their fellow human beings, and rejoice in the diversity of God's people.

Alan Sheard
England

Growing Up Gay and at School: The Stories of Two Survivors

What is it like to be gay and still have to go to school? Since the equal-isation in the Age of Consent in 2000, today's reality is that not only do we recognise that lesbians, gay men and bisexual men and women have gone to school but that many are still going to school and need our support. Despite the constant round of statements condemning homophobia in all its guises from politicians and pundits, it is clear that there are many harsh lessons that we still have to learn. The les-son we have to learn most is that lesbian and gay young people are in our schools now and need to be recognised, supported, appreciated and valued unconditionally. When I began my research into bullying behaviour among school children one phrase continually reared its ugly head: *Children are cruel!* In recording and reporting the school experiences of over 190 lesbian, gay and bisexual people over the past seven years, I have continually had to ask myself: Are children really cruel? Today, as before, my gut reaction is that they are not. To suggest that a child or young person has innate desires to hurt or otherwise depreciate the value of another human being is to suggest that society and the institutions therein have no role to play in the shaping of all of our attitudes, beliefs, customs and behaviour. Children are products of the family, community and culture in which they are raised, educated and socialised. A child is cruel because we allow her/him to be cruel. In the wider world, if one person hits another, dependent upon the circumstances in which such an altercation occurs we will decide whether or not such behaviour is justifiable on moral, religious, legal or political grounds. It seems that historically we have judged bullying in the same way.

History tells us that nearly two thousand years ago the Greeks of Asia Minor chose an individual – a *pharmakos* – upon whom they would transfer the blame for all of society's woes. This *pharmakos* or *scapegoat* would be kept at the city's or state's expense until such time as famine, war or any form of hardship fell upon its citizens. They would then be fed, paraded and ultimately sacrificed in order to placate the deities to which the city or state prayed for protection. Today it would seem that lesbians, gay men and bisexual men and women are the modern representations of the *pharmakos*: vilified by politicians, shunned by society, the subjects of laws and decrees that seek to criminalise the love two people share for one another. If a society or culture is able to brutalise such love, then is it not surprising that children learn this also, and act out such brutality in their own environment – the school?

In 1994, when I began gathering data on the experiences of lesbians and gay men at school, I had no idea that I would be an active participant in a debate that continues to this day surrounding the social inclusion of those who do not identify as heterosexual. Through my own research and that of many colleagues around the world, we have seen a gradual recognition that homophobia is a pervasive and destructive influence that infects us all. It separates families, divides communities, alienates faiths and contaminates cultures. Young people are told that homosexuality is not only wrong, but that it is sinful. Until 1992 the World Health Organisation still classified it as a mental disorder, and today debate continues around the curability of homosexuality. In such a climate of hostility, it is no wonder that some children feel justified in victimising those whom they perceive to be lesbian or gay, and it is no wonder that those who are lesbian or gay seek to hide as Paul, a 27 year old gay man recalls:

> For almost a year of my school life I spent every break and every dinner break sitting in the back of the toilet area reading because I knew I was safe there, that I was isolated, and no one would give me any hassle.

The fear of disclosure, of victimisation and ultimately of societal censure can have detrimental consequences for young people as Paul goes on to say:

> I don't think anyone who isn't gay can ever understand the complete 100% humiliation you feel because all you know is you are yourself. You have no other way of expressing yourself because it's simply you.

Such humiliation can lead to anger and frustration and self-blame. Susan, a 30 year old lesbian, recalls:

> I blame myself that it [bullying] went on so long because I didn't do anything to fight back.

Susan's criticism of herself is not uncommon. Hindsight can be just as destructive as the experience of bullying itself. To look back on a child-hood episode with the wisdom of adulthood is often unhelpful. What could Susan have done differently that would have had an effect? How would her parents, her teachers or her peers have reacted to her fighting back? As she said:

> I spent the first two or three years in secondary school frightened on most days to go in. I was frightened of a certain group of girls.

In reality Susan faced a wall of indifference or silence when she approached her teachers:

> I think the thing that was certainly missing when I was at school was that none of the teachers responded negatively to me telling them I was gay, but nor were they supportive in the sense that they had no advice, no information, nowhere to offer. I wasn't necessarily expecting them to solve my problems, but had they – any of them – told me there was anything like a gay switchboard or a gay support group, or anything like that [it] would have been an enormous help.

Paul found that there was little he could do to enlist the support of his parents and siblings, they were, in his own words, *ashamed* of him:

I just hated myself so much because I didn't know what to do to make myself appear better so that people wouldn't pick on me so much, so my family wouldn't feel ashamed. Even my brothers and sisters were ashamed because I was such a puff.

Silence, indifference or shame were perhaps the best reactions a young lesbian or gay man could hope for from her/his teachers or family. As Paul recalls, sometimes teachers can play an active part in further humiliating a young person because of their actual or perceived sexual orientation:

I do remember one time with him [a PE teacher]. It was in the hall, we were doing gym and he asked me the time and I responded *'quarter to ten'* or something and I heard the other kids laugh. I didn't hear what he said but I just heard the other kids laugh and then he asked me again, and then he made me come out and say the time and every time I said the time he repeated it and did a John Inman act. I just had to stand there and keep repeating it while he did 'puffy' interpretations and then the class fell about. It affects me more now as an adult to think that that man was in authority and he did this and the school did nothing about it.

The one desire that is common to many young lesbians and gay men at school is that of inclusion: being a member of the 'in' group rather than an outcast. For some, like Paul, this means denying one's own feelings or emotions towards members of one's own sex, repressing all of those things that adolescence allows other young people to explore fully:

I remember I had a girlfriend for about a year and it was a completely useless time for me because I would like meet [her] at barn dances but really I just wanted others to see me with my girl-friend so I would look – you know – peer pressure. It was that wonderful freedom of living in the countryside and in a good community atmosphere, and then the private torture of knowing that you would never be part of that community. You were alien to it.

Paul saw himself as an alien, as someone who was not allowed to play a full role in his community because he was and is gay. He attempted to live a lie in order to feel that he had a place within his local community. He sought the approval of his peers by being seen with a girlfriend rather than a boyfriend because at no point while he was growing up had someone turned to him and said, *'it's OK to be gay'*.

But, how OK is it to be gay? How does a young person reconcile the inward desires with the outward tensions? For Susan, her first sexual experience was very positive – a defining moment in her development:

> I mean afterwards I thought 'brilliant!' It's like 'Yeah, at last!' because by then I had some concept of being gay.

For Paul, his first attempt at a relationship brought with it confusion:

> I was in love with him, but physically I didn't want him to be there because I was scared people would know and you know the relationship kind of fell apart because of that – because of that extreme pressure.

Growing up lesbian or gay is not a simple process. It does not involve simply taking a different path on the route to adulthood. The skills with which society equips the young heterosexual to help them on their way are not the same skills required by young lesbians and gay men. In a climate of fear, intolerance and, often, overt hostility, those skills that lead a lesbian or gay man to adulthood require expertise in subterfuge, secrecy, self censure and the ability to cope with solitude. The young woman or man who is able to follow this path and overcome the obstacles that society has placed before her/him will ultimately be strengthened by the experience. It should not have to be like this, but for the time being it is.

Eventually things will change, the collective conscience has already been pricked. It is right and proper that at the beginning of the 21st century we abandon the practices of two thousand years and stop looking for scapegoats.

Ian Rivers
England

Prevention of Anti-Gay Violence Starts in Your Congregation

This morning, October 12 1998, I heard on the radio that Matthew Shepard has died. He's the gay University of Wyoming student who was brutally assaulted, lashed to a fence and left to die. He was 21 years old.

Even though I didn't know Matthew Shepard I'm in touch with grief today. A tragic loss of a young life – brutally and savagely taken by two men whose girlfriends were accessories to the crime.

And on a personal level, I'm finding myself this morning having to reprocess the time when I was also the victim of a hate crime. I was 22 years old then and like Matthew was in a bar. I left alone and was assaulted on the street a few doors away. There were twelve or fifteen of them. I never got an accurate count or really a good glimpse of any of them. Acid was sprayed in my face and my left contact lens dissolved in my eye. A week later when the patch was removed I was relieved that I could still see. At the time I was too afraid to even report the crime to the police.

Over ten years have passed. This crime against Matthew Shepard was much more severe than the attack I experienced. Matthew was deliberately abducted and pistol whipped. One report I read said that his skull was bashed in more than two inches by the pistol. He was tied to a fence post and left to die. A passer-by saw him and thought at first that he was a scarecrow but he was found too late. He was on a respirator in the hospital for several days before he died.

I'm also remembering that during a workshop I gave on lesbian, gay, bisexual and transgender concerns I was continuously heckled by a man who was not open to anything I said. He was convinced that my intention was to make fun of the Bible. During the workshop I made reference to the assault I had experienced and tried to make a connection between it and similar attitudes. I don't think that man was willing to understand the link but I think the rest of the audience did.

I wonder about the upbringing and the education of this man, of those who assaulted me and of those who murdered Matthew Shepard. What were their experiences as children? Where did they learn that it was acceptable to physically and verbally assault someone? Did the church never challenge these beliefs? Were teasing, taunting and hitting gay students in their youth groups and Christian education classes overlooked? Also, I wonder what could possibly motivate someone to celebrate the death of this student and to laud his murderers by sending hateful e-mail?

The good news – if anything positive can be said to come from this tragedy – is that there may be hate crimes initiatives. And maybe our churches will seriously examine the role they play. Maybe as persons of faith we'll all be forced to take a serious look at our own congregations. When we hear a racist slur, more than likely we'll all take appropriate action, no questions asked. How many of us do the same for homophobic slurs? Maybe, if Matthew Shepard's murderers had been challenged along the way, they would not have come to be so hateful. How many of us stop children of any age from hitting each other? If a child is being punched by another kid for being a lesbian do we overlook this? When such actions are overlooked, the silence on the part of the teacher condones and reinforces the hatred, which, if unchecked, can grow to the level which enables people to kill – and not simply to kill, but to torture brutally.

Members of the United Church of Christ have the power to do something 'official' about homophobia in their churches. The General Synod took the initiative to openly state a specific welcome to lesbian and gay persons by passing an Open and Affirming resolution in 1985. I suggest we all look at our own congregations and examine whether we tacitly allow homophobia to grow, or if we speak the truth and name it for the bias and hate it is. It's too late for Matthew Shepard but it's not too late for our other youth and young adults. Start now. Start today. Start when you finish reading this article. Make a commitment to yourself, to your congregation, to humanity, that you will not allow anyone to be harassed, verbally or physically, or put down because of their sexual orientation or gender identity. It starts with each individual, one congregation at a time.

Timothy Brown
USA
(slightly adapted by Geoffrey Duncan)

In Honour of Rev. Dr Martin Luther King, Jr.

Martin Luther King Jr. was a man with a dream; a man with a vision; a man with the commitment and drive to make that dream come true. He was a man who embodied his faith and called forth, in others, a renewed faith, a sense of spiritual urgency and mobilisation for justice. He knew the cost of discipleship yet he was willing to pay the price. He took the road of justice, following his God. That faithfulness cost him his life.

The impact of that life changed millions of lives and the course of the future. The dream was no longer just a dream. With committed actions for justice, the dream could become a reality. Martin Luther King, Jr. was not the only leader of the Civil Rights movement in the USA but his presence, his words, his unrelenting stance and action for justice drew peoples together across race, gender and class lines. His legacy is a non-violent justice model for *all* peoples seeking equal, not special, rights.

The work is not done. The dream has not been fully realised. We cannot let the vision of Martin Luther King, Jr. die. The Word of God compels us to Christian Social Action. For gay, lesbian, bisexual, transgender and questioning peoples, we must position ourselves for justice. This justice is not just for ourselves but for *all* people, *all* around the world of every race, class, gender, sexual orientation, and physical ability, until all of us can say, 'Free at last! Free at last! Thank God Almighty, I'm free at last.'

Response In Memory and Action

One: We have been challenged to action; to act out the gospel of Jesus Christ; to be peacemakers and bridge-builders; people of faith, of justice and integrity. Our worship is not limited to this time and space. We worship God with the fullness of our lives.

All: **We give God thanks for the powerful witnesses that have gone before us. May we learn from their lives and faith. May all who come behind us find us faithful. As we go out today, we go in worship and praise of God.**

Colleen Darraugh
USA

Violence and the Gay Question

I have tried to shift the subject I was asked to deal with, from 'violence and the gay question' to 'creation and cowardice'. This is because I think that violence is not a 'they' question. Violence is the 'we' question, and it is a question of no interest at all in itself. Sound and fury, signifying nothing. Violence is the clinging on to old being when, in the midst of our world and giving it great birth pangs, the Creator is bringing forth the new creation starting from those who are not. We are all formed by, and tempted to, violent belonging, violent association, violent loyalty, and we are all masters at hiding it from ourselves. I've talked about cowardice, because that has been my problem, my way of holding on to the old paternity and not daring to allow myself to be held in being by the new. But in as far as unwittingly gracious persecutors have conspired to push me in directions I would never have dared to tread by myself, I've started to look at this not as an issue to do with violence and gay people, but as one where faith in the Creator has begun to make possible an equal-hearted fraternity which defied all definitions of identity.

To come back to the occasion of our conversation. Think of those murders. What do you see? I see Matthew Shepard, the Redding couple, Billy Jack Gaither, Scott Amedure and the other victims, all in the hand of God, beyond the need of our ministrations. But in whose hands are their murderers? And how will we use those hands? I've seen something of the guys on television, in news articles and so forth. What do I see; I see trailer parks, dusty pick-ups with gun-friendly bumper stickers, worn-in jeans and cheap white underwear. I see heads filled with kooky bits of Bible-talk, dwellers in conspiracy theory and all the intellectual dead-ends of resentful poverty. I see kids silently howling for manhood, when everything of manhood except its cheapest and most vulgar accoutrements is permanently, grindingly denied them. If I can't beat up a faggot, then who the fuck can I beat up on except myself? The sort of world that only a great soul like Flannery O'Connor could do justice to with both realism and a respect bespeaking love.

But I see more than that. I see the same kids that I have been and I have known in gay clubs, in dark rooms and bath-houses, fumbling for a fix of manhood, a sense that in the middle of all this shit I may have some value, be of some worth, be able to be loved, just be. I see kids scandalised by a changing world with upside-down values, where we all try to find an identity, and all feel our failure. We too flail around in relationships which we don't know how to sustain, we write off our aggression in articles, we look for a 'politically correct' pack with which to hunt, we deplore guns as violently as others defend them. I'm learning to see brothers: straight, gay, what the hell, scandalised brothers who have to grab being from each other since we can't let go and learn to receive it from only the giver.

And beneath and in the midst of that I see the Sacred Heart of Jesus, palpitating and bleeding with pain and love because these are his brothers: the weak ones, the fatherless ones, the shepherd-less ones, the murderers and traitors and the simply confused, who can, oh yes who can, be nudged into a story of being held in being beyond all the flailing around, the bravado, the cover-up of a life out of control. And he's saying, and it cuts me to the quick: Feed my sheep, feed my sheep, feed my lambs.

James Alison
UK/USA/Latin America

Statement of Solidarity On Religious Intolerance and Sexual Diversity

(From the organisers and speakers of the International Gay and Lesbian Human Rights Commission's Conference (July 2000): 'Separation of Faith and Hate: Sexual Diversity, Religious Intolerance and Strategies for Change', Rome World Pride 2000)

Preface

We, people of diverse sexuality and spiritual, religious and secular communities, come together from around the world. We issue a call for solidarity to end religiously motivated and perpetrated intolerance based on sexual orientation, gender identity or HIV status.

We recognise the complexity of sexuality and reaffirm that sexuality is an intrinsic part of our lives as human beings.

We call attention to how religious intolerance directed at those who do not conform to dominant norms of sexual expression results not only in their exclusion but also in human rights violations. We recognise the interdependence of all lives and believe that an affront to the dignity and integrity of one is an affront to all human beings.

Purpose

We reaffirm the worth and dignity of every human being.

We express our deepest commitment to all human rights emphasising that some rights cannot be privileged over others since human rights are indivisible and that a person's sexual orientation and identity should not interfere in the full exercise of their human rights.

We affirm that sexual rights – including bodily integrity, sexual health and freedom from sexual coercion and violence – are integral to human rights. In this light we condemn victimisation and discrimination based on certain lifestyles, appearance and cultural/social stereotypes.

We recognise that many people of marginalised sexualities belong to religious groups as both followers and leaders and they often suffer discrimination and alienation from expression of their spirituality. We call for reconciliation and healing of the relationship between spirituality and sexuality within these communities.

We express concern that many individuals are disinvited from their religious communities because of their sexual orientation. We call upon these communities to respect, honour and celebrate gifts of sexual diversity and recognise that the presence of these individuals further enriches their communities.

We call upon religious bodies and leaders to respect the rights of individuals to live a fulfilling life and not encourage violence or victimisation of individuals – especially young people, within educational institutions, within families and in other social institutions.

We call on religious establishments to join us in the recognition that all people are born free and equal in dignity and rights.

International Gay and Lesbian Human Rights Commission
USA

Oracle for YHWH's Rainbow People

The vision of Diane, the ordinand, mother of Jessica, daughter of Patricia the teacher, daughter of Jessie of the long arms and black eyes, daughter of Lilly the poor: concerning the people of the rainbow in the days of John of the 150th – husband to Sheila; Duncan the crazy – husband to Shirley; John 2 the Scot – husband to Rachel; Graeme the evangelist – husband to Shirley; Margaret the mystic – widow of Warren – champion of the people of the rainbow; Peter, husband of Beryl and 'wisher that Scripture was different'; and Bruce of the many woes: all Moderators of Assembly.

Whakarongomai O cosmos, titiromai O collective unconscious – for YHWH has spoken again.

Woe to the false prophets who rashly proclaim in the name of YHWH!

Be appalled, O cosmos, be shocked, be utterly desolate, says YHWH. For the Assembly has forsaken me; it is not my Temple, not my Temple, not my Temple!

My rainbow children, those who make my Word a cracked cistern are your oppressors. Did I not form you wholly nephesh and in my image? O my people, these shepherds mislead their flocks over precipices and into the mouths of lions. They do this for the promise of a halo and a harp (in Sheol).

This says YHWH: Because of their unfaithfulness they will be a laughing stock in paddock and pavilion. Their churches will be desolate, large and beautiful without worshippers. People who know my mercy will flee from them.

They have devised shame for my houses by cutting off many people, they will forfeit their place until they repent.

Even though they offer me their piety, I will not accept it.

Hear the word of YHWH my people of the rainbow: did I not bring you up out of the shadows and into the light, and lead you forty years in the wilderness after the law was passed. I have been YHWH, your God, even since the darkness, you know no other God but me.

It is I who answer and look after you, your faithfulness comes from me. Forget your parades and sing a love song to me. For those who oppress you, those who proclaim as unclean what I have created – shall stumble.

Those who handle my law do not know me.

Now YHWH rises to argue his case against the elders and dignitaries, against prophets who teach lies about his love and his image.

Have I not parted the waters of the voting continuously so that the heart of their Moderator shook like the trees of the forest before the wind? Have I not clouded all eyes until they let go of their pretence to righteousness? I do not want their righteousness, it falls apart like rotting meat. I want their humility before me.

Therefore says YHWH, God of hosts, O my people of the rainbow in Aotearoa. Do not be afraid of the Assembly when they beat you with a rod and lift up their ignorance against you as did the bigots of the ages.

On that day, your burden will be removed and the yoke will be destroyed from your neck. So there shall be a highway from the Assembly for the remnant that is left of the rainbow, as there was for Israel when they came up from the land of Egypt.

My people, you will say in that day: we believed you were angry with us for loving in our image, but now we love with the faithfulness learned at the breast of YHWH.

Righteousness shall be the belt around our waist and faithfulness around our loins. Though we may lie down with those like us – we are YHWH's children. Now your anger has turned away from us and toward our oppressors. We will trust in YHWH and not be afraid in that day.

Let this be known in all the earth. On that day YHWH will assemble the outcasts of the Assembly from the four corners of Aotearoa. The stereotyping of Sheol's mouth shall depart, the hostility of his prophets shall be cut off.

This is the plan that is planned concerning the whole earth. For YHWH has given birth to it. Who will bury this placenta in the holy place? Who can undo what YHWH has done?

Diane Gilliam-Weeks
Aotearoa New Zealand

Wisdom
(Luke 23:24)

O Holy One, with Sophia – Wisdom,
Your partner in the creation of the world –
Teach us partnership rather than power-over relationships.
May we listen to one another
in our pain and in our fear.
May our hearts and minds be open to change
so we may value one another
and listen to everyone's life story.
Deliver us from hurting each other
     in your name,
        we kill one another's soul by slapping everyone with our
            definitions,
        our 'isms' that exclude rather than include,
        divide rather than unite,
        wound rather than heal.
        Forgive us but teach us what we do so
        we may truly repent of the evil that continues
        to crucify you on crosses of misunderstanding
        prejudice
        and even 'purity'.

Chris Glaser
USA

Our Gay Youth in Our Church
(Acts 10:27–8, 34–5)

Holy Father and Mother, teach us to be truly inclusive of all your
children, especially those who are growing up in every congregation
and becoming aware of their homosexual feelings.

Save them from literal suicide, as well as suicide in its multiple guises:
substance abuse, unsafe sex, denial and repression that often leads to
depression or opposite-gender marriage. Give us a vision of the sacred
nature of same-gender love and unions so that our gay children will
know the holiness of their feelings.

Chris Glaser
USA

Birthing a Revolution

Holy Mother of God,
she's a gay activist
yet doesn't have that for which she fights:
a lover.
Like you, Holy Mother,
she births a revolution alone.

Dear Mother of God,
as she did for you, may the Holy Spirit
bless the fruit of her womb
that it may bring down the mighty
and exalt those of low degree,
that those who are hungry may be fed
while the rich learn poverty,
that her daughters may enjoy
the embodied love that has eluded her.
Bless her with this vision
when reality disappoints her.

Chris Glaser
USA

Chavrusa[1]

Must we not seem to ants as gods,
All out of scale, too vast to see,
Pursuing unknown, godlike ways
With arbitrary, awful steps,
Destroying worlds, disbursing crumbs,
Capricious, brutal, grand, aloof?

The ants are not deceived, bright friends:
They work and praise the only One God,
Repeat along their lines the Name
That we forgot to speak aloud,
Those holy, unremembered vowels
Stuck like our tongues to palates mute.

[1] *Chavrusa* or *chavruta* is a pair of study partners in a Torah class.

Art Addington
USA

Who Will Stop the Cart?

See how the crowds are gathering
To watch the final kill;
They line the fearful roadway
That leads to Tyburn Hill.
And who will ride the gallows cart
Beside the lonely one,
To share the jeers and bear the scorn
Until the work is done?

There's always one more sinner
To send to Judgement Day;
There's always one more other,
One enemy to slay.
But who will speak for mercy,
Who'll plead the sinner's part,
Take on the condemnation
And ride the gallows cart?

And once I saw Christ Jesus,
Led on that way to die;
His face was pale with anguish,
I heard his lonely cry,
'O who will tear the gibbet down,
And who will stop this cart,
And when will love, not hatred rule
In every human heart?'

Colin Gibson
Aotearoa New Zealand

Scripture is a Conversation

Scripture is a conversation,
Ezra, Jonah, Peter, Paul;
hidden is God's revelation,
told to some but meant for all.

Like a conference many speakers,
vie to make their voices heard,
only to the eyes of seekers
is disclosed the living Word.

We are called to be discerning
as we eavesdrop on the text;
not for answers but for learning
may the Spirit richly vex.

Move me from my fixed opinions,
axe laid to the frozen sea,
Lord, I long for your dominion,
liberated from my 'me,'

Thus unthreatened by the other,
unconcerned with being wrong,
may we add with sister, brother,
to your all-inclusive song.

Tunes: All for Jesus or Drakes Broughton

Kim Fabricius
USA/Wales

A Blessing for a Lesbian, Gay or Heterosexual Relationship

The blessing of the ground of being be upon you.
The blessing of the incarnate and risen one be upon you.
The blessing of the maternal spirit be upon you.

May you live in the covenant of love so long as God wills it.
May the Sun of Righteousness shine on you all your days.
May the Spirit fill your home with welcome and affirmation.
May you be a blessing to those who are welcomed into your home.
May you not be ashamed of your love.
May your love shine as signs of Christ the loving one,
    so long as you live as one.

Peter Colwell
England

Welcome to the Rainbow World

Fancy Noah sailing in the Ark,
Ploughing through the wind and rain and dark;
All of a sudden, feel that bump,
Landed safe on Ararat's hump.
Welcome to the rainbow world.
Rainbow people, every creature too,
Rainbow people, well what a motley crew,
With a snow-white dove to guide them
And an olive leaf their sign,
Rainbow people in a rainbow world.

Some folk want a world of this or that,
(Mostly this, if that is what they're at):
All God's plenty is our store,
Open wide the old Ark's door,
Welcome to the rainbow world.
Rainbow people, bridging earth and sky,
Rainbow people, God's promise in their eye,
And a shining arch to point them
To the harmony of all things,
Rainbow people in a rainbow world.

Some folk want their world all black and white,
Some folk like their world just wrong or right;
We like colour, we like hue,
We like me and we like you:
Welcome to the rainbow world.
Rainbow people, children of the light,
Rainbow people, declaring God's delight
In the multitudinous colours of a multifarious world,
Rainbow people in a rainbow world.

Some folk want a world of wrath and flame,
We prefer the gentle falling rain;
Black clouds gather, still it shines,
Pledge of seed and harvest times,
Welcome to the rainbow world.
Rainbow people, joyful, full of mirth,
Rainbow people, all colouring the earth
With the love and grace and laughter
Of a plenitudinous God,
Rainbow people in a rainbow world.

Colin Gibson
Aotearoa New Zealand

Go Out Into the World

Go out into the world in holy anger.
Put on the whole armour of God.
Grasp the sword of the Spirit.
Work and speak with courage and informed conviction.
Stand beside victims of hate and prejudice,
Share their pain and fight for their liberation.
Carry the cross you are given along the way of Christ.
Build, heal and lead with love.

John Cornwall
England

Be A New Creation

May you be a new creation,
Christ for those
to whom Christ shall
send you;

and the blessing of God our Creator,
Redeemer and Giver of Life
Be with you always.

Go in peace to love
and serve the Lord
In the name of Christ.
Halleluia,
Halleluia.
Amen.

A New Zealand Prayer Book
He Karakia Mihinare o Aotearoa

This Day is Ours!

People of God, this day is ours!

> **A day to acknowledge our hunger; hunger for love,**
> **hunger for respect, hunger for justice.**

People of God, this day is ours!

> **A day to proclaim that all God's creation –**
> **Gay, Straight, Bisexual, Transgender –**
> **must be affirmed**
> **and made to feel welcome in our communities.**

How deep is your hunger? How long can you wait
in order to be fed the bread which will sustain you?

> **Our hunger is deep!**
> **Yet even as we gather for worship,**
> **we begin to feed one another with the bread of life,**
> **a bread that will not run out even in times of scarcity.**
> **Let us seize the day and make it count.**
> **Let us seize the day and proclaim the good work**
> **that is taking place here and now.**

Reconciling Church Programme
USA

We Wait in Praise and Freedom

We wait in praise and freedom,
Both children of God's grace;
Anticipating passion,
Love in each other's face.

We seek the gift of insight,
In need of human care,
In hope, anticipating
The joy we long to share.

The partnership we marry,
The depth of faith we seal,
Are witness to the knowledge
The love we have is real.

Then God please bless this union,
This meeting of two minds,
This fusion of two bodies,
With all that heaven finds.

Andrew Pratt
England

To A Gay Christian

I have heard so many people say to you –
And, I confess, I must have said it too –
Yes, Jesus loves you as you are,
Yes, you'd be welcome in our church,
BUT . . .
Of course you know you'll have to change
Your lifestyle, at least, if not your orientation,
Because, you see, the Bible says . . .
Or does it?
And if it does, do I conveniently ignore
Those other things it says, about casting stones,
About motes and beams,
And who am I to judge you anyway?

So before God, who knows both you and me inside out,
Whose welcome has no shadow of a 'but',
I promise to love you as my fellow traveller,
And let God decide what or whom to change.

Jenny Dann
England

SPIRITUALITY AND
SEXUALITY

To Enhance Our Delight

O God who has created us as sexual beings,
help us to use our sensuousness responsibly,
that rejoicing in our bodies and our imagination
we may use them to nurture our love,
to enhance our delight
and to increase our awareness of oneness with all things.

W. L. Wallace
Aotearoa New Zealand

Grounded Angel

He was a grounded angel
given wings by God
taken away by humanity.
He was going to soar
fly high and float on his love
sail on the breeze of his passion
but they dragged him down.
They said
'you can't fly'
it's not right,
it's immoral,
it's evil
flying is wrong.
They clipped his wings
but he held on to them
kept them in a box
took them out and looked at them
flapped them for take-off
and dreamed of flying again
flying far, far away
to another place,
a place where flying was good and right
where he could
fly high and float on his love
sail on the breeze of his passion
stare into the eyes of his love
and kiss them
and no one would tell him it was wrong.

Naomi Young
England/USA

Zacchaeus
(Luke 19:1–10)

You are spiritually self-satisfied, she said,
you need to be broken open.
A community is what you need
to be pierced to the heart.

Well it didn't take a community.
It took only one woman
to fall in love with.
And then I was broken,
sliced in two,
divided neatly down the middle.
On one side, sexuality,
on the other, religion.

And it has taken many years
to piece these two sides together,
using God as glue.

My rosaries and masses,
prayer-cards and promises
lie, discarded,
along with, I hope, my self-satisfaction.

Because like Zacchaeus,
I have been called down from my tree,
and I can't for the life of me, climb back up.

Suzi B.
England

Is There a Gay Men's Spirituality?

Is there a Gay Men's Spirituality? As a gay man I believe there is. I
cannot speak for gay women but the points made include all people of
a homosexual orientation. Contemporary spirituality must learn from
the growing insights and understanding of sex, sexual orientations,
sexuality, sensuality and spirituality. Efforts need to be made to accept
our sexual orientation, our sexuality, our sensuality and our
spirituality.

I believe we can talk about 'spiritualities' in general and of
spirituality in particular. I say this because I have a sense that every

person is embodied in his or her own spirituality. This may or may not be associated with a particular faith journey. I believe that we can talk about Gay Spirituality as gay men and women who are living the process of becoming who we are in truth for ourselves and others. By owning our own spirituality within the gay community we are recognising the oneness of all creation.

The spiritual life of gay men is the interior life embracing and nurturing the exterior actions of our lives. How we think about ourselves, others and life. Spirituality relates to the whole complex by which we come alive to the fact we matter as gay men. The spirituality of the gay man is recognised by the way he asserts himself, not only as an individual having a religious dimension but as a man whose very differences are the defining sign of his spirituality. In my own efforts to work towards the 'white heat' of spirituality I must try as a gay man to keep in mind the following:

Sexual orientation is a gift to be accepted and shamelessly honoured throughout our lives.

Sexuality is not always about genitals; it is part of who I am. It involves more than a physical act; it is a powerful erotic energy force. It is meant to be co-creative and liberating.

Sensuality is about the innate senses; is about the co-creative gratification of the senses. It is not abusive; it is an inherent human quality.

Spirituality is a process of loving in depth. It is a way of releasing my compassion for self and others. It demands that I be radical; it recognises that I am sexual and sensual.

The integration of these enables us to live our lives as gay men relating physically, emotionally, intellectually and with the spirituality that is unique to gay men individually and collectively as members of the gay and greater community. This is creating a more positive awareness of homosexuality and the gay community. What is needed now is encouragement to recognise a 'homospirituality' that is central to gay men and women in our community. Yet being part of the greater community of humanity. This empowers us to embrace a spirituality that nurtures our values, guides and supports us and affects the way we respond to the all of life as gay men. Yes, there is a gay men's spirituality alongside other spiritualities.

Bill Kirkpatrick
Canada/England

A Renewed Vision
(Revelation 21:3–5a)

> God of Revelation,
> Reveal to your church yet more light to illuminate the glory
> and the mystery of sexuality and the sensuality with which you
> have blessed us to better love one another and to better love
> our earth.
> May our sexuality and our spirituality
> teach each other,
> touch each other,
> love each other as soul –
> the very life that is the starstuff of your cosmic image revealed
> in us
> as we follow your Light that has entered this world.

Chris Glaser
USA

Our Senses

O God,
we glorify your name
and enjoy you forever.
You have immersed us in your world
and baptised us with your Spirit.

We see your beauty reflected
in our community and in your world.
We enjoy you forever.

We feel your love in the warmth of sun,
the smiles of strangers, the hugs of friends,
the bodies of lovers.
We enjoy you forever.

We taste your refreshment
of sleep, of breath, of food and drink.
We enjoy you forever.

We smell your fragrance
of flower and field, of flesh and flavour.

We enjoy you forever.
We hear your voice
from the winds of nature to the winds of spirit.

O God, open our eyes so we see your goodness.
Sensitise our numbed senses
so we may feel your goodness.
Overcome our blandness
so we may taste your goodness.
Break into our vacuum
so we may smell your goodness.
Unstop our ears
so we may hear your goodness.

O God, our God,
we glorify your name
and enjoy you forever.
Alleluia!

Chris Glaser
USA

To Offer Our Inner Wealth

May we, O God,
cease to imagine our value lies in isolation
but sacramentally, sacrificially, sensuously
offer our inner wealth to the whole
and in that offering open ourselves
to its gracious hospitality.

W. L. Wallace
Aotearoa New Zealand

The Spirituality of Friendship

The prime source of celebration in life for me is that of friendship. This
is the most human and sacred relationship. Friendship cannot be
manufactured. The seedling of friendship must be given space and
time to mature. It begins with recognition of a shared stillness within.
It appears as if from nowhere and yet there is a recognition of a hidden

past being awakened to new life. It is as though two souls recognise each other at an unexpected meeting of a kind that will open the way towards the renewal of a friendship. It is as though the exile of loneliness is over in the awareness that there is more than just a mutual presence of one to the other.

In the Celtic Tradition there is a beautiful understanding of love and friendship. One of the fascinating ideas is that of 'soul love'. The old Gaelic term for this is 'Anam Cara' – Anam is the Gaelic word for soul and Cara is the word for friend. With our 'Anam Cara', our Soul Friend, we share an innermost heart and mind. This was and is a friendship of mutual recognition and of belonging that cuts across all convention, morality and category. It implies that through a true friendship we were linked to an ancient and eternal way with the friend of our soul. They are drawn together by the divine energy that flows between the two friends from a source beyond their comprehension.

When old friends re-meet there is a touch of expectancy as soul meets with soul with all they are for each other. These friendships of love form the most real and co-creative meeting of human presence with one another as they stand at the threshold where divine and human presence ebb and flow into each other. A friendship of this kind is ready to reach out towards others and draw them into the orbit of this friendship of love. This friendship is being nurtured by the fact that we matter to each other and any other person who comes into the enlarging circles of friendship. The greatest gift we may offer to another is the gift of ourselves with no strings attached. We do so in the awareness that friendship is about 'bonding' rather than 'binding'. Its main gift is nurtured by the spiritualities of friendship. It is very affirming and reminds us of how we relate to our perception of the truth and goodness as friends one to another. In this way we enable each other to celebrate lives worth celebrating and dying for.

Bill Kirkpatrick
Canada/England

A Basic Human Characteristic

Sexuality is a basic human characteristic; it is part of our being human. Hence, it is part of the handiwork of God.

. . . God did not find aloneness good and that is why God created friendship and companionship. I believe that for as long as every relationship is just and loving, mutually affirming, and mutually enriching, God will surely bless it and say, 'This, too, is very good.'

Hope S. Antone
Malaysia

Sexuality and Spirituality

Christianity owes its origin to the 'Word made flesh'. 'The Word was made flesh and dwelt among us' (John 1:14) describes love being humanised. This love is to be experienced and lived through the gifts of sex, sexual orientation, sexuality, sensuality and spirituality. There is no doubt that sexual health and spiritual health are joined; both are needed for sexual integrity and spiritual wholeness if any committed relationship is to be nurturing of each other.

'Sex' is biologically based and is orientated towards procreation, for pleasure and the release of tension. It can also be perceived negatively and this in turn can lead to fear and a denial of one's sexuality. Basically it is the inner drive yet is a longing for connection, for affirmation of one's self, of others and of all creation.

'Sexual Orientations' are not a choice. They are gifts from our creator to be fully integrated into our lives and spirituality. Can any of us recall the time when we chose to be homosexual? No, but we do remember when we discovered the truth of our sexual orientation to be honoured as a vital aspect of our lives.

'Sexuality' includes sex and the biological systems. It has more to do with being co-creative than procreative. It has to do with total offering and receiving. Our sexuality and its orientation unites body, mind and soul with each other. We should never be afraid of our sexuality. It is the raw material for nurturing our wholeness potential.

'Sensuality' is related to the notion of 'sense' and sense experience. If it is left at that and if sexuality is used merely in a physical way then we are no more than physical beings. It is also a bridge between our sexual and spiritual selves. Our selves need to be brought together in some form of harmony, otherwise we fail to develop the fullness of our potential. Sensuousness is about being open to experiencing fully our senses of hearing, touching, seeing, smelling and tasting. The more we are open to our senses the more we are alive to ourselves, others and the all of creation.

'Spirituality' is a capacity rather than an actuality. We are first and foremost a spiritual species due to the fact we belong to a physical world but are embodied in the spiritual world of all creation. Spirituality is the attempt to live our lives to the full in such a way that it will encourage others to realise that to be spiritual is to be fully alive to life with all our co-creative potential. Yet also with our imperfections.

The spiritual life involves our exploration of life in all its fullness, including our imperfections that in some way nurture our journey into the mystery of life and death. This insight enables us to recognise and accept the fact that our spirituality enables transformational change through our acceptance of the gifts of sex, sexuality, sensuality and spirituality along with other gifts that enable us to enjoy our lives to the full.

Bill Kirkpatrick
Canada/England

Intrinsically Sexual

. . . sexuality is crucial to God's design that creatures do not dwell in isolation and loneliness but in communion and community.

Through the incarnation, God not only participates in human sexual experiences but God is intrinsically sexual.

Ng Chin-pang
Hong Kong

In Church

We crept in the side door
And moved softly up the aisle;
We touched each other so gently,
Trembling from desire or the cold,
I don't know.
We lay down in the chancel
Close to where the choir sings,
And we made love
With angels keeping watch,
Protecting us from harm.
As the dawn
Rainbowed through glass
On to your sleeping body
I heard god cry out
With joy

Rosie Miles
England

A Factor in Salvation History

People's sexuality is sometimes expressed positively and sometimes negatively, even cruelly, but it is always a factor in salvation history.

Why does the church think it has done anything about sexual morality by condemning homosexuality? Is homosexuality wrong or is the violation of the human rights of homosexuals wrong?

Ann Wansbrough
Australia

Charis

You touched my flesh
with infinitely tender embrace:
the touch of charis,
the caress of grace,
the chrism of bliss.

You sought my face
with your lips,
came closer than breathing
to give me the kiss of peace.
No one loved me like this.

You opened my body
like rain parting leaves,
like the blessing of oil
on a dying man's brow.
You blessed, broke and offered
the bread of your body.
You ate of my flesh,
you drank of my juice.
You forsook every other
and cleaved unto me.
We are flesh of one flesh.
We are forged of one will.
We are still,
in the heart,
in the bone,
in the dark,
in the tongueless,

wondering place
where two are made one.
We are gift,
we are grace,
we are the face of love.
We are one, we are one.

Nicola Slee
England

Cherish

If someone offers you their body
To love,
Only cherish it.
Treat it with as much
Passion and care and tenderness
As you would have them
Treat your own.
If someone shows you their scars
And offers you such vulnerability
Only ever touch them healingly:
We are all wounded
Somewhere, somehow,
Holding within this gentle flesh
Signs of the body's struggles.
If someone offers you their body
To love,
They are giving you
Such a gift.
Cherish it with your life.

Rosie Miles
England

To Reflect Upon . . .

The boundary between healthy sensuousness
and unhealthy sensuality
is the fine line which only love can determine.

Within the psyche of each person
there is both a feminine
and a masculine dimension.
Do not be afraid
of your opposite
for you need it
to complete your personality.

W. L. Wallace
Aotearoa New Zealand

Sexuality

God our lover,
whose embrace is fierce
and ever expanding;
we hold before you those who are unloved

Name people known to you

Give us the Spirit
to work diligently for their inclusion
as we enlarge our understanding of your kingdom.
We hold before you those who are loved

Name people known to you

May we learn from all your lovers
of the endless bounds
and infinite variety of your love,
and celebrate it with you forever.

Janet Lees
England

Making Love With You

Is being born again
Is dying and rising to a new world
Is heaven come on earth

Is softness
and sweetness
and soaring
and the silence of holy prayer

Is wetness
and warmth
and wonder

Is tenderness
is trembling
is a torrent

You are the ground on which I stand
You are the air I breathe
You are the sky towards which I climb

You are my holy sacrament
      my sacred food
      my only good
We are the eucharistic feast
This is the divine mystery
of God made manifest in flesh
She is with us
in the body
in the blood
We are holy good
We are fecund god.

Nicola Slee
England

Extravagant Love

Setting: *The room has a centre table on which are set handcrafts, a jar of perfume, a vase of flowers, a silk scarf draped over and partly in the jar.*

Music is playing, quietly.

Readings: John 12:1–5, 7–8; 13:34–5

Reader: Six days before the Passover, Jesus came to Bethany, the home of Lazarus, whom he had raised from the dead.

Leader: We join Jesus and the disciples as they journey to Jerusalem. They are on foot, walking the dusty, rough tracks of Israel. Bethany is the home base of Mary, Martha and Lazarus, lifetime friends of Jesus. Friends whom Jesus has stayed with many times and received hospitality from them. Lazarus whom Jesus called from the tomb and bid his bandages be unwrapped.

Response: **Jesus, friend of Mary, Martha and Lazarus.**
                Christ who opened the tomb and called Lazarus to life.

Silence

Reader: There they gave a dinner for him, Martha served and Lazarus was one of those at the table with him.

Leader: Lazarus has joined the guests at the table for the meal that has been prepared for Jesus and the disciples. Lazarus whom Jesus called back to life. Friendship would hardly begin to describe the depth of relationship between these two men.

                Martha is serving as she had been on a previous occasion, giving her love in the preparation and offering of hospitality.

Response: **Lazarus sits with his friends at the table, Martha offers her love in service but what is Mary doing?**

Silence

Reader: Mary took a pound of costly perfume made of pure nard, anointed Jesus' feet and wiped them with her hair. The house was filled with the fragrance of the perfume.

Leader: *(picking up the jar)* This jar is symbolic of the size and amount of perfumed nard that Mary used. It is more than enough to cover Jesus' feet, legs and body. Did Mary begin at his feet, proceed to his legs, then to his body? This is an action of extravagant personal love, publicly declared.

Jesus does not rebuke Mary or refuse her gift.
Her gift is received, accepted.
An extravagant, sensual gift of touch, massage, emotion and love.

The perfume has filled the whole house, all present are drawn into Mary's action as they breathe in the lovely fragrance.

Response: **Can our love for Christ be so extravagant, so public? Does our love waft like perfume to draw others in? Can our love for each other be acknowledged and public? Can we receive, accept when a gift of love is given to us?**

Silence

Reader: But Judas Iscariot, one of the disciples (the one who was about to betray him), said, 'Why was this perfume not sold for three hundred denarii and the money given to the poor?'

Leader: Judas' words betray an embarrassment about what Mary was actually doing; about the sensual, sexual nature of her actions. Costly perfumed nard, anointing the man she loved, wiping him with her hair, touching and massaging him, mixing her tears and her love in an intimate action of service. Was Judas also embarrassed at Jesus' acceptance of her actions; at the interaction of this man and this woman?

Response: **Are we embarrassed by acts of sensual-sexuality? Do we stop and count the cost before an extravagant act of love?**

Silence

Reader: Jesus said, 'Leave her alone. She has bought it so that she might keep it for the day of my burial.'

Leader: Jesus approves of Mary's action and tells Judas to back off. More than just approve, Jesus gives her action a startling new meaning, that Mary had deliberately, knowingly, purchased and kept the nard to anoint Jesus with on the day of his burial. Did he mean that Mary knew and anticipated his violent death?

Response: **How can I support those people whose public actions challenge prejudice and oppression?**
Can I give extravagant acts of love, to those I love publicly?
Can I accept extravagant acts of love, from those I love?

Silence

Reader: You always have the poor with you but you do not always have me.

Leader: Jesus replies to Judas and all the disciples that there will always be opportunity to serve the poor – but not to love me – the human Jesus. Mary has participated in Jesus' death with an act so extravagant and so loving that we remember her, honour her, love her still.

Response: **May we be open and free to give extravagant gifts of love to one another.**

Silence

Reader: I give you a new commandment, that you love one another. Just as I have loved you, you also should love one another. By this everyone will know that you are my disciples, if you have love for one another.

Leader: At the Last Supper, Jesus gave his disciples this great commandment, to love. Mary has already anticipated and given Jesus the greatest of all gifts, of love, of herself.

We are disciples of Christ, we are known as such when we follow this great commandment. Hear it again, 'I give you a new commandment that you love one another. Just as I have loved you, you also should love one another. By this everyone will know that you are my disciples if you have love for one another.'

Affirmation of Faith

All: I believe in God who called Lazarus from the tomb,
  the same God who calls me from my closets of
  fear, self denigration and despair.

  I believe in God who shared table fellowship
  with the disciples, Mary, Martha and Lazarus,
  the same God who offers hospitality to every
  human being,
  the great 'I am' who created who I am.

  I believe in Jesus the Christ whom Mary anointed,
  with touch, with tenderness and with love,
  the same Jesus Christ who commands me to
  love,
  love God, to love each other,
  extravagant, personal public love.

  I believe in the Holy Spirit, gift of God,
  fragrant, flowing perfume of delight,
  breathed deeply into my whole being,
  liberating, energising, joyous, sensual.

  Come Holy Spirit, that I may be your disciple,
  when the closet doors are shattered,
  when every human lives to fullest potential,
  when I am full to overflowing with
  extravagant love,
  love for living, for life and for loving.
  Amen.

Leader: Go in Christ's name, to honour who you are by the gift
of God
Go in Christ's name, as God's disciples.
Go in Christ's name, following Jesus' great command-
ment that you love one another as God has loved us.
God's blessing go with us all,
Shalom
So be it
Amen.

Margaret Donald
Aotearoa New Zealand

Creation

(Inspired by Psalm 8)

Why are you mindful of us, O God?

An opened eye, an opened hand
Stealing away the hurt and confusion;

An opened heart, an opened mouth
Forming praise and hope and healing.

We've been taught that
   Our words are inadequate
      Our flesh is limiting and finite,
Yet you have made us
   slightly less than you
      and have given all the world
         into our care.

We celebrate you by feeling . . . fully,
   by opening eyes,
      by opening hands,
         by opening hearts,
            by opening mouths.

When I look at the heavens
   and the works of your fingers
   I know why you are present with us.
   And I laugh.

Marcie N. Wexler
Canada

Lovemaking

Dear Creator,

Create our lovemaking flesh,
Live in our desires.

Blossom and sing
in our bodies
as we join

as we close the gap
between two of your creatures.

Draw us out dear God,
out of our skin and bones
and stamp this
   with your caress and smile,
   your covenant.

Bring the words out of us, God,
your words,
that describe and grasp
that canonise
the shapes we make

the shapes whose parts are male
like knotty wood
whose parts are female
like piles of leaves

canonise
our gay and lesbian shapes
dear God
with breath and tears
with colour and smell
with words.

Clifford Frasier
USA

A Love Poem to God

You are multiple, huge, bellowing,
blowing bubbles, waiting to burst,
birthing dreams and desires
not spoken by your mouth
to mouth you hold me,
longing to mingle
your multitude with mine,
by clinging and letting go,
by singing and being silent.

In you there are no opposites.
There is no us and them.

There are only your hands,
your soul,
your laughter,
which hold
all contradictions,
all polarities,
all loves,
together,
without tension.

Suzi B.
England

The Rich Tapestry of Creation

Pious people talk so easily about 'God's will', as though in every instance of life what happens must be what he wants to happen. 'One day we shall understand'; 'there's a purpose in it all'. Can God never be crossed, frustrated by the recalcitrance of the evolving universe he willed into being? 'It's all a part of the rich tapestry of creation', we say, and no doubt in one sense everything must be. But does that make everything good? Do we really believe that God manipulates every event – mega-tsunamis, viruses, solar flares, black holes – the way that in specific details, for some inscrutable reason, he has decided it should be? A good deal of the Bible assumes so but does that automatically make it true?

From a human-centred standpoint we can say this and no more. In the universe God has created and sustains, much in life is problematic. Some of it can be used by us as the raw stuff from which to make something good. Some cannot. Only by taking up the cross this lays upon us may we, crawling along the Way of Suffering, create from it some positive spiritual power. Spiritual discernment is the gift of being able to see within which of these two categories each change and chance of life belongs.

Christian thinking on sexuality has too often lacked this discernment. For cultural and psychological reasons some kinds of sexuality have been lumped with the things that have no good possibilities and so must simply be endured as a sacrifice when in truth they belonged on the positive side. Not all sexual conditions, desires or actions belong there. But certainly more than tradition has supposed have the potential for goodness, godliness, Christlikeness.

Were the Church readier to listen, to learn to use its imagination, it could see the face of God in unexpected places.

John Austin Baker
England

Thou-She, Thou-He

'I will never forget you,'
says the Infinite Lover,
Thou-She, Thou-He.
'I will penetrate your being.
'I will hold you alive,
and growing in my womb space.
'I will firmly steady and contain you all.
'I will send you forth transformed.'

Mary Robins
England

Could Jesus Have Been Gay?

Could Jesus have been gay?

The question is, apparently, provocative. According to comments and letters in the media this week, even asking the question is sacrilege, blasphemy, a vilification of Christianity, and a mockery of people's deepest beliefs. The Priests Anti-Defamation League is on alert, the Australian Family Association is outraged, George Pell is being 'kept informed', and even the Moslems are appalled – and all because of a play called 'Corpus Christi' which re-imagines Jesus as a tender, thoughtful and gutsy young gay man in modern day Texas. Why all the fuss?

Some years ago I taught a Religious Education course entitled: 'Jesus: Man, Myth, or Magic?' Each year I would tell my Year 12 students about the Church's teaching that Jesus was 'truly man', and we would then list some of his human characteristics. They were fine with the dark eyes and the long hair and beard, but things got tricky when his human digestive system and his male reproductive organs were mentioned. Some students were embarrassed, some shocked, and a few flatly refused to accept that Jesus was built like a normal man. Something in Christian culture and piety had instilled in these 20th century teenagers a kind of revulsion at the idea of Jesus Christ, True God and True Man, having to go to the toilet or cope with sexual arousal like any other human male.

Mind you, these students were not the first to feel this way. Some early theologians speculated that Jesus would have perfectly regulated his intake of food and drink so that he satisfied his nutritional requirements without ever needing to urinate or defecate. Some of the desert monks tried this themselves, with sadly predictable results. Even more common was the claim that Jesus had 'perfect' control over his sexual responses, so that he would never, for example, have had to cope with an inconvenient erection.

Most modern Christians would chuckle at these ideas, yet the smell of a pious, shame-based, anti-physical moralism has lingered long in Christianity – and my students sniffed it out. I suspect that beneath this week's outrage at the suggestion that we might validly imagine Jesus as gay, is a persistent horror at the idea of him being truly human – sensual, emotional, sexual, physical. The same outrage erupts when a film-maker like Martin Scorsese depicts Jesus' love for Mary Magdalen, a theologian like Bishop John Spong questions the physical virginity of Christ's mother – or when gay Catholics line up to receive Holy Communion. The sacred and the sexual, spirituality and sensuality, prayer and physical pleasure must never be merged or celebrated together. Yet this is precisely what happened when the Divine became human in Jesus.

And when we look at the sort of man Jesus actually was, we see that the 'Incarnation' was not some ethereal epiphany, but more like a sweaty, heartfelt bear-hug between God and humanity, indeed, more like the passionate, profound, joyous inter-penetration and mutual surrender that happens in really great sex.

The Gospels show Jesus as a man who understood and treasured the sensuality of human living. He brought the fine 'new wine' of celebration, both literally and figuratively. He loved parties, dinners and weddings, and was accused of being a 'drunkard and a glutton' and of partying with 'prostitutes and sinners'. He responded by claiming that the Kingdom of God would be one great feast where the poor, the prostitutes and the ritually unclean would have pride of place. He healed with spit, clay, touch and breath. He cuddled children, hugged lepers and delighted in a tender foot massage offered him by a woman of ill repute. He taught using images of earth, weather, animals, flowers, birds and house building. He revealed the secret of his identity to a woman from a despised religious sect who had been married five times and was 'living in sin'. He revealed his resurrection to his apostles over breakfast on a beach. He left bread and wine – those essential elements of dinner parties ancient and modern – as living symbols of his abiding presence. He referred to himself the 'Bridegroom' and called everyone to an eternal banquet of love.

Considering all this, could Jesus have been gay? The Gospels tell us nothing about Jesus' 'sexual orientation' – in fact the concept itself has only been explored in modern times.

They are equally silent about whether he was ever married or had ever had sex. What they do show us is a man who lived with passionate freedom and who loved fearlessly and without regard for cultural norms or religious rules. The love he shared with Mary Magdalen was clearly intimate, tender and committed. The people he made his 'family of choice' were three unmarried adults – Martha, Mary and Lazarus – and if Jesus too was unmarried they must have been viewed as a somewhat shocking little community in a culture strictly regulated by 'traditional family values'. Jesus himself was always telling people to leave their families, homes and properties to form a new community of equality, love and justice.

Jesus was also deeply comfortable sharing intimate love with members of his own sex. Two men were especially close. John, 'the disciple Jesus loved', would lay his head on Jesus' chest at that final dinner and, alone of all the apostles, stand by him during his crucifixion. Lazarus was referred to by Jesus' friends, when speaking to Jesus, simply as 'the man you love'. He was so dear that Jesus would weep openly at his tomb and perform, for him, his most astounding miracle, raising him from the dead in the very shadow of Jerusalem and provoking the fatal wrath of the religious authorities.

There is also a rarely explored Gospel story that reveals Jesus' attitude towards same-sex lovers. One day a Roman centurion asked him to heal his dying servant. Scholars of both Scripture and Ancient History tell us that Roman centurions, who were not permitted to marry while in service, regularly chose a favourite male slave to be their personal assistant and sexual servant. Such liaisons were common in the Graeco-Roman world and it was not unusual for them to deepen into loving partnerships. Now the Jewish people were not ignorant, and like oppressed people everywhere they would have gossiped about their conquerors, especially the local battalion. This particular centurion was well known in the Jewish community, so when he humbled himself and pleaded with Jesus to heal 'my beloved boy', everyone would have known exactly what he meant.

Undoubtedly Jesus, who knew the secrets of human hearts, also knew. Jesus offered to go to the servant, but the centurion asked him simply to speak a word of healing, since he was not worthy to welcome this itinerant Jewish teacher under his roof. Jesus responded by healing the servant and proclaiming that even in Israel he had never found faith like this!

So, in the one Gospel story where Jesus encountered people sharing what we would call a 'gay relationship', we see him simply concerned about – and deeply moved by – their faith and love.

(The history of this story contains a deep irony, noted by Fr John McNeill, the gay theologian expelled from the Jesuits on Vatican orders. The words of the centurion, 'Lord, I am not worthy that you should enter under my roof. Say but the word and my servant shall be healed' form the basis of the prayer said by Catholics over many centuries just before they receive Holy Communion. They come from the lips of a man we would call gay.)

So, to return to our original question, could Jesus have been gay?

I believe the answer is yes, but I don't think it ultimately matters. What does matter is Jesus' revelation that tenderness, passion, generosity and overwhelming love are the very heart of God. What matters is that we lesbian, gay, bisexual and transgender people claim the grace of seeing, in the face of Christ, our own true face reflecting the image of God. What matters is that our heterosexual sisters and brothers learn to see shining in our eyes and in our loving, no less than in theirs, the light and love of the God we both worship.

Each of us must be able to say to the other, in the words that open the play 'Corpus Christi': 'I bless you and honour your divinity as a human being'.

Michael B. Kelly
Australia

Prayers Inspired by the Works of Derek Jarman

Sweet Garden of Pleasures
In which we wander
Not afraid to be naked
Having lost the fig-leaf
Hiding the handle of the closet door
Some time past

There's a wisdom in pleasure
A happy yet wise acceptance of our natures

Praise to the giver of all good things
For disturbing, exciting pleasures
For the ecstasy where we know as we are known

*****

We fear oblivion
Yet sometimes desire it
Weary of our identities
Yet not having anyone else to be

Losing ourselves in you, O wisdom
May it be to us –
A root growing into the earth
A roaring ocean
A transforming fire
A rushing wind

Amen

*****

Our bodies are our own
But not our own

Beauty blossoming, with a price of gold
Marketed, faked, possessed and sold
A precious possession
But neither beauty of body or mind
Is really ever possessed but rather
Reflected light

Incarnate icon of human beauty
Suffering servant of no loveliness
Caught between our desires and our realities
We ask for your intimate touch of truth

*****

Is it the sensation of geological time
Or is it the harmony of the spheres
That makes us sense our own death within us?

Feel ourselves both here and alive
Yet feel, at moments, that we are already long past
And time has compressed us wafer thin

Communion of saints
Holy immortal Trinity
Find me and shelter me in this time of eternity
Amen

*****

At the breaking open of a closet
At the switching on of pink neon
We shall remember them
Those that didn't make it this far
That got lost in the labyrinth of self-pity
Or cut themselves out of history
In a moment of desperation
Drowning in a sea of hatred

Wisdom of earth and air, fire and water
Let those unspoken bodies experience the touch
Of the love and wisdom that's deeper than any ocean
That inhabits inter-stellar space and the depth of every soul

*****

God of the rainbow covenant
Whose delight is in difference
Let us know the joy of contrast
The Other who impels us to friendship

Let us pray 'pink'
Because it colour contrasts
With the world we're living in

Draw us into you
Difference without end

*****

Friend and divine lover
In our exodus from 'church'
As we cross our red sea
And watch the deserts widen around us
May we stand in the downpour of grace
And see a thousand blossoms grow around us
The gifts that wisdom gives to its true lovers

Steve Carr
England

What Would I Say To Christ?

My Father was a Presbyterian minister and my Mother a passionate believer. It was my Mother who often said to me 'If you become a homosexual, it will break my heart' and 'To your own self be true, and it follows as night follows day, that you cannot then be false to any one.'

My Mother died when I was twenty leaving me somewhat confused. Before I married at twenty-one I told my fiancée that I thought that I was gay. I tried to be heterosexual, but the propensity was always there, so I settled for being a provider rather than a lover. My wife died when I was forty.

Jesus came eating and drinking and some said of him, 'Here is a glutton and a drunkard, a friend of tax collectors and sinners.' But wisdom is proved right by her actions.

Of the unrepentant cities, Jesus said, 'If the miracles that were performed in you had been performed in Sodom, it would have remained to this day.'

Jesus also said 'Woe to you teachers of the law and Pharisees, you hypocrites! You shut up the kingdom of Heaven in men's faces.'

My Mother also said to me 'If in whatever you are doing, you are not afraid to meet your Maker, then whatever you are doing is not wrong.'

Should Christ appear, when I am making love to a man, what would I say to Christ? What would I reply to Christ if he asked 'Mind if I join you?'

Hector Cumming
USA

Rainbow Steeple

We are a church with a rainbow steeple
This is a place for rainbow people
Make the windows wide, let the light inside
To proclaim the truth of God.

Turn the world upside down
Colour in that gloomy gown
Ev'rybody, straight or gay
Follow Jesus Christ's own dancing way.

We are a church with a rainbow Bible
'Love' is the Word that we read, not 'liable'
Here the human race is in no disgrace
We proclaim the love of God.

We are a church with a rainbow banner
Sample our wine, taste our rainbow manna;
Let the children play in the yard all day
To proclaim the joy of God.

Colin Gibson
Aotearoa New Zealand

LISTENING:
LEARNING WITH LITURGY

You Are Love

Dear Lord
You are the Way
Help us to find new ways of Walking
You are the Truth
Help us to find new ways of Talking
You are the Life
Help us to find new ways of Living
You are Love
Help us to find new ways of Loving.

Michael Reiss
England

To Be . . .

Be bold in doing justice,
be generous in loving tenderly and
be prayerful in walking humbly with God.

Ted Dodd
Canada

To Love More and More
(Philippians 1:9–10)

Dear Lord,
The grace and love that you offer us as your children
    is so pure and inclusive.
When we hurt,
        we bring our pain and disappointments to you,
            anxious to know that you will understand and forgive us
                for our inadequacies and shortcomings.
Lord, help us to be more like you.
Teach us to be more understanding and loving
        to our brothers and sisters
            who face personal challenges as a result of 'being'.
Being lesbian, Jewish, Afro-American, Hispanic, Catholic,
        homosexual, Caucasian, male, heterosexual, Asian,
            female, differently-abled – and the list goes on.

All of these things are 'distractions':
    they cause us to miss out on relationships
        that can bring the joy and love that you have promised.
We are all really much more alike than we are different.
    All of us have special needs.
        All of us, your children,
            face challenges in our society and our world.
The task we face
    in trying to understand and accept each other
        will come through love.
Love and only love
        will give us the desire to fully accept each other.
Help us to look beyond the distractions and differences
        and begin to see the true beauty in humankind.
I know, Lord, that I will be rewarded,
        my mind and my consciousness will be elevated.
It will be easier for me to love, share with and understand
        my brother and sister
I will live my life closer to you.
    I will have evolved.
        In the name of Jesus, I pray. Amen.

Susan S. Nimmo
USA

I Sing the Spirit's Life Within You

I sing the grace of God within you,
I know that grace within my soul,
And when we honour God in each other
We bring together one gracious whole.

I sing the love of Christ within you,
I know that love within my soul,
And when we honour Christ in each other
We bring together one loving whole.

I sing the Spirit's life within you,
I know that life within my soul,
And when we honour life in each other
The Spirit forms one living whole.

Colin Gibson
Aotearoa New Zealand

Our Gifts

Pray that the church accepts the gifts of those of us who are gay, lesbian, bisexual and transgendered

Thank you, O God, for the gifts you have given us to offer the church.
May those who have something against us be reconciled to us before approaching your altar.
May they not block our way or impede our access by their failure to rejoice in the way you have made us,
the talents we bring and the devotion we offer.
Keep us from failing to rejoice in the ways you have blessed us, this and every day.

Chris Glaser
USA

Dialogue Together
(Ephesians 3:18–19)

Creative Conversationalist,
You speak to us through Scripture,
Even today;
You cry to us through the oppressed,
Even today;
You rejoice with us through the uplifted,
Even today;
You pray with us through the church,
Even today.
Remind us through your incessant chattering
that we do not need to stop talking among ourselves,
no matter what conclusions we seem to arrive at.
Keep us talking.
Keep us listening.
Speak to us and through us:
Cry, rejoice and pray with us,
Even now.
In Christ.
In Spirit.

Chris Glaser
USA

The Love of God
(based on Psalm 36)

Your love, O God, breaks the small boundaries of our understanding.
Your faithfulness is not constrained by etiquette and protocol.
Your righteousness is as firm, yet as fluid as the ever-changing face of
    the mountains.
Your justice can plumb the depths of our humanity and raise us up to
    new heights.

You, O God, have created both the Gay and the Straight.
You love and nurture us all.
You preserve and honour our lives.
In you we find refuge and strength,
    inspiration and courage,
From the abundance of your spirit, without partiality,
    you give of yourself to us all.
For with you is the fountain of life,
    in you we find acceptance and renewal.

Liz Styan
England

Maker of Love

Giver of life,
Infinite God,
penetrating and containing,
gestating and birthing,
open our being to Yours.

Bearer of pain,
Gracious Beloved,
seeded with truth,
yearning, dying for new life,
open our being to Yours.

Maker of love,
hungry and passionate,
refining and enlivening,
guiding and inspiring,
open our being to Yours.

Holy Trinity,
looking at one another,
earthing and impregnating,
evoking life between You,
open our being to Yours.

Mary Robins
England

Love is a Miracle

Love is a miracle
and friendship a wonder,
let's spread more miracles
and wonders around;
open the floodgates
and water the dryness
till wonders and miracles
of friendship abound.

Love is a mystery
and friendship a marvel,
boundless as ocean
and deep as the night;
love is completion,
and friendship fulfilment,
simple, profound
as a bird taking flight.

Let us dance miracles
of friendship together;
let us dance wonders
of love in God's sight;
friendship and love
are the keys to the kingdom:
friendship and love are
our steps to the light.

Love is a miracle
and friendship a wonder,
let's spread more miracles
and wonders around;

open the floodgates
and water the dryness
till wonders and miracles
of friendship abound.

Colin Gibson
Aotearoa New Zealand

Wise and Wonderful Creator of Infinite Variety

Wise and wonderful Creator of infinite variety,
   forgive our petty striving to squeeze you
   and your creation into our conventions.
Sophia, flower of richest and rarest beauty,
   forgive our ignorance and prejudice
   that has kept us from seeing your sacredness.
Though you created us with wondrous diversity,
   we have tried to restrict one another
   into limited ways of being and doing,
   and we are all the losers.
Forgive us and heal us of our racism,
heterosexism, sexism, classism,
and all other evils that keep us
from appreciating your abundant, manifold creation.
Amen.

Jann Aldredge-Clanton
USA

Ground of Being

God, ground of our being,
Life-giver and Love-maker:
we praise you for you give us
a law not written in stone or on paper,
but a law of love in our hearts.
May we trust that law of love;
may we not be afraid to hear its voice
and may we know of its liberating power.

God of our laughter and God of our loving,
God of our anger and God of our tears:
We look for you in the theatre that we know as the church –
Whether it be Mad Scene or Love Scene
May your justice flow and may your kingdom come.

Holy Spirit:
voice of Wisdom and energy of change.
May that energy flow through us;
giving us the pride of our proclamation,
and trust in the God who sets her people free.
Amen.

Peter Colwell
England

Embrace Every Layer of My Being

May God strengthen your spirit, renewing that inward spring of life
that enlivens you, where the Holy Spirit, wedded to your spirit, gives
you access to all the riches of God.
May God embolden your will, encouraging perseverance and the
resilience to endure, especially in adverse circumstances, so that, held
by the One who keeps faith with you, you may persist in prayer,
generosity and hope.
May God renew your mind, filling your vision with the Divine desire
for peace, plenitude and joy, that you may have confidence in the love
that sustains you.
May God lift up your heart, catching all your longings and dreams
into the rainbow thread of Love's holy, playful, creative purposes for
all people.
May God refresh your body, renewing your relaxation and rest, for the
acting – and the waiting – asked of you this day.

Julie M. Hulme
England

Coincidental God

God of chance meetings and coincidental happenings,
help us to recognise where your hand has played its part.
We never know who we will meet,

or what is around the corner.
We cannot be sure which of our new encounters or experiences
will make a difference to our lives.

All we ask
is that you keep us alert to the possibilities
and aware of the opportunities
that you offer us.

We pray for the people we will meet today –
> for those we will greet with pleasure and recognition;
> for those we do not yet know but may discover unexpectedly;
> for those who will challenge us, or teach us something new;
> for those who will need our help;

and especially we pray for those we would rather not meet,
that we may greet them with the same openness that Jesus used in his
dealings with others.

Forgive us Father, those times when we fail to recognise the angels
you have sent to us,
but please keep coming back,
so that one day we may become aware of the ways in which you are
trying to reach us.

Help us to greet friend and stranger in your name.

Marjorie Dobson
England

Pride – Call to Worship (1)

One: In the name of the Creator who made us,
Many: **we celebrate the goodness of our lives.**
One: In the name of the Christ who came to set us free,
Many: **we rejoice in our diversity of love and life.**
One: In the name of the Spirit who sustains us,
Many: **we challenge ourselves to grow and to dream.**
One: God, in your presence we gather,
Many: **be among us now!**

Justin Tanis
USA

Pride – Call to Worship (2)

One: Sing praises to our God, who has done wondrous things!
Many: **We thank God for the gift of bisexual people, who teach us
        that love is boundless.**
One: Sing praises to our God, who has done wondrous things!
Many: **We thank God for the gift of transgendered people, who
        teach us the beauty of change and courage.**
One: Sing praises to our God, who has done wondrous things!
Many: **We thank God for the gift of straight people, who teach us
        to seek community beyond the ordinary and accepted.**
One: Sing praises to our God, who has done wondrous things!
Many: **We thank God for the gift of lesbians, who teach us to love
        that which is like ourselves and to celebrate the goodness
        within.**
One: Sing praises to our God, who has done wondrous things!
Many: **We thank God for the gift of gay men, who teach us to look
        for love beyond the expected and to love beyond the every-
        day.**
One: Sing praises to our God, who created us, redeemed us and
        sustains us.
        Thanks be to God!

Justin Tanis
USA

Pride – Call to Worship (3)

One: From the East and the West, the North and the South,
Many: **We gather in the presence of the Holy One.**
One: Bringing our joy and sorrow, with comfort and with
        trepidation,
Many: **We come together in this place.**
One: To those who love us and those who fear and despise us,
Many: **We proclaim the power of God working in our lives.**
One: Once we were not a people,
Many: **Now we are a people of God.**

Justin Tanis
USA

Pride – Call to Worship (4)

One: For all who have taken the risk of loving another,
Many: **We thank you, O God of Courage.**
One: For all who integrate their sexuality and spirituality,
Many: **We praise you, O God of Life.**
One: For all who have coloured outside the lines that society has placed around us,
Many: **We rejoice with you, O God of Creativity.**
One: For all who have lived true to the inner voice within,
Many: **We celebrate with you, O God of Integrity.**
One: For all who proclaim their pride at who you created them to be,
Many: **We dance with you, O God of Joy.**
One: For all that you are in our lives, and all the gifts that you have given us, and most especially, for the unique creation that is each one of us,
Many: **We honour you, O God of All.**

Justin Tanis
USA

Blessing for a Pride Parade

O Holy One, known to us in many ways,
be present with us now.
We ask for your blessings
as we rejoice as a community this day.

Bless our pride
that it be a humble reflection of gratitude
for who it is you have created us to be.

Bless our celebration
that it be an expression of our joy
in love and in health.

Bless our laughter
that it herald the building
of friendships and relationships.

Bless those who may come to oppose us
that our happiness may be contagious.

Bless our differences
as a source of our strength
and a sign of our respect for one another.

Bless those for whom it takes great courage to be here
that they may feel the abundance of life.

Bless our calls for equity and freedom
that we may both speak and hear
your vision of justice and peace.

Bless each one of us here today
with your presence
and our presence, one with another.

All this we ask of you, O Holy One,
for you are ever faithful to us.
Rejoice with us today! Amen.

Justin Tanis
USA

A Series of Pride Litanies Based on the Psalms

God Is Our Source
(Psalm 1:1–3)

One: As streams come together to form a single river,
          you, O God, bring us together to be one people, united.
Many: **We are all human, one people, made in your image.**
One: As many trees draw life-sustaining water from a single river,
          you, O God, are the source for many people, each one
          unique.
Many: **We are all different, many people, made in your image.**
One: We are bisexual, lesbian, gay and straight.
Many: **Made in your image.**
One: We are transgendered, female and male.
Many: **Made in your image.**
One: One people and many people, made in God's image.

Many: God of differences, God of unity, be with us as we worship you.

God is Our Guide
(Psalm 25:1, 4–10, 21)

One: Lead us in your paths, O Holy One.
Many: Guide us on our journeys of self-discovery.
One: Forge in us your ways of truth and hope.
Many: Shape in us pride in who you created us to be.
One: Form us as your justice-bearers in the world.
Many: Make us know your ways, O God; teach us your paths.

God Is With Us
(Psalm 56:1–6a, 8–13)

One: To those who shout with bitter words and prejudiced hearts, we say,
Many: In God I trust, I am not afraid.
One: To the voices within that doubt and fear, we say,
Many: In God I trust, I am not afraid.
One: To the forces of prejudice, to homophobia, biphobia and transphobia, we say,
Many: In God I trust, I am not afraid.
One: To the diseases of the heart, mind and body, we say,
Many: In God I trust, I am not afraid.
One: God of Justice, God of Beauty,
Many: Holy Creator of us all,
One: In you we put our trust; to you we call this day.
Many: Be with us as we worship.

God Is Our Refuge
(Psalm 61:1–5, 8)

One: O Loving God, we long for the day of dominion when your people will take to the streets, pouring out of homes everywhere, in celebration.
Many: We will march, banners flying, declaring our pride in who you created us to be.
One: We will dance in sheer exuberance and irresistible joy in your presence.
Many: We will be a living vision of your justice and equity; all will be welcomed, all will be included, all will be safe.

One: We will be every size, colour, gender and type, each with the right of self-expression, each with the right to love and live and be free.

Many: **We will look around and see the beauty of your creation, O God, on every face and in every heart.**

One: We will feel uncontainable wonder at the beauty that surrounds us and is within us.

Many: **May we, O Creator, make your living presence known on earth. May we march, dance, sing and love to glorify your name.**

Justin Tanis
USA

A Gay Psalm

Give praise to God
Give praise with all your being

Let lips that have not dared to speak
Shout words of praise

Let hearts restrained through hurt and fear
Share love in praise

Let hands rejected, tied, ignored
Build works of praise

Let minds by silent torment crushed
Create new praise

Let every life, constricted, cramped
Release its praise

Give praise to God
Give praise with all your being

Sigrid Rutishauser-James
England

Litany of the Eternal Word:
Interfaith Gay and Lesbian Worship

One Voice: Eternal and Everpresent One, we praise you for your word of love and life. We are grateful for all those people you have given us as a sign. For this Eternal Word:

All: **We give you all our thanks and praise.**

One Voice: We remember Ruth who broke all the traditions of her culture to be with the woman she loved. From Ruth we hear the words of love: 'Wherever you go, I will go too. Your people shall be my people.' For this Eternal Word:

All: **We give you all our thanks and praise.**

One Voice: We remember Naomi who accepted the love of a younger, foreign woman, contrary to all her society taught. From Naomi we hear that Ruth did more for her than seven sons. For this Eternal Word:

All: **We give you all our thanks and praise.**

One Voice: We remember David who loved a king's son. From David we hear the words: 'How wonderful was your love for me, better even than the love of women.' For this Eternal Word:

All: **We give you all our thanks and praise.**

One Voice: We remember Jonathan who loved his father's enemy. From Jonathan we hear that he loved David as much as he loved himself and that when the men parted they cried and kissed each other farewell. For this Eternal Word:

All: **We give you all our thanks and praise.**

One Voice: We remember John, the beloved disciple. From Peter we hear that John was the disciple that Jesus loved and trusted and who laid his head on Jesus' shoulder. For this Eternal Word:

All:	**We give you all our thanks and praise.**

One Voice: We remember the Christ, who formed a new family with his beloved disciple. From Christ we hear the words that named John as the son of Mary and thus Christ's brother and partner. For this Eternal Word:

All: **We give you all our thanks and praise.**

One Voice: We remember the words of the prophet Hosea that in the very place we are called not beloved, not of God, we will be called My Beloved, you sons and daughters of God. For this Eternal Word:

All: **We give you all our thanks and praise.**

One Voice: We remember all those people who have spoken to us of your love. We remember John McNeill, Chris Glaser, Carter Heyward . . . *(name other people known to you)* . . . and hundreds of unnamed people in history who show and tell us of your endless love and care for all of us. For this Eternal Word:

All: **We give you all our thanks and praise.**

Ken DeLisle
Canada

A Litany of Blessing

Women:
We bless the Teacher,
Who leans into the light looking for love, honesty, truth.
Who breaks down the barriers of stale tradition.
Who channels wisdom through cracks in staid authority.
Whose ear yearns for the experience of compatriots.
Who leads us to kinder days and gentler ways.

Men:
We bless the Teacher,
Who leans into the warm places looking for love, honesty and truth.
Who pounds on the barriers built by tradition.

Who is unafraid to ask, or answer the hard questions.
Who is unafraid to change her mind when she learns something new.
Who shares the stories of each generation.
Who leads us to kinder days and gentler ways.

Women:
We bless the Lover,
The God given blending of bone and blood.
Whose lovemaking on the mountaintops and grunting in the gutter manifests male energy
in embraced bodies of sweaty flesh and muscle entwined.
Explorer of fantasy and fetish.
Who opens the heart and quiets the mind.
Creator of new relationship models, forming families formerly unimaginable.
Circles of brothers overlapping, inviting acquaintances and strangers within.
And the touch of a friend,
Who leads us to kinder days and gentler ways.

Men:
We bless the Lover,
The God given blending of spirit and body.
Who embraces all in the womb, her milk let down to nourish each and every one.
Curve upon curve joining in sacred circles sending love inward and outward.
Explorer of fantasy and fetish.
Creator of new relationship models, making her own families, in many forms.
Who loves herself.
Circles of sisters, holding one another as lovers and friends
Who leads us to kinder days and gentler ways.

All:
We bless ourselves and the dear love of our comrades.

Steve Marlowe and Terri Echelbarger
USA

An Adaptation
(John 9:1–7)

As he went on his way, Jesus saw a woman who had been gay from birth. His disciples asked him, 'Rabbi, whose sin caused her to be lesbian? Hers or her parents' sin?'

Jesus answered, 'Neither she nor her parents sinned; she was born that way so that God's work might be revealed in her. While the day lasts, we must carry on the work of God; night is coming, when no one can work. While I am in the world I am the light of the world.'

With these words, he spat on the ground and made a paste with the spittle; he spread it on the disciples' eyes and immediately her pain eased and she was able to be herself.

Helen Garton
England

Through Touching and Loving
Our Faithfulness Shows

Through touching and loving our faithfulness shows,
We're drawn to each other, encouraged, love shows,
But even the depths of our human desire
Are cold to the furnace of God's hidden fire.

In every relationship where we are known
Some facets are covered and others are shown;
But God will enlighten, expose to our view,
A depth of compassion that we never knew.

So great is God's faithfulness, seasons of care
Will merge with each other and endlessly share
The touch and the tenderness, love's strong embrace,
A sensual expression of consummate grace.

Andrew Pratt
England

A Prayer of Approach (1)

God of Love we come together to meet in your name.
We come as a church family.
We aren't alike.

We don't look alike.
We don't think alike.
We don't act alike
and we don't all like the same things.
Despite our diversity
and our faults
we are all made in your image.
May we never forget whose image we reflect.

We pray for an inclusive church
and yet we don't always like each other.
It is hard to accept
that other good people can hold views that differ from ours.

Not all of us can walk a straight and narrow path.
Not all of us would want to.
We know there are many worthy paths to travel
and you can be found on them all.

Provision us with hope and joy.
Enable us to walk tall
and move forward valuing otherness.
Help us to seek good in everyone
and in that seeking there find you.

Rosalie Sugrue
Aotearoa New Zealand

A Prayer of Approach (2)

Word of God, human face,
We arrive at this place, this time,
Our paths merging,
To join in praise to you.

You spoke your word,
Spoke creation into being,
Spoke love into life,
Spoke chaos into peace.
You said, 'I am for you'.

You became your word,
Earth's fond guest,
Displayed a human face,
Became one with humankind,
You said, 'I am for you'.

You invite us to embody your word,
Speak our lives into love,
Speak our individualism into community,
Speak our complacency into action,
We say, 'We are for you'.

Lis Mullen and Clare McBeath
England

A Prayer of Adoration

Passionate God,
At the dawn of creation
and at dawning of all our creations,
You are present.

You dance the lover's dance,
whirling with the touch of tenderness,
nervously anticipating closeness,
making space for naked insecurity.

You discover unimagined possibilities,
embracing our tentative exploring,
caressing our broken vulnerabilities
delighting in unadorned beauty.

You kiss the world into being,
expending energy and effort,
drawn by all-consuming desire,
into the joyful abandonment of self-giving love.

Gary Gotham and Clare McBeath
England

A Prayer of Forgiveness

We come before you knowing hurt.
To suffer hurt is part of being human.
This we understand.
You know suffering too.
We know you understand.
We come to you nursing our hurts.
Some hurts have become so much a part of us
we are reluctant to let them go.
Forgive us.

We all know the pain of being different
for each of us is unique.
We want to rejoice in our uniqueness
but cannot.
Some of us fear difference
and in our fear
despise those
we brand as 'very different.'
Forgive us.
Save us from fear.

Others of us believe we have good reason
to take the moral high ground.
Forgive us.
Save us from arrogance.

Heighten our awareness of otherness.
Keep us sensitive to the pain of difference –
difference caused by gender, sexual orientation,
ethnicity, culture,
physical or mental impairment,
age, experience and status.

And now we bring our hearts to you
the Pain Bearer.
Accept the hurts we name . . .
Free us from our pain and save us from causing hurt to others.
Help us to be like Jesus
caring a little for Scripture
and a lot for people.

This we ask in His name.
Amen

Rosalie Sugrue
Aotearoa New Zealand

A Prayer of Confession

Out of my pain
I confess my hate-filled days.
Out of my anger
I confess my wish for death.
Out of my fear
I confess my distortion of truth.

> O God who knows us in our weakness
> and befriends us in our chaos,
> free me from hate and fear;
> turn pain and anger
> into tools for healing;
> open the door to reconciliation
> and restitution of right relationships
> between friends and neighbours,
> between lovers,
> between
> nations and peoples,
> that your truth may reign
> in our hearts,
> and your peace
> welcome us home.

Kate McIlhagga
England

A Prayer of Intercession at the Beginning of a Year

God of our yesterdays
and
God of our tomorrows
We ask that you be with us now,
God of our today.

We stand on the brink of a new year
uncertain and unprepared
but if you are with us
we are unafraid.
We know not what to expect.
Our desire is to be equipped for what is to come.
Our hope is to travel light
and carry what is best
from the past
to the future.

God of Vision and New Possibilities
open our hearts and minds
to the reality of your presence.
God of Light illuminate the dark places of our lives.
We are not perfect people.
Come through the cracks of our imperfections and fill us with your
light.

We pray for all marginalised people.
Those who suffer discrimination because of
gender, sexual orientation,
race,
physical impairment
or their beliefs.
Give them strength and belief in their worth.
We pray for those active in discrimination
and those who allow it to happen.
May they know what they do.
May they understand the hurts they cause.

We gather our thoughts in this sacred place
Knowing that you have heard each sincere desire.
We long for a time when all people are valued.
May our unconditional love flow from us to others
may it swirl and curl
Through the year embracing all who seek a better life.

Rosalie Sugrue
Aotearoa New Zealand

O God, Who Conceived Me

O God, who conceived us and created us
Who nurtures and cares for us
Who stands alongside us as we grow and develop
Who models for us the way to be,

> May we revere Your name
> May we stand in awe of You
> May we speak of You with unqualified respect.

Let what we do and build, and create
Be more and more in line with Your governance.
May your creative Spirit flow ever more freely
Through our lives, powering our actions and shaping our words,
Here where we live, in our homes,
> at our work
> and in our leisure.
Even as Your Spirit flows throughout the universe.

> Give us today the things we need
> To sustain us, to help us grow:
> Food for our minds and emotions as well as our bodies.

And forgive us for getting things wrong
For overstepping the boundaries of freedom
For taking to ourselves things that do not belong to us
For robbing others of what is rightly theirs.
And may we forgive those who trespass in our space
Who rob us of our due
Who wound by their mistakes.

> O God, lead us today and into our tomorrows
> But remember we are human:
> There are limits to our coping.
> We trust You not to put upon us that which is beyond us.
> Rescue us when our lives are threatened.
> Save us from real harm,
> As we embrace the challenges and risks of Your life in us.

For all things belong to You, O God.
Your Spirit empowers and sustains all that is.
And the celebrations in honour of it all, are for You.

Sigrid Rutishauser-James
England

The Divine Feminine

May the wine of the Divine Feminine
be created in you,
as it was in Christ,
as it was in Mary of Magdala.
Her beloved died.
Her desire for him,
and her newly healed self,
descended to ferment.

May the wine of the Divine Feminine
flow through you,
as it flowed through Christ,
as it flowed through Mary of Magdala.
She knew him still,
in her own separateness,
and from her depths
new wine rose.

May the wine of the Divine Feminine
send you forth,
as it helped send Mary of Magdala.
They touched for a moment –
companion lovers –
and she is free to tell,
'Love is Risen'.

Mary Robins
England

We Are Part of the Church

Voice One: We are part of the church universal –
faithful people of every colour,
gender, class, sexual orientation,
age and ability,
gathered to love and serve God.

Voice Two: We are an Opening and Affirming church[1]
Together, let us worship God,
rejoicing in the good news which we celebrate this day!

All: There is a place in God's heart,
there is a place at Christ's table,
there is a place here and in every welcoming church
for all people – Lesbian, Gay, Bisexual and straight.

Voice One: Christ who gathers us,
bids us follow in the ways of love and justice.

All: May our hearts be open to Christ's leading in our worship
and our living, this day and always.

[1] The denomination or local congregation can be named here.

Ann B. Day
USA

We Are the Body of Christ

Voice One: We are the body of Christ.

Voice Two: The hand clapping, toe tapping, heart pumping, mouth tasting, arms embracing,

Voice Three: Justice seeking, hymn singing, love making, bread breaking, risk taking

All: **Body of Christ!**

Voice One: Baptised by one Spirit, we are members of one body,

All: **Many and varied in gender, colour, sexuality, age, class and ability,
we are members of Christ's beautiful body.**

Voice Two: None of us can say to another, 'I have no need of you.'

All: **For only together can we find wholeness.**

Voice Three: None of us can say to another, 'I will not care for you.'

All: **For we are connected like muscle and bone.
If one suffers; we all suffer. If one rejoices, we all rejoice!**

Voice One: Thanks be to God who in Christ has made us one.

All: **Let us worship God!**

Ann B. Day
USA

A Prayer of Affirmation

God who made me in your image
Teach me to love myself as you love me.

God who made me in your image
Allow me to show that image to the world.

God who made me in your image
Help me to see your image in all those I meet.

God who made me in your image
Teach me to conserve and protect all your creation.

God who made me in your image
Bless, protect and keep me and all your children safe.

Anna Cory
England

Statement of Faith

God is hearing what we hear
God is seeing what we see
Urging us
With others
To make fresh
That which is in decay
God is crying when we cry
God is laughing when we laugh
We are known
In community with believers
In ministry with the marginalised
Encouragement and support

Are the gifts we exchange
In our places of rest, work and play
In our speaking of dreams and vision
In our physical, emotional and spiritual relating
Being loved
Empowers lesbian women and gay men
To, in turn, minister in love.

Ken DeLisle
Canada

We Believe in a Sacred Power

We believe in a sacred power within and around us – a divine spirit
that we call by many names and experience in many ways – that
empowers and heals – that calls us forth.

We believe in our creativity.

Making and transforming beauty out of words and notes, images and
colours, lines and pictures – and silence.

We believe in doing justice.

Justice that compels and empowers us to risk whatever we must risk
to create a climate in which all people can be who they are.

We believe in our dreams.

We experience the world as it is – in both its ugliness and beauty – and
we see what it can become.

We believe in making peace.

A peace that is based on openness, honesty and compassion.

We believe in hope.

We expect changes to continue to occur in our world. We rely on our
courage to continue to bring about these changes.

We believe in love.

A passionate love within and around us that laughs and cries, challenges and comforts, a healing love that perseveres.

We believe in potential.

We know who we are – painful as that can be at times – yet we continue to call each other to become more of who we are.

We believe in celebrating.

We remember and we commemorate. We create rituals. We play and dance and sing and love well.

We believe in our diversity.

We affirm our many shapes and sizes, colours and traditions, emotions and thoughts, differences and similarities.

We believe in life.

Life that wells up within and flows out of us like a streaming fountain.

We believe that we are good and holy – a sacred part of all creation.

Susan Kramer
USA

We Are God's Choice People

We are God's choice people,
One in every ten.
Gathered round Love's table,
Gay and lesbian.

Firstfruits of the vineyard,
Grafted from above.
Twigs a-bending inward,
Leaning on God's love.

Grace of Love's endeavour,
Tithe from God's own heart.
Called to live forever,
Charged with life on earth.

Brimful with fine vintage,
Pearls of greatest price.
Coins of dearest mintage,
Lavished, spent in grace.

Yes, we claim Thy Promise,
One in every ten.
Pour Thy spirit on us,
Gay and lesbian.

Bind us all as brothers,
Bless our sister-soul.
Strangers not, nor others,
Families now whole.

We are God's choice people,
One in every ten.
Gathered round Love's table
Gay and lesbian.

Tune: North Coates

Edward Moran
USA

Companions Let Us Pray Together

Companions let us pray together,
in this place affirm our faith.
God who made us is here among us,
we stand together in God's grace.

We are *whanau*[1] we are one,
brothers, sisters of the Son.
We are reaching for our freedom,
the prize that Christ has won.

The broken Christ stands here among us,
shares our suffering and our pain.
In breaking bread we find empowerment
to live in *aroha*[2] again.

The risen Christ brings light and laughter,
celebrates the life we share
The poured out wine of Christ's self-giving
inspires us to reach out and care.

Now let us sing to God who loves us
and accepts us as we are.
Go out from here and live that message,
proclaim our oneness near and far.

[1] *whanau* – family
[2] *aroha* – love

David Clark and Witi Ihimaera
Aotearoa New Zealand

Praise My Soul, the One Who Gives Life

Praise my soul, the One who gives life,
Fills your heart with joy and peace,
Touches, heals, renews, forgives you,
Speaks the words that bring release.
Alleluia, alleluia,
Words of life that cannot cease.

Praise God for the Spirit's working
Through our forebears' faith and love
Praise God still the same as ever,
Gifting us with grace enough.
Alleluia, alleluia,
Faithful Spirit, Holy Dove.

Loving God, Your grace enfolds us,
All our hopes and fears You know.
In your hands You safely keep us,
Rescue us from every foe.
Alleluia, alleluia,
Through Your power we live and grow.

Come you saints, cry alleluia,
Celebrate God's grand design:
Through Christ's gift all life re-birthing;

Eat and drink this bread and wine.
Alleluia, alleluia,
Living Word, God's gift and sign.

Tune: Praise My Soul

Sigrid Rutishauser-James
England

Psalm of HIV Lament

O loving God, wrap Your arms around me
for those who see me fear to touch me.
I take comfort in Your everlasting love
when doctors examine me with sterile gloves and masks
and Your priests bless me from the doorway.
My wanderings have others counted
but You, O God, behold my desire for intimacy.
They label me intrinsically evil and disordered
yet You know my nature and love me because You made me so.
When they call me sick, sinful, and criminal,
you see their fear and know my heart.
The fundamentalists say I am an abomination,
the right-wing deny my civil rights.
The ignorant believe I recruit their children,
the fearful call me a threat to the family.
In Your loving mercy is my solace, O God;
your knowledge of my soul brings me peace.
Give me Your compassion to forgive my accusers,
your kindness to see their lack of vision.
In You, O God, are my hope and my trust,
my weakness, as well as my strength, gives You praise.
As I close my eyes each night to the hostile world,
I feel the peace of Your glorious light.
I give You thanks for the supportive friends you give me
through whom Your eternal love shines.
You are my refuge, my loving, best friend,
I give You thanks and glory and praise.

Jeannine Gramick
USA

A Litany

From fear and ignorance;
Good Lord, deliver us.
From indifference and detachment;
Good Lord, deliver us.
From prejudice and pity;
Good Lord, deliver us.
From selfish and speedy judgements;
Good Lord, deliver us.
From shallow and simple answers;
Good Lord, deliver us.

Silence

With hope and wisdom;
Living God, inspire us.
With compassion and involvement;
Living God, inspire us.
With openness and love;
Living God, inspire us.
With full and prayerful generosity;
Living God, inspire us.
With courage to face the reality
and complexity of life;
Living God, inspire us.

Silence

Living God,
so inspire us with the depth of your love,
that we bear it on our lips and in our lives;
for your name's sake.

Amen.

Richard Watson
England

A Collect

Stigmatised God,
in Christ you tasted the bitterness of rejection
and bore the fear and prejudice of others.
Give strength to those who carry
that same weight today,
living hope to those in despair,
and the fullness of your love to the exhausted.
And give your people grace
that we may see in others the marks of your Son,
Jesus Christ our Lord.
Amen.

Richard Watson
England

Sharing Pain and Peace

We are the body of Christ.
In the one Spirit
we were all baptised into one body.
We are one body.

We affirm all that is good in each other:
our God-given dignity and integrity,
our companionship, and common pilgrimage:
We are one body.

We acknowledge the wounds we share:
in our society and in ourselves,
our brokenness, and our dis-ease:
We are one body.

We are one body.
We are the body of Christ.
The peace of the Lord be always with you.
And also with you.

Let us share the peace of Christ . . .

Richard Watson
England

A Thanksgiving
(based on 2 Corinthians 4)

Creator God, we give you thanks and praise.
In your mercy you have given us
the light of the knowledge of your glory
in the face of Jesus Christ.
But we have this treasure in earthen vessels,
so that it may be made clear
that power belongs to you alone:

Creator God:
we give you thanks and praise!

We are afflicted in every way, but not crushed;
perplexed, but not driven to despair;
persecuted, but not forsaken;
struck down, but not destroyed:

Creator God:
we give you thanks and praise!

We know that as you raised the Lord Jesus
you will raise us also with him,
and bring us into your eternal presence.
So we do not lose heart
as we are renewed day by day.

Creator God:
we give you thanks and praise!

We look not at what can be seen;
for what can be seen is temporary,
but what cannot be seen is eternal.

So we join with your people in heaven and on earth
in the unending song of praise:
Holy, holy, holy Lord;
God of power and might!
Heaven and earth are full of your glory.
Hosanna in the highest!

Richard Watson
England

I Hold a Memory Within My Heart
(This hymn may be used at times of parting, bereavement and funerals)

I hold a memory within my heart
of sunny days and bright,
when we would love to laugh and share
in special moments, without care.
I promised that we'd never part,
to hold you in my heart.

I hold a memory within my heart,
of days without the sun;
the stormy nights and constant rain,
when I would reach to share your pain.
I promised that we'd never part,
to hold you in my heart.

I hold a memory within my heart,
a gentle thought of you:
a precious jewel that grows more rare,
each time I turn . . . and you're not there;
and yet . . . I know we'll never part:
I hold you in my heart.

Tune: Repton

Anonymous

Neti, Neti
(Not This, Not That)

The church cannot be uniform, just as its members are not uniform. I came across a lovely idea in an American journal. It is about the Hindu idea of Lilla: Differentiation, Hindus believe, is a demonstration of Lilla, the cosmic, joyful, playful creation of God. But their word for the Almighty is Neti, Neti (not this, not that), a designation that reminds humans of their limits in power and understanding. Mortals too can participate in this joyous play, acknowledging and affirming the vast particularity of the universe.

I do not see why the church cannot reflect this kaleidoscopic view of creation in its worship, in its acceptance of the diversity of talents, forms of expression and sexualities and sexual orientations, for this diversity reflects the nature of divinity. But the church is the people so the church will only accept this when individual people themselves do. And this means accepting ourselves. I don't mean tolerating, although heaven knows how difficult that is, I mean rejoicing in diversity. For in rejoicing in diversity, insights are shared and one doesn't have to feel the need to make a uniform system to entomb what can be best described as 'not this, not that'.

Harvey Gillman
England

We Are So Slow

Throughout history the followers of Jesus, like the followers of Moses, are slow to recognise the gift of the Spirit in others. The Spirit is no discriminator of persons but is the source of all inclusivity. As women and men and communities we divide to rule, we break down rather than build up. We confess:

that we place upon the Spirit of God, who will blow where she will, as we try to confine our Spirit/God in the structures we create and the walls we erect;

Sing Kyrie Eleison

that we fail to hear the throbbing cries of marginalised people as women and men, as communities and nations we perpetuate the burden of debt for developing nations;

Sing Kyrie Eleison

that we do not repent for the structures of societies which create inequality and suffering and for our part in them, in the world, the church, our communities and our lives;

Sing Kyrie Eleison

God of boundless mercy you show the beauty of your power in constant forgiveness. As we follow the pattern of Jesus, may this powerful love be in our hearts so that we are motivated to bring about change and release for humankind.

Amen.

Roman Catholic Caucus
Lesbian and Gay Christian Movement
England
(adapted by Geoffrey Duncan)

The Desert

Leader: Like the deer that yearns for running streams
so we are thirsting for God, the Living God.
In the desert we search for the Thread of God.

All: **In the desert we search.**

Leader: Because of who we are, we are excluded from churches and communities.

All: **In the desert we search for the Thread of God.**

Leader: To you giver of life, we call in faith, in search of love, truth and wholeness.

All: **Be with us, hear us, we pray.**

Leader: We light this candle to remind us of the fear we experience in the world in which we live:

A candle is lit and placed on the communion table.

All: **May the Light of Christ dispel our fears.**

Leader: Let us remember all those who have been victims of violence because of who we are:

All: **May the Light of Christ bring peace to the world.**

Leader: Let us remember those who live with HIV and AIDS, those who have died with AIDS and those who fear:

All: **May the Light of Christ heal us and remove our fear.**

Leader: Let us remember all the ways that we as lesbian, gay, bisexual and transgendered people remain caught in our inner struggles:

All: **May the Light of Christ break all the chains that bind us.**

Roman Catholic Caucus
Lesbian and Gay Christian Movement
England

Bad Verse Prayer

rainbow in the moonlight
figure in the haze
tingle in the touching
years are glimpsed in days

covenant for freedom
failure not a sin
making, not restoring
hatred wearing thin

debt of full acceptance
giving God's to give
respect without obeying
earning, but not to live

dancing to the silence
opening to the closed
laying down in risk
and, trampled,
winning letting go.

Jesus, make it so.

Make it so.

David Coleman
Wales

God of Our Fathers?

I can no longer bow before the King in his Majesty,
                    the Lord who is to be obeyed,
                    the Almighty Out-There-God –
although instinctively I kneel before the Mystery . . .
                    the Depth . . .
                    the More-ness . . .
                    at the heart of all life.

I can no longer feel awed by a Conquering Warrior God or a Christus
Victor –
but I do feel drawn by a Vulnerable God and a Wounded Christ.

I can no longer pray to my Father in heaven –
                    nor even to my Mother in Earth –
although I do throw open the door of my life
                    in waiting expectancy
                    to being . . . to OM . . . to Love . . .
                    to the Mysterious Spirit . . . the Breath of Life . . .

I can no longer engage with a God who exerts power *over* me –
                    and locks me into rule-keeping, guilt and servility;
but I do exult in One who is both the power within *and the power* between,
                    you . . . and you . . . and you . . . and me . . .
                    as we strive to be fully present to one another,
                    to be authentic, reverent, respectful and loving . . .

I can no longer love a God beside whom I am a miserable sinner –
not a Christ who wants, from his heavenly goodness, to rescue me
from darkness –
but I cherish the God who gives me worth and helps me fulfil my potential;
                    and I am moved by the down-to-earth Christ,
                    whose fidelity to his deep inner feelings
                    promptings
                    lights up for me what 'life more abundant' can
                    mean.

I no longer relate to the God who is depicted in many of the hymns,
                    prayers and sermons of the church –
but I know that without the God who wakes me up to my deepest self,

and to the riches in all other creatures,
who astounds me with compassion,
and challenges me to live in the present moment
and attend to the wonder of the everyday,
I would be more shrivelled,
more selfish,
more violent
than I am,
with little to contribute towards the New Community
of justice and peace,
hope and celebration.

Kate Compston
England

A Good Friday Blessing

Bless you, Wise and Holy One,
for your enduring Word – the Word
that endures the cross of
words heard
but not understood;
palms bestowed
for the wrong reason;
laurels withheld
by home and family;
friends with us only
until the cock crows;
peers who condemn our I-am-who-I-am –
denounce our integrity
as blasphemy.
Bless you, Wise and Holy One,
for your enduring Word from the cross –
   whoever is true to I-am-who-I-am,
   who risks I-am for others,
   rises from affliction
   rolls away despair
   endures beyond
   even death itself.

Norm S. D. Esdon

Canada

A Liturgy to Celebrate a Saint's Day

Worshippers should gather in a circle.

Reader: You shall be my witnesses
                   through all the earth,
                   telling of all you have heard
                   and received,
                   for I arose and am with you,
                   and you have believed!

Leader: Let us pray:

                   God of Good News,
                   God of surprises,
                   surrounded by a cloud of witnesses,
                   queer men and women in history
                   and our friends,
                   named and unnamed,
                   known and unknown,
                   we drink deeply of their
                   wisdom and fidelity,
                   the faith of our foresisters and brothers
                   who showed us how
                   to love what we believe.
                   when driven to doubt,
                   when close to despair,
                   they taught us to believe in miracles.
                   we gather to thank them and
                   pledge ourselves to take our turn
                   as courageous witnesses
                   to your liberating love
                   through all the earth.

All: Amen.

Leader: Let us now proclaim our saint – our friend, companion
                   and guide upon the way.

*A person takes the picture, symbol or name of the saint and places it in the
centre of the circle. When they have done so they say the name of the person*

out loud and anything else they would like to say to or about that person.
They finish saying: Hail, (name)!
To this all reply:

All: **Your name is written in the book of life!**

Reader: In each generation Wisdom passes into holy souls;
                  making them friends of God and prophets;
                  She is indeed more splendid than the sun,
                  outshining all the constellations;
                  compared with light, she takes first place,
                  for light must yield to night
                  but over wisdom evil can never triumph.
                  She deploys her strength from one end of the earth
                  to the other,
                  ordering all things for good.

Leader: Those who work for change suffer resistance.
All: **So make us strong.**
Leader: Those who do new things sometimes feel afraid.
All: **So make us brave.**
Leader: Those who challenge the world as it is arouse anger.
All: **So grant us inner peace . . .**
Leader: Those who live joyfully are envied.
All: **So make us generous.**
Leader: Those who try to love encounter hate.
All: **So make us steadfast in you.**
                  Amen.

Elizabeth Stuart
England

A Prayer for Our Bodies

*This is a type of guided meditation. One leader takes people through praying
for their bodies. Time should be given to allow people to pray silently. All
parts have not been listed but be sure, dependent on your time, to be as
detailed as possible. Do not avoid the breasts and genitals. It is important that
we pray for erogenous zones, reproductive organs, and especially our
sexuality. Only a few suggestions for prayer should be given. Basically this
is a guided time for personal prayer. Given the frequent discomfort talking*

about sexuality in church in a positive way, this is one area of the body where some guidance is encouraged. These prayers for the body apply equally to the dis-abled and temporarily-abled. The following is offered as a guide for the leader.

We are invited today to take time to pray for our bodies. This is a time to pray with thanksgiving and intercession acknowledging our places of comfort and dis-comfort, ease and dis-ease with our own bodies. This is a time for private prayer and meditation in a communal setting. It is a time to be in touch with various parts of our body and to know that God loves every single part of us. This is a time for healing whether physically or in attitude towards our body. For some, this prayer may unlock painful memories. Know that God is with you and loves you. This is a time to acknowledge our strengths and weaknesses and to know that our bodies, just as they are, are the temples of God.

I ask you to close your eyes as a way of creating a safe space, a private space for this individual yet communal prayer for our bodies. You will be invited to pray over your own body. You may lay hands on the part of your body we are praying for or hold your hands over it. Please respect your own privacy, each other's privacy and enter into this time of prayer as much as you are comfortable.

We begin by placing our hands on the top of our heads.

Feel your hair or your thinning hair or your baldness. Smile as you remember some of the hairstyles you once sported. Feel this crown chakra and the energy that flows from the top of your head. If you suffer headaches, take time to pray for healing. If your brain works so much that you have a hard time sleeping, pray for quiet and calm for your brain and head.

You know what you are thankful for. You know what you need. Pray.

Place your hands on your eyes.
Pray for your eyes. You know what you are thankful for. You know what you need. Pray.

Place your hands on your ears. Pray for your ears.
You know what you are thankful for. You know what you need. Pray.

Nose . . .

Mouth
Throat
Shoulders
Arms
Hands

Place your hands on your chest/breasts. Pray for your breasts, your chest.
Pray for this sensitive place of your body, this nurturing part. Be aware not only of the heart and lungs that lie below, but your breast itself. Share with God your comfort or your discomfort praying for this part of your body. Share what you are thankful for. Tell God what you need. Pray.

Give this a little more time. For some people this unlocks some emotion.

Stomach . . .
Hips
Thighs

Place your hands on or over your genitals. Give God thanks for your sexuality. Give God thanks for the physical aspects of love. Pray for your sexuality. Give your sexuality to God. Remember that God knows everything already. In the privacy of this moment, with all eyes closed, talk with God about your feelings about your body and your sexuality. Pray.

Again, give this a little more time.

Legs . . .
Knees
Ankles
Feet

As you finish talking to God about your body and praying for your body, stretch upward, with your arms open offering all of yourself to God. Know that God loves you, all of you! Know that you are created in the image of God. Know that your body is sacred! Know that you are the temple of God. Give God thanks for the joy of being an embodied spirit!

Open your eyes. Look around the room and give God thanks for the diversity of bodies. Know that everyone is made in the image of God.

Know the sacredness of every body in this room.

God, we thank you and bless you. Continue to teach us to bless our bodies, our whole body, and to be responsible stewards of our bodies. Thank you for this time of blessing and healing. Amen.

Colleen Darraugh
USA

Celebrate a New Day Dawning

Celebrate a new day dawning, sunrise of a golden morn;
Christ Sophia dwells among us, glorious visions now are born,
Equal partners 'round the table, we make dreams reality;
Calling out our gifts we nurture hope beyond all we can see.

Christ Sophia lights the pathway to a world of harmony;
Sister Brother Love surrounds us, nourishing our synergy.
Earth joins in our rich communion, grateful for our healing care;
Leaping deer and soaring eagles, all Earth's fullness now can share.

Sing a song of jubilation, dance with joyous revelry,
Clapping trees and laughing rivers join our call to liberty.
Free at last to blossom fully, flow'ring forth in beauty bright.
We become a new creation, bursting open into light.

Tune: Hymn to Joy

Jann Aldredge-Clanton
USA

EUCHARIST

The Ritual of Welcome

In the name of God the creator who has made you in the divine image
and delights in the diversity of creation,
in the name of God the liberator who breaks the bonds of oppression,
in the name of God the love-maker who rejoices in true love
wherever it is found,
we welcome you into the lesbian and gay community and promise to
do all we can to support and sustain you in the days to come.
With you we commit ourselves to integrity and promise to fight
ignorance, injustice and fear wherever it is found.

We now share together bread and wine. These are the symbols of
God's commonwealth where all shall live together free from pain,
exploitation and oppression, delighting in the diversity of God's
creation. By sharing the bread and wine today we recognise that what
we are celebrating today takes humankind one more step along the
road towards that goal.

Bread and wine are shared.

Elizabeth Stuart
England

A Service for Eucharist

Leader: May God be with you.
Response: **And also with you.**
Leader: Open your hearts.
Response: **We open them to God and to One Another.**
Leader: Let us give thanks to God.
Response: **It is right to give God thanks and praise.**

Leader: It is right and our joy to give you thanks
                hope-breathing, love-giving God, our creator,
                for you have made us in your own image
                shaping us with infinite care, as creatures
                of delight and passion, setting us
                in a world of every good thing, a world
                of our giftedness.

It is right and our joy to give you thanks
world-gazing, vulnerable God, our Cherisher,
for you sent Jesus to walk among us, sharing
our humanity, knowing with us the bodily pain and hurt
as integrity is trampled in the dust,
and justice dissolves in empty words,
One whom even death could not stop from loving us.

It is right and our joy to give you thanks
encouraging, hope-cheering God, our Companion,
for you are present with us in the Spirit,
provoking us, lifting us, nudging us
to work for the healing of this world's brokenness,
to keep alive the dreams and visions of a world
where all are valued, where God may look
from heaven and see that all is good, that all is very
good.

And so today, in the company of each other, and
in company with people throughout the world
we declare as generations before us have declared

Response: **Holy, holy, holy,**
hope-breathing God,
Heaven and earth are full of your glory;
hosanna in the highest.
Blessed is the one
who comes in the name of God;
hosanna in the highest.

Leader: Blessed is God who has brought us to this table.
We, who have come, remember that night among
friends,
the night of deathly betrayal, when Jesus took bread,
blessed it, broke it, and shared it, saying
    Take, eat, this is my body
    which is given for you.
    Do this to remember me.
And taking the cup, gave thanks and shared it, saying
    Drink this all of you;
    this is my blood of the covenant
    poured out for you.

Come, unsettling spirit of hope.
Be present in the mystery of this Eucharist
and lead us out to follow the risking Christ.

The Lord's Prayer (sung)

Leader: We break this bread
remembering
the brokenness of our world
and declaring
our hope of wholeness and shalom
is in Christ.

Response: **By eating this bread we become one in the hope.**

Leader: We pour this wine,
remembering
the pain and bloodshed of our world
and declaring
our hope in the overflowing love
of Christ.

Response: **By drinking this wine we become one in this hope.**

The distribution

Leader: Blessed be God who has raised us and shaped us from
the dust.
Response: Blessed be God who has brought us to this table.
Leader: Blessed be God who has given us the bread of life.
Response: Blessed be God who has fed us with the food of love.
Leader: Our hands and our hearts were empty.
Response: Blessed be God who has filled us with hope.
Leader: Let us go out risking the reality of the Gospel.
Response: We go in the name of Christ.

Judith E. McKinlay
Aotearoa New Zealand

Invitation to Communion (1)

God says:
'Everyone who thirsts, come to the waters; and you that have no money,
come buy and eat!
Come buy wine and milk without money and without price:
Listen carefully to me, and eat what is good and delight yourselves
in rich food.
Incline your ear and come to me; listen so that you may live.'

(Isaiah 55:1–2)

**We will bring bread and wine. We will bring ourselves and we
will listen to the Spirit so that we may live.**

God invites us to this most joyful of feasts.
We are invited to share this bread and wine;
The body is broken and blood poured out.
We are invited to come as we are.

**We will come and receive as we are and we cannot exclude anyone,
for this is the Lord's table.**

In thanksgiving we come, for Christ is known in this meal of grace.
In remembrance we share, for Christ broke bread and shared wine
on the night before he died.

Peter Colwell
England

Remember Me
(A meditation for World Aids Day)

This is my body . . .
Weakened by chronic fatigue,
Wracked by stomach cramps,
Wasted by daily vomiting and diarrhoea.

This is my blood . . .
Tainted by an alien virus,
Tightly sealed for testing in laboratory phials,
Taken and touched by protected, plastic skinned hands.

This is my life . . .
Wrung out, washed up,
Lonely, labelled,
Trickling away too soon.

Remember me and pray for me
At your communions,
As you share the bread
And drink the wine,
That I may die believing
His body was broken,
His lifeblood shed,
To hallow and redeem
your life and mine.

Jean Mortimer – for Matthew and many of his friends
England

Preface for the Thanksgiving Prayer in the Holy Eucharist
(Written for a House Eucharist for a local gay group)

The Lord be with you
And also with you
Lift up your hearts
We lift them to the Lord
Let us give thanks to the Lord our God
It is right to give thanks and praise

It is indeed right, it is our duty and our joy
to give you thanks in all places and at all times.
But on this day we give you especial thanks
that you have brought us to life,
made us in your image
and enriched us with the gifts of your love.
As your Son Jesus Christ taught your people
that we should see the gifts of grace
in the context of love and mutual regard,
may we so affirm what we are,
rejoice in your love for us and for our brothers and sisters,
have strength to face those who despise us,
have compassion for those who misunderstand us,

and have confidence to stand with the
community of all the baptised around your table
that with joy we may receive the gifts of new life.
Therefore with angels and archangels
and with the whole and holy company of earth and heaven
may we join in their eternal song of praise.
Holy, Holy, Holy Lord, God of power and might,
Heaven and earth are full of your glory,
Hosanna in the Highest . . .

Christopher Wardale
England

Invitation to Communion (2)

Jesus said, 'This is my body.'
Take, hold, remember.

Remember the women who loved him:
Who birthed him,
Who touched his clothes,
Who wiped his feet,
Who shared their resources,
Who cradled him after death.
Take, hold, remember.

Remember the men who loved him:
Who birthed him,
Who touched his clothes,
Who wiped his feet,
Who shared their resources,
Who cradled him after his death.
Take, hold, remember.

And together with those who still love him
Who birth him, touch him,
Share with him and cradle him still,
Come to this feast!
Take, hold, remember.

Janet Lees
England

We Give You Thanks for Your Call To Love the World and to Change It
(Eucharistic Prayer)

Loving God, we give You thanks and praise,
for the calling You have given to each of us,
the call to leave the City and go on Exodus with You,
the call to new ways of being,
new ways of loving, new ways of living,
we give You thanks for Your call to love the world
and to change it.

Even though the World cannot understand us,
even though we are often killed
by the eyes and guns of human hate,
because they do not understand or are afraid of us,
despite this we thank You
and claim Your strength and pride
to be who You have created us to be.

And now we remember one
who also was not afraid to be different,
to show a different way of living and loving,
we remember Jesus,
the Clown of Glory who tumbles, juggles
and leads us through dance, song, play and fireworks
into Your glorious realm of equality, love and justice.

We remember the night when he was betrayed by one
who loved him,
and was led out of the City's gate to die for love.
On that night he shared a meal with his friends.
During the meal he took bread, blessed it, broke it
and gave it to his friends saying:

'Take this all of you and eat it, this is my body, which is given for you.
Do this and make me real in your lives.'

In the same way after supper, he took the cup filled with wine,
gave thanks and gave it to his friends saying:

'Take this all of you and drink from it, for this is my blood,
the blood of the new and everlasting promise of God,

for you and for all people.
Do this and make me real in your lives.'

Let's allow Jesus to become real for us
as we celebrate the central mystery of our faith.

Come Holy Spirit of our God,
Spirit of integrity, tenderness, joy and dance,
set this bread and wine apart from all common use,
and transform them and us, into the Body and Blood of Jesus,
whose love and life we seek to share.
Transform us into truly being the hands and feet of Jesus,
allow us to love and to serve,
give us the passion and
the energy to transform our world into Your Reign,
and give us strength and pride in ourselves as
we need to show the diversity of Your love.

This we ask through Jesus, with Jesus, in Jesus. Amen.

Come and share this meal
for this is not the table of the church or the establishment.
This is the table of God and the meal of the Exodus.
It is to give us strength and pride for our journey.
So come and receive with us,
eat the bread of salvation and drink the wine of passion.
Taste and see that Our God is good.

Andy Braunston
England

And Now We Remember One Who Gave Up Power
(Eucharistic Prayer)

Eternal One, we give You thanks and praise
For all Your many gifts to us,
We remember how, throughout the ages,
You have called us to be Your people.

As the people of God, we have, in many ways,
allowed You to change and challenge us.
We have learnt of Your care for all people,

of Your nurturing, mothering love,
we have learnt of the way
You take power from the powerful
and lift up the poor and oppressed.
We have learnt, despite the silence,
of the many women You have used
to spread Your New Realm of peace and joy.

And now we remember one man who gave up power
and who became like us in all things but sin.
We remember Jesus, who washed his servants' feet
and who, before dying, took some bread,
said the blessing, broke it, gave it to others and said,

'Take this all of you and eat it.
This is my body which will be broken for you,
do this and make me real in your lives.'

Later on he took a cup filled with wine,
said the blessing, gave it to the others and said:

'Take this all of you and drink from it,
for this is the cup of my blood,
the blood of the new and everlasting promise of God
which shall be shed for you and for all,
do this and make me real in your lives.'

As the people of God, let us proclaim the mystery of our faith.

Eternal One,
We ask You to send Your healing and wise Spirit,
Upon these gifts of bread and wine.
Bless them and make them holy.
We ask that You transform them
Into the Body and Blood of Jesus,
And to continue to transform us into truly being the
People of God.

Therefore, with the entire company of Your people
throughout the ages,
We join with those who are oppressed and excluded
To proclaim Your love and liberty for all.

Through Jesus, with Jesus, in Jesus,
All glory and honour belongs to You,
Our Loving God, for ever and ever.

Andy Braunston
England

To Celebrate Communion

Come to this table,
>for God is revealed here.

For in this place,
>God's promise is made known to us all.
For at this table,
>God's presence is made real among us,

offering food and refreshment
>for our journey,
food to nourish us
>on the way we are called to go,
refreshment to revive us
>when we long to turn back.

For here, God offers us the bread of life,
>the nourishment we need,
the reminder that the presence of the holy
>lives deep within our being,
giving us all that we need to become the
>people we are created to be,
giving us the affirmation to
>live fully, and love wastefully.

So come, for God longs to meet us here
>and feed us for our journey.

A Song

Prayer

In the beginning,
>the Word called creation into being.

Darkness was called to see light,
light was called to know the darkness.

Chaos was called to order,
order was called to acknowledge chaos.

Life was called to live in the face of death,
death was called to know the reality of life.

Beauty was called to be there in ugliness,
ugliness was called to know real beauty.

Hope and potential were called to see pain and despair,
despair and pain were called to dare to embrace hope and potential.

And the creator saw what had been made,
    and said,
        'This is good'.

And deep in the heart of creation
    lay the life of the creator,
a deep yearning,
    calling all to live fully
        and love wastefully.
And all this
    expressed uniquely in the life of one man
in whom the holiness of the creator,
    and the potential of the creation meet,
expressing completely what it was
to live fully
and love wastefully.

And in the place, at this table,
we meet, to remember one night of his life.
The last night of his life,
the night on which he was betrayed
    and handed over into the hands
        of human hatred and cruelty.
And we remember how, on that night,
he shared a meal with those closest to him.
And as they ate, he took some of the bread
    said a prayer of thanks,
and broke it, saying,

'This bread is broken, as my body will be'.
And he handed it to them,
        and invited them to eat saying,
'Remember all that I have been for you.'

And then, later, he took some wine,
        said a prayer of thanks,
and offered to them saying,
'This is poured out,
        as my blood will be poured out.
As you drink,
        give thanks for all I have given.'
For his body was broken,
        his blood was shed,
                and his life was taken
                        by cruel hands,
                        in a harsh world.

But his presence was not gone.
for after his death
        he was made known among them.
                And the power of his life
lives on today,
        in those who seek to follow,
and to them is given
the power of his spirit,
        given strength and wisdom
that they too may live fully,
        and love wastefully.

So, eat this bread and share this wine,
        and remember the one
who gave himself that we might know
                the true meaning of love.

And drink this wine,
        and give thanks for the one
who did not stop loving and calls us to follow.

And let us pray that
        by the power of the Holy and life giving Spirit,
this bread and wine here
        may be transformed

into signs of the life of Jesus, given for us,
    offering us all we need
        to sustain us on our journey.

All glory be to God,
in whose image we are made,
    who is known among us and within us,
and who is present with us in this place,
    in this time
        and forevermore.
Amen.

Anne Sardeson
England

Mother and Father of Us All
(Opening prayer at the Eucharist)

O God, true source of humanity,
mother and father of us all.
You renew us so we may grow like you.

We gather together:

from corner or limelight,
from fears or from sadness,
from hope or from gladness
in close relationships
or from separate lives.

We gather together:

who long for the nourishment,
the company,
the levelling
and the deepest joys,
found at your feast.

We gather together:

to meet you, to share your meal,
to celebrate your love,

and to rejoice in the possibilities that arise
when we honour all the diversity of our humanity.

We gather together – with you.

St James's Church, Piccadilly
London, England

A Candle Prayer

Reader: Give me a candle of the spirit, O God, as I go down into
the depths of my being. Show me the hidden things, the
creatures of my dreams, the storehouse of forgotten
memories and hurts.
Take me down to the spring of my life and tell me my
nature and my name. Give me freedom to grow, so that
I may become that self, the seed of which you planted in
me at my making. Out of the depths I cry to you, O God.

We are sometimes lonely and the world seems cold and
hard.

All: **In our loneliness we light a candle of thanks.**

Reader: We have known awe, wonder and mystery;
glimmerings of perfection in our own imperfect world.

All: **In our wonder we light a candle of praise.**

Reader: We bring together many uncertainties, many sorrows,
many joys, much wonder.

All: **We bring together many candles, many lights.**

Reader: May our separate lights unite in one that together we
may be nourished by one flame, in the name of our Lord,
Jesus Christ.

St James's Church, Piccadilly
London, England

A Post Communion Prayer

O God, Giver of Life, Bearer of Pain, Maker of Love,
affirming in your incarnation the goodness of the flesh,
may the yearnings of our bodies
be fulfilled in sacraments of love,
and our earthly embracings
a foretaste of the glory that shall be,
in the light of the resurrection of Jesus Christ.

St James's Church, Piccadilly
London, England

Living in the Spirit
A Eucharist

Please respond using the words in bold.

Invocation

Send forth your Spirit, Eternal God,
   and renew the face of the earth.
Move amongst us, Holy Spirit;
   surprise and unsettle us.
Grant us your peace, Spirit of Jesus;
   Let love and justice pour down like rain on the parched earth.
Amen.

Hymn

Litany

The Spirit of God moved over primeval waters . . . light appeared and
God's creative work began.
   Brood over us, Creative Spirit.
The Spirit of God energised prophet voices . . . and God's passion was
loosed upon humankind.
   Disturb us, Vigorous Spirit of God.
The Spirit of God stirred in Mary's womb, heaven sang of peace and
God delighted in human flesh.
   Stir within us, Deep Spirit of God.

The Spirit of God beat in the heart of Jesus of Nazareth and God's good news was heard by the broken and wounded.
Lift us up and heal us, Strong Spirit of God.
The Spirit of God breathed into disciples and apostles and God's love was displayed to the whole world.
Grant us new birth, Restoring Spirit of God. Amen.

Reading

Hymn

Reading

Sermon

Hymn

Offering

The Bread and Wine are presented together with the gifts of the people and everyone says:
Eternal God,
We offer this bread, made from the grain of life
We bring this wine, symbol of life poured out;
We give this money, the work of our hands
Receive them for the renewal of the world. Amen.

Intercessions

After each bidding, the responses will be:
Come, Spirit of God,
Renew the whole earth.

Lord's Prayer

Great Eternal One,
Creator of the universe, Holy is your name.
Your kingdom stretches across the face of the earth, embracing us all;
Glory and power are yours for ever.
We seek to know your will – help us.
We seek to do your will – guide us.
The fruits of the earth come from your hand;
We thank you for your mercy.

We are surrounded by your compassion and love;
Your generosity knows no end.
Give us grace to be generous to others.
You forgive us when we fail you.
Help us to forgive each other.
and bring in your kingdom of justice and love
that all people may sing of your power and glory
for ever and for ever. Amen.

The Peace

God's Spirit is healing this broken world and restoring to us our humanity. Let us then be healed and restored ourselves and live in peace. The Peace of God be with you.

And also with you.

We greet each other.

Hymn

We Remember

Let us recall how this sacrament began:
The Lord Jesus, on the night of his arrest, took bread; and, when he had given thanks, he broke it and said to his disciples,
'This is my body, which is broken for you. Do this in remembrance of me.' In the same way, Jesus took the cup after supper, and said, 'This cup is the new covenant sealed by my blood. Whenever you drink it, do this in remembrance of me.'
So let us, who are the people of God, do as our Lord Jesus did. Let us give thanks and so share in his life, that we may bring life to others.

Thanksgiving

We thank you, God, Mother and Father, for giving us food for each day and for every generous gift which sustains our lives;
We thank you for the love which comes to us through friend or lover, parent or child; and for strangers, through whom we catch glimpses of the fresh new world you are creating.
We thank you for Jesus, your Son and our Brother, in whom heaven and earth met; he who was friend of the friendless.
We thank you, Giver of all Life, for the Spirit which sustains our world, breathing into every living thing.

With sun, moon and stars and all creation, we worship and adore you, Gracious and Eternal God. Amen.

Breaking And Sharing

Jesus took bread; he gave thanks and broke the bread
His life is our life.
Jesus took the cup and said: Drink from it all of you.
His life is our life.
See, here is your God coming to you in gifts of bread and wine.
The gifts of God for the people of God.

Eternal God, breathe life into us as we eat these holy fragments. As this bread was once scattered seed and became one loaf; so gather all peoples together into one humanity. Heal this damaged world and bring all things into unity.
Through Jesus, your Son and our Brother. Amen.

Bread and wine are shared.

Prayer after Communion

Creator God,
You have fed us with symbols of Eternal Love.
We thank you for daily provision for our needs.
Renew us by your Spirit
and through us bring life to the world.
Hasten the day when the earth is renewed and all humankind can eat at one table.
For Jesus' sake. Amen.

Hymn

The Blessing

Go now; energised by God's Spirit.
Live out your lives in love and peace.
Thanks be to God.
Amen.

John Simmonds
England

CELEBRATE! REJOICE!

We Embrace

We embrace the notion that all people are embodied, sexual creatures. And in this embodiment, we rejoice.

We proclaim our faith that there is a divine welcoming for all people into spiritual community. And we profess our belief in the role the Gay, Lesbian, Bisexual and Transgendered community plays in the divine community.

We proclaim our faith that there is a divine calling for all of us to be in spiritual community. And we profess our belief that all of us – Gay, Lesbian, Bisexual, Transgender and heterosexual – are called to help create that community.

As a people of faith, hope and love we rejoice in the spiritual community gathered here today. And we pray we may continue to gather and profess our belief in the radical inclusiveness of divine love.

Andy Ulman
USA

Our Flesh

Our flesh
     is the temple
         of the Holy Spirit –
therefore do not be afraid
     to look at it
         delight in it
             celebrate it,
for it is something to be wondered at –
     a seat of mystery
         and worthy of all
             the appropriate caressing
that can be bestowed upon it.

W. L. Wallace
Aotearoa New Zealand

Your Body

Your body is a book that I would read,
With your permission,
As I invite you to read mine.

Part of the reading will be with my eyes
But most of it will, like reading Braille –
Be with my fingers and my body.
I do not seek to read your body by myself
As if it were some object
But to read it in mutual dialogue
Of playful reverence.
Together we shall explore with wonder
The line and mass,
Texture and colour
Of our sculptured complexity
And delineated simplicity.
In the exploration
Our spirits shall intertwine
Our life forces merge
Until with abandon
We shall dance within
God's unfenced
Eternity.

W. L. Wallace
Aotearoa New Zealand

A Celebration of Love

I have had
many beautiful encounters
with love
in my life –

Sometimes it has been
the love of nature –
the soft lines,
strong trunks
and the mossy smell of bush.

Sometimes it has been
the tenderness of another person –
a oneness in relationship,
shared silence,
the mingling of tears,
the fragile flower of romance.

Sometimes love has been
a passion for justice,
the fight for equality,
a concern for others,
grief at the Church's divisions,
anger at its petty-mindedness.

Sometimes love has been parenting
of child and adult,
of others and self,
of nature and ideas.

Sometimes love has been creating
words and music,
colour and form,
line and texture,
buildings and gardens,
one's own kind
and one's own life.

Sometimes love has been pain and sorrow,
sometimes dream and fulfilment,
sometimes tearful ecstasy,
sometimes common-sense practicality.

But at all times
love has nurtured me
enlivened me
fulfilled me
wooed me
and drawn me on
into the oneness
of God
divine lover
creator
liberator
never dying life
the source of all our loving.

And now
in the knowledge
that no love is ever wasted
and that all love

becomes part of God's love
I thankfully celebrate
all the loving
that God
has graciously
allowed me to partake
create
or enhance.

W. L. Wallace
Aotearoa New Zealand

A Celebration of Coming Out

'And alien tears will fill for him pity's long broken urn, for his mourners will be outcast men and outcasts always mourn.' These words are written on the tomb of Oscar Wilde, one of the most famous 'out' gay people of all time. He is buried in France in permanent exile, unwelcome in his own country. We are here today to show that it doesn't have to be like that, that despite living in a society and being part of a Church in which we are often unwelcome and feared we are not doomed to a life of mourning. We come here to give witness to the fact that our sexuality is a gift from God and that we rejoice in the opportunities it gives us to love and relate and enjoy friendships unshackled from the bonds of conformity and socialisation. We today declare our pride in belonging to a community of lovers who co-operate with God in building up the divine commonwealth of peace, freedom, love, justice and equality. We come here today refusing to be victims, refusing to be disempowered and marginalised into a life of mourning. And we come to welcome N into the lesbian and gay community. We pay tribute to his/her courage in coming out and we pledge to support him/her through all the joys and pains of being lesbian or gay in our world today. We pray for God's blessing upon him/her and upon us.

Elizabeth Stuart
England

A Liturgy for Coming Out

The room should be darkened.

The person coming out:

As Eve came out of Adam, as the people of Israel came out of slavery into freedom, as the exiled Israelites came out of Babylon back to their home, as Lazarus came out of the tomb to continue his life, as Jesus came out of death into new life, I come out – out of my desert into the garden, out of the darkness into the light, out of exile into my home, out of lies into truth, out of denial into affirmation.
I name myself as lesbian/gay/bisexual/transgendered.
Blessed be God who has made me.

All: Blessed be God who made you so.

The person coming out lights a candle and all present light their candles from it. Flowers are brought in. Music is played. The whole room is gradually filled with light, colour and music. Bread and wine are then shared.

Elizabeth Stuart
England

A Promise

In the presence of God and God's people, I, *N*, declare my love for you, *N*, and seek God's blessing on our friendship. I will continue to love you, care for you and consider you before my own needs, in good times and through periods of difficulty; I will rejoice when you are happy and grieve when you suffer; I will share your interests and hopes for the future; I will try to understand you even when I do not agree with you; I will help you to be your true self – the person God wishes you to be. In all this I ask God's help, now and in the days to come. In the name of Jesus Christ.
Amen.

Hazel Barkham
England

Covenant to Celebrate Diversity

Reader One: Sophia, our wise and marvellous Creator, fills the earth with amazing diversity.

All: **We covenant with our Creator and with one another to celebrate and nurture diversity.**

Reader Two: Innumerable living beings fill the earth, beyond our ability to fathom or classify.

All: **We covenant with our Creator and with one another to celebrate and nurture diversity.**

Reader Three: Mountains and valleys, forests and oceans, sing forth the abundance of creation.

All: **We covenant with our Creator and with one another to celebrate and nurture diversity.**

Reader Four: Ostriches and otters, amphipods and anteaters, show forth the playful prodigality of our Creator.

All: **We covenant with our Creator and with one another to celebrate and nurture diversity.**

Reader Five: Human beings of rich colours and shapes show forth the lavishness of our Creator.

All: **We covenant with our Creator and with one another to celebrate and nurture our diversity.**

Reader Six: Our Creator loves variety, and so created people to express sexuality in different ways.

All: **We covenant with our Creator and with one another to celebrate and nurture diversity.**

Reader Seven: Families and communities of diverse forms and cultures fill the world with joy and grace.

All: **We covenant with our Creator and with one another to celebrate and nurture diversity.**

Jann Aldredge-Clanton
USA

A Covenant Commitment to the Single Life

Single Person's Commitment

Today, in the presence of God
and all those gathered here,
I, N, make my solemn commitment
to the single life to which I am called,
in which I have proved and tested my calling,
and which I joyfully and freely embrace.

I commit myself
to sharing generously with others the spaciousness in my life
and to guarding and cherishing the solitude which is its core.

I commit myself
to serious work, undertaken wholeheartedly, with singleness
    of purpose
and to the making of merriment, joy and celebration.

I commit myself
to a freedom of heart which is open to the stranger, the little ones,
    the outsider,
and to a steadfastness of heart which keeps faithfulness with my
    chosen friends.

I commit myself
to the joy and labour of prayer and contemplation
and to the drudgery and delight of housework and menial tasks.

I commit myself
to a freedom of spirit which is ready to explore, travel and journey
    wherever the Spirit is leading
and to a stability of life which knows itself deeply rooted and centred
    in God.

I commit myself
to living singly
    and seriously
    and passionately
    and simply
    and wholeheartedly

and freely
and generously
and faithfully
and joyfully
within the limits and the loveliness
of this single state I have chosen.

I call on all here present
to witness and affirm this calling,
to honour its capacity for human becoming and divine glory,
to hold me in my commitment to it
and to help me realise its gift and potential.

I make this commitment
this Nth day of the Nth month
in the presence of those I have gathered as friends, companions
    and supporters,
and in the presence of God my Companion, my Guide and my Goal
whose strength I call upon,
whose grace I plead
and whose faithfulness I trust
this day and forever.
Amen.

Congregational Commitment

We witness and we celebrate your commitment.
We affirm your chosen calling
and we believe in its beauty, its holiness and its dignity.
We will stand by you in your singleness.
We will offer our friendship, our love and our solidarity.
We will seek to be faithful in supporting you
and to be sensitive in caring for you.
We will pray for you, work with you and learn from you.
We will give to you and receive from you.
We will respect the way that you have chosen,
and we will delight in the fullness of life into which we all have
    been invited,
single and partnered,
childless and child-bearing,
living alone or living with others,
knowing ourselves all to be God's children and God's chosen.

N, this day we make our pledge to you,
and we call on the grace and goodness of God
to sustain us in our promise.
Amen.

Blessing

May the God of all life and all love,
who delights in the variety of our patterns of living and loving,
sustain and support us each in our common and distinctive callings.
Amen.

Nicola Slee
England

The Open Road to the Open Table

We think of pilgrimage as a journey towards the 'centre', the holy place . . . towards a new illumination . . . towards Life. And the journey home is an enriched journey: we are changed: we bear gifts.

The story of what happened between Jerusalem and Emmaus seems to be an upside-down, inside-out pilgrimage. Cleopas and his companion are journeying away from the light: feeling hang-dog and helpless, with their expectations dashed, they're coming away from the Holy City, empty-handed – shambling towards an unremarkable little village, to what is (presumably) their home. And it's in this unremarkable, *non*-sacred place – and in gathering *darkness* – that the epiphany takes them by surprise. And then how they dance! They leap and prance with the others the boon, the grace, the amazing mystery of Christ Alive.

Unless research on the matter has passed me by, we know very little about Cleopas and even less about his companion. If where they 'went in' was indeed their home, then the likelihood is that they were partners. It is anyone's guess whether they were same-sex or opposite-sex partners. Knowing so little is, in a way, helpful. We can be imaginative. The story – and the not-knowing – allows us all in on the action. On that open road, where at first these broken ones travel so despondently, we can join them.

For we too – some or most of the time – get it wrong. We miss the moment; we fail to discern the golden thread; we look and listen in the wrong places or at the wrong times, so we fail to see and hear. Consequently, we carry burdens that weigh us down almost to the ground. And we travel in the wrong direction.

We're all there on that open road . . . sad, mixed up, self-important or self-despairing, helpless silly clowns with all our nice starched ecclesiastical clothing now mud-stained and tattered and hanging off us – pretty vestments looking more (the further we drag our tired feet) like the motley of the fool . . . Fat ones, thin ones, shorties and giants; wise ones and zany ones, the musical and the tone-deaf; female ones, male ones and those who don't quite know; straight ones and gay ones; hairy ones and smooth ones; woolly liberals and fiery fundamentalists; scholarly ones with M. and D. Phils., and the ones who left school when they were fourteen or four . . . Wordy ones and silent ones; smelly ones and fragrant ones; the ones who could be models, and the ones made when the Creator's hand slipped a bit on the wet clay . . . Rich ones and poor ones; flighty ones and steady ones; activists and contemplatives; efficient ones and chaotic ones; the multi-talented, and the ones who struggle to find anything they're good at . . . We're all there, on that open road. All – in one respect or another – going in the wrong direction.

But equally: all so much loved by the Source of our Being – whose exuberant love was responsible for such diversity – that we're pursued and turned around again by love: for us broken ones, God's Christ is broken to pieces.

And still we don't get it, even though – in Christ's brokenness – our healing has begun. We didn't sign up, did we, for uncertainty and suffering and doubt and death. We thought he was going to be a big-shot, this Messiah, who'd be a great ruler and lay down a set of neat black and white rules, so that we could get it right every time . . . perhaps so that we could give ourselves a little pat on the back by looking down our noses at all those other people on the road, and know that *we'd* made it, *we* were on the right tracks, *we* would be saved . . . Jesus! What a disappointment!

But that broken strange one comes along to us, and he explains it again. He's a bit mad that we didn't get it the first or second or third time round – but he tries again. And gradually, wonderfully, amazingly, our hearts warm up . . . something is alight and brewing in that hearth inside: something's about to happen.

And then the stranger consents to come into our home.

Jeeze . . . and we forgot to dust around before we left – and there are tea-stains on the carpet – and there's our flatulent dog to contend with, too . . . the neighbours are only too glad to dash around and return him to us as soon as they see us going through the gate. Well, at least they also bring round a fresh loaf – and a bottle of their home-made wine . . . Thank goodness, actually, because what we left in the larder has gone a bit stale and flat now. Not to put too fine a point upon it, our own bread is growing whiskers . . .

And so we sit down around the table, slightly on edge, with this dithery, uncertain, excited feeling in our stomachs; because we're good hosts, we offer the bread to the guest first . . .

And those strangely familiar hands reach out and take the loaf and a suddenly familiar voice offers words of thanks and then the pilgrim looks at us as he breaks the bread, and – in the breaking – our hearts leap up, and the scales fall from our eyes. Good Lord! It's him.

And just as the road widened and opened up to accommodate us all, so the table is open to all God-seekers, all who come looking – desperate ones and hopeful ones . . . all who feel called by the Mystery of the Way. An open road to an open table. An open Christ greeting all who – with an open heart – come running or stumbling to be fed.

That's the amazing good news: we do not have to be perfect (or even good enough) before we're welcomed into open arms. Christ doesn't say: 'Have you fulfilled these conditions: Do you believe these edicts and dogmas? Have you signed on the dotted line?' What seems to count is our longing to catch a glimpse of life's meaning, an appetite for deepening experience, and a desire to love and be loved extravagantly . . . When we reach out, there is an answering response: 'Come closer, my friend: this is your home.'

And though such amazing love creates great difficulties for us – because we're quite sure that not everyone should be so favoured, nonetheless that's how it is. That's God for you. Thank heavens! Alleluia! Three cheers for the open road, and an open table.

Kate Compston
England

Like a Star . . .

Like a star should your love be constant.
Like a stone should your love be firm.
Be close, yet not too close.
Possess one another, yet be understanding.
Have patience each with the other.
For storms will come but they will go quickly.
Be free in giving of affection and warmth.
Have no fear and let not the ways or words
Of the unenlightened give you unease.
For the spirit is with you.
Now and always.

Source unknown

Prayers for a Couple
(For a period of growing together, of testing, of sounding the depths)

Minister: N and N, God loves you. How do you respond?

Couple: **We wish to grow in love, sharing our lives with each other and we ask God's blessing.**

Minister: Will you recognise each other's freedom to grow as individuals within your life together?

Couple: **We will.**

Minister: Your relationship has not yet been tested by time or trouble. Will you try to make it a strong and permanent one?

Couple: **We will.**

Minister: If you decide not to stay together, will you part in good-will and mutual forgiveness?

Couple: **We will.**

Minister: God is the source of all love. Will you accept his gift, sharing it with each other and with those around you?

Couple: **We will.**

The minister then prays with the couple and blesses them.

Lesbian and Gay Christian Movement
England

A Service of Affirmation and Blessing

Music or hymn (optional)

Introduction

Minister: Brothers and sisters, we meet here in the presence of God to celebrate and affirm the commitment of N and N to each other. May they, through the assistance of the Holy Spirit, commit themselves today to each other; promising to live together in love, faithfulness, trust and forgiveness. While they make this solemn covenant we remember that our Saviour Jesus Christ shows us the path of courage and selfless love. We ask God's blessing on their lives. We join in rejoicing with them and offer them support with our love and prayers. Let us hold them in our hearts as we commit their lives to the love and grace of God.

Pause for a moment of silence before the minister continues.

Loving and gracious God, who made us in your image and sent your son Jesus Christ to welcome us home; protect us in love and empower us for service. Through the power of the Holy Spirit may N and N become living signs of his love and may we uphold them in the promises that each will make this day, through Jesus Christ our Lord.

All: **Amen.**

Minister: Jesus told us to 'Love the Lord your God with all your heart, with all your soul, with all your strength and with all your mind; and love your neighbour as yourself.' For the love that we receive and give let us all thank God, saying together . . .

All: *Either:*

Almighty God, source of all being, we thank you for your love, which creates and sustains us. We thank you for your unique and personal gifts to every one of us in our minds, our bodies, and our spirits; and for the blessings of companionship and friendship. We pray that we may use your gifts so that we can ever grow into a deeper understanding of love and of your purpose for us, through Jesus Christ our Lord. Amen.

Or:

Almighty God, source of all being, we thank you for your love, which creates and sustains us. We thank you for the physical and emotional expression of that love; and for the blessings of companionship and friendship. We pray that we may use your gifts so that we can ever grow into a deeper understanding of love and of your purpose for us, through Jesus Christ, our Lord. Amen.

Music or hymn (optional)

Reading from Scripture

This should be announced as 'A reading from . . .' *and ended with* 'This is the word of the Lord.'

Questions of Intent

Minister: N and N, is it your intention to enter into a solemn covenant with each other in love and trust?

Couple: It is.

Minister: Do you offer your lives together for God's blessing?

Couple: We do.

Minister: Will you be to each other a companion in joy and a comfort in times of trouble; and will you give each other opportunity for love to deepen?

Couple: We will, with God's help.

The Promises

Minister: *(to each partner in turn)* Will you N give yourself to N, sharing your love and your life, your wholeness and your brokenness, your success and your failure?

Partner: I will.

Couple: We, N and N, witness before God and this congregation that we have pledged ourselves to each other. We offer you, Lord, our souls and bodies, our thoughts and deeds, our love for each other and our wish to serve you. Take us as we are, and make us all that we should be, through Jesus Christ our Lord.

All: Amen.

Exchange of Rings and Tokens

Minister: God in heaven, by your blessing let these rings/tokens be to N and N symbols of unending love and faithfulness to remind them of the solemn covenant and promise made today.

All: **Amen.**

Then each partner in turn presents the ring/token and says:
N, I give to you this ring/token as a symbol of my promise and with all that I am and all that I have, I honour you in the name of God.

Music or hymn (optional)

During this time the couple may sign their wills and/or certificates marking their vows and promises to each other (optional).

Address

Prayers as appropriate concluding with the Lord's Prayer if there is to be Eucharist.

These might include the following or something similar.

Loving God, whose son Jesus Christ welcomed strangers and called them his friends, grant to N and N such gifts of grace that they may be bearers of your friendship and their home a place of welcome for all.

All: **Amen.**

Jesus, our brother, inspire N and N in their lives together, that they may come to live for one another and serve each other in true humility and kindness. Through their lives may they welcome each other in times of need and in their hearts may they celebrate together in their times of joy, for your name's sake.

All: **Amen.**

Holy Spirit of God, guard and defend N and N in their life together, protect them from evil, strengthen them in adversity until you bring them to the joy of your heavenly kingdom, through Jesus Christ our Lord.

All: **Amen.**

Creator God, the source of our being, bless the lives of N and N. May they be faithful and true, generous in the gift of forgiveness, patient and understanding as they grow together, and may they become living witnesses to your restoring love. We ask this in the name of Christ, who heals and sets us free.

All: **Amen.**

The Lord's Prayer *(not when a Eucharist follows)*

Bidding to the Company

Minister: Will you the chosen witnesses of N and N do all in your power to support and strengthen them in the days ahead?

All: **We will.**

Minister: God has called us to live with each other in the spirit of love, joy and peace. Let us all share a sign of God's peace. The peace of the Lord be always with you.

All: **And also with you.**

Minister: Let us offer one another a sign of God's peace.

The company greets N and N and each other.

Music or hymn (optional)

(A Eucharist may follow, the form to be agreed between the presiding priest and the couple.)

The Blessing

Minister: N and N have now given themselves to each other by solemn promises and the making of a covenant. Let us now pray that they may be sustained by God's love.

              Spirit of God, you teach us through the example of Jesus that love is the fulfilment of the Law: help N and N to persevere in love, to grow in mutual understanding and to deepen their trust in each other; that in wisdom, patience and courage, their life together may be a source of happiness to all with whom they share it; and the blessing of God Almighty, Creator, Redeemer and Sustainer be upon you to guide and protect you and all those you love, today and always.

All: **Amen.**

Dismissal

Minister: Go in peace to love and serve the Lord.

All: **In the name of Christ. Amen**

As the couple and their friends leave, music may be played.

Jeffrey Heskins
and members of the congregation at St Luke's Church, Charlton
London, England

An Act of Confirmation and Commitment
(Written for the blessing of a lesbian relationship but could be adapted for other partnerships)

We have come here today to create a space –
> A space where love can be celebrated
> A space where passion can be honoured
> A space where commitment can be affirmed.

We have come together to share this time –
> A time of recognising friendship old and new
> A time to gather strength for our journey
> A time to celebrate women loving women.

For each of us, there has been a separate journey which has brought us to this point. Let us spend a few moments sharing something of what that journey has meant for each of us.

A time in which any member of the group can offer a personal statement, reading or poem on the theme of our own journey towards affirming ourselves and our sexuality.

The journey towards celebrating ourselves, our sexuality and our interdependence is not an easy one. Sometimes we are restricted and constrained by the society in which we love; sometimes we hold back from all that could be. We learn to recognise strength and vulnerability, passion and tenderness, grief and delight. Let us spend a few moments in silence, seeking forgiveness for our failure, courage for our living, and hope for our intentions.

Silence

Members of the group anoint one another with oil, saying:

> **You are good.**
> **You are whole.**
> **You are beautiful.**

Statement of Intention

N and N, you have chosen to continue your journey together. You have invited us, as your friends and fellow travellers, to witness your commitment to one another. We give you this time, our attentiveness, and our love, as you make your promises to one another.

The Promises

Spoken by each of the couple in turn:

N, I have chosen you as my partner.
I love you and I delight in you.
I promise to share my life with you
in tenderness and passion
holding to you in good times and bad,
in anger and forgiveness
in pain and in hope.
Forgive me when I fail;
support me when I am weak.
Please go on trusting me,
as I grow in love and trust you.

All: In the name of all that is loving
In the name of all that is holy and just
In the name of all that moves towards freedom
We honour the promises you have made.

The Blessings

Spoken by each of the couple in turn:

I bless you with this ring
It is a gift and sign of our love.
May we be held together within its circle
in joy, faithfulness and trust.

Spoken by one of the gathering who presents the couple with flowers:

We bless you with these flowers
They are the gift and sign of joy and laughter in your life,
of your delight in each other,
of tenderness and vulnerability
and the blossoming of your hopes.

Spoken by one of the gathering who presents the couple with a bowl of fruit:

We bless you with this fruit.
It is the gift and sign of the work which you do, separately and together,
of the home which you are making,
of strength and nourishment
and the ripening of your hopes.

Closing Blessing

All: **We go forward on the journey**
rejoicing in all that we have
and open in trust and faithfulness
to all that is to come.

Jan Berry
England

Service of Commitment for a Same-Sex or Common Law Relationship

Organ Voluntary

Introduction

We celebrate this service because N and N have made a decision for each other. Now they wish to stand before God and the community gathered here to ask God's blessing for the path they intend to go together.

Psalm 139 or Meditation Psalm 118

God –
You wanted me and created me as the one I am.
I have not always been aware of this reality.
Often I felt as if it was not me you were speaking to,
left at the margins,
misunderstood – excluded.
I was driven by questions about the meaning of life.
There was no room for joy.
My heart was in chains;
why, God, why me of all people?
And you heard me –
maybe it was just a dream –
or was it a miracle?
I cannot fathom it yet.
A door has been opened
and I will not go through it all alone.
Merciful God – I thank you.
Amen.

Margot Michaelis
Germany

Or:

Meditation Psalm 118

Thank the Lord, for he is gracious and his mercy shall endure forever.
Yeah, I will give thanks to our God; he is good! His goodness towards me has no beginning and no end. I may end up deeply in trouble but when I call him, he answers and puts my feet on wide and

firm ground and wraps me into his closeness.

Human beings do such terrible things to each other. They deny each other their homes, their rights, their dignity. You cannot trust those who are in power.

But when I seek refuge in God, I am at home. When I am struggling for my dignity, he does not compromise but is on my side. Nothing is more valuable to him than my happiness, even in the smallest things. I was lonely and rejected, nobody bothered to speak to me; I was discouraged and in despair, nobody stood by me. But God is faithful to me. My whole life is safe with him, nothing is forgotten, nothing is in vain. Therefore nothing and nobody can take away the unique meaning of my life, its greatness, its poetry, its completeness.

On many occasions everything seemed to be over, on many occasions I had already lost all hope, all my strength seemed to be spent. But I am alive. Heights and depths are part of my life, but not a single day is without purpose, even if it sometimes remains hidden from me. All my days are part of the grand handiwork of his creation. About that I shall not be silent.

I shall speak about unexpected happiness, even luck. I will speak about the wonders of new beginnings. In the trash of misspent days I found a stone which I had already cast away. In a wonderful way just this stone became the cornerstone which was the foundation of my liberation. This is the day which God has made; let us rejoice and be glad in it. The warmth and the light of the new day came towards me, they were meant for me. Today, I want to start again, as if I was born anew. The day lies before me like a gift and so many new beginnings are hidden within it. I will dedicate this day to joy and rejoicing.

Give thanks to the Lord, for he is good and his mercy shall endure forever.

Cornelia Kenke
Germany

Suggested readings: Ecclesiastes 4:9–11 or 5:1–4; Song of Songs 8:6–7

Romans 12:9–13 (after Cornelia Kenke)

Let your love be without falsehood, avoid anything which could be the source of evil, but be passionate about increasing what is good. Regard each other with the eyes of the heart, full of admiration and respect. Do not put off from one day to the next what has been left unsaid or undone. Entrust yourselves fully to the Spirit of God which carries you through life safely.

Be glad in hope, remain patient in times of trial and do not cease to seek what really matters. Be there for each other not just in familiar circles but be open for all whom you meet and open your fellowship even to strangers.

1 Peter 4:8b–11 (after Cornelia Kenke)

Nothing is more important than that your love for each other shall remain alive. For love covers all failures. She finds a way across every abyss. She is the inexhaustible source of forgiveness.

Be open and free for everything you encounter; open your doors and your hearts without many words. And stand up for each other with all your strength, everyone with their own gifts which God has given them. Let one empower the other with all their talents so that your many gifts may not be hidden and enrich all of you.

Philippians 2:1–5 (after Cornelia Kenke)

Let me invite you to dare live with each other in the wisdom of Christ: regale each other with love; trust the spirit which has led you to each other; regard each other with eyes of love which judges everything with mercy.

Be of one mind in those things which matter; do not compete with each other; join up together and be a source of strength for each other. Do nothing seeking your own reward or your own glory but be humble and make sure that the other one can be a person in their own right. Do not care for what is for your own good but for what opens up a future for others. Let me invite you to let your lives together be guided by the wisdom of Jesus Christ.

Sermon

Hymn

Vows

You have made a commitment to each other. Therefore, I ask you before God and before those gathered here, families, friends and relations:

N: Will you take N as a gift of God? Will you protect and conserve the love that is between you and do everything in your power to ensure that your relationship will endure? Will you care for N, encounter him/her with honesty and respect and stand by him/her for better or for worse, in sickness and in health? And will you renew your relationship through the strength of forgiveness again and again?

Answer: Yes, I will.

So God may go with you to transform your will into completion.

Or:

I accept you as a gift from God. I will protect and conserve the love between us and do anything in my power to ensure that our relationship may continue. I will always be responsible for you and will encounter you with honesty and respect and stand by you for better or for worse, in sickness and in health. I will renew our relationship through the strength of forgiveness again and again.

Blessing

May God bless you, care for you and protect you from all harm. Never shall you feel rejected and left helpless in adverse circumstances. May he put at any time good people by your side.
May his face shine upon you, may he be merciful towards you and regale you out of the wealth of his goodness. May he give you open eyes and ears that you may see his mighty acts and miracles in the small things of everyday life.
May he give you strength and courage to go your own way, to seek and find the path of life that is yours. May he free you from all pressures and compulsions, from 'you have to' and 'you ought to'; from all expectations of others, 'one does' and 'it would be expedient if'.
May he give you peace and salvation. May he give you self-confidence and trust. Let rejection not fret you or numb you. May you not constantly be guided by fear.
May he give you a gladsome heart, a smile on your face, even laughter which is contagious and liberating and a gift not to take yourselves too seriously, even to laugh about yourselves. May he send you a leading star in times of darkness; in sadness someone who will comfort you.
May he give you sufficient time for rest. Though there should also be challenges, bright ideas and great surprises as ingredients in your lives together.
May he be near you at all times with his blessing, surround you with his closeness, so that you may grow and mature and find your own way.

So may God keep you who called you into life and desires for you to live and be happy.

Or:

God, bless us, when we look back and when we look forward.
Bless us, so that we may not only hear the roaring but also the still small voice of the wind which blows where it wills.
Bless us, so that the fragrance carried towards us by the wind may spread the aroma of a new world.
Bless us, so that hope for justice and love, longing for tenderness and peace may ride towards us on wings of the wind.
Bless us, that we may be grappled by the winds of the future which blow towards us.

Hymn

Intercessions/Our Father

Blessing

Cornelia Kenke
Germany

Litany For A Same-Self Couple
Celebrating An Important Anniversary
(Originally written for a lesbian couple celebrating their 10th anniversary)

Response for the couple after each verse:
We give thanks to God and to each other

For the years that we have been together . . .

For good times and bad times . . .

For easy times and hard times . . .

For the times we have loved each other and the times we have fought . . .

For the times when we kept faith in each other even when we didn't understand each other . . .

For our home and all who have been welcomed there . . .

For our families, our neighbours and our friends . . .

For all who have 'been there' for us . . .

For all who have laughed with us and cried with us . . .

For those who stood with us against those
who sought to separate us . . .

For those who comforted us in the face of hostility from those
who would not see God's face in our love for each other . . .

For times of being together and times of letting go . . .

For all who have enriched our lives in any way . . .

For all the blessings we have received . . .

Christopher Wardale
England

Blessing of a Relationship

N and N have now committed their lives to each other. I wish them love as we all do but then they have love already. There are two things though that are sometimes overlooked.

The first is friendship. I really do wish them friendship. We all know that love affairs come and go and so, sadly, do a lot of marriages. However, and I expect that it's the same with many of you, our friendships last a whole lot longer. Most of my closest friendships were made first when we were students together. I conducted a funeral recently of a very old lady who had been married for nearly sixty years. 'You see,' said her husband, 'we were best friends.' To be best friends, as well as lovers, as well as partners; that is a very sound basis for a marriage.

The second thing I wish for you is kindness. I'm really as serious about kindness as I am about friendship. I don't wish for you any kindness that's mushy or uncritical, or cowardly or appeasing or lazy. No conspiracy of mutual back-scratching or a sort of unspoken bargain struck between you to tell each other only half truths to protect yourselves from reality. That would be to exhaust each other's strength and humanity for the sake of safety.

I wish for you kindness that starts from the realisation that the other person has put the power of his/her happiness right into the other person's hands to see what they do with it. What is needed, demanded, in response is kindness; kindness to meet and cherish the real vulnerability, the openness to being hurt that always comes when you love or allow yourself to be loved. That's the real nakedness, the real trust.

I think that sort of kindness, that trust, that generosity of the naked heart is where maturity begins. It is the point at which unprotected except by each other's kindness you start to share and lose your private pride, and private shame and your private guilt. You can begin to grow and mature together; growing in the exchange of tolerance and strength, irony and amusement, affection, respect and acceptance. It is then that we become fully human and as Jesus said two people can become one.

So my two young friends, be good mates and be kind to each other.

Neil Dawson
England

Blessings from the Netherlands

You have come into our midst,
because you have chosen each other,
and in doing that you are aware of God's choice for you.
That which has grown and become between you,
fills you and all of us with joy and hope:
the chance to see in our fellow human beings
what love can make possible.
Therefore you have come here
to promise each other your shared lives
and to ask for God's blessing on them.
You wish to share each other's lives in love and faithfulness,
close to each other in liberty,
to search for the other one again and again,
even in spite of pain and resistance,
different and yet at one with each other unknown and yet familiar.
You have come here to promise before God and other people
to honour one another and stand side by side

as God's creation in God's image,
to share each other's stories
and to explore the future with and for each other.
From today onwards you wish to be called and known together,
responsible for those who are entrusted to you on the way.
You say to each other: 'I will be there for you.'
This is what God says to all those
who want to follow his path.
Therefore we can know that the promise which we give to each other
is born by God's love
which purifies and deepens our love,
renews it and strengthens it again and again.
May the Spirit of God turn your promise to each other into his blessing.

The Remonstrant Fraternity
The Netherlands

Hymn for the Blessing of a Relationship

Praise you Creator, the Spirit, the Son,
Giver of life through which two become one,
Bless all that is in them and all that they share,
Their lives joined together embraced in your care.

Lord God be with them as they journey through life,
Bless their commitment through good times and strife,
Give strength in their weaknesses, give hope to their fears,
Give voice to their longings, give laughter through tears.

Grant us the courage to change and to grow,
Wherever you lead us the wisdom to go,
Our homes will be your home, your peace to reside,
A welcome to others as we live side by side.

Tune: Slane

Karen Hutt and Clare McBeath
England

A Selection of Vows

Day by day I promise
to love and to honour you
to treasure you and to respect you
to walk with you side by side
in joy and sorrow

Day by day I promise
to hold you in my arms
to grow with you in truth
to laugh with you, to cry with you
to be with you
and to love you with all that I am and all that I shall become

This I promise you from the depth of my heart,
my mind and my soul
– for all our lives together.

*****

No one has touched my life like you.
No one can compare with you,
No one has made my heart leap and my soul dance,
nor set my mind alight with joy.
In your presence I have found my rest,
my home,
my self.
In your arms I have known such peace.
Today I give myself to you.
I am yours and ever shall it be.

*****

You are so beautiful/handsome to me,
You are my life, my light, my hope, my joy.
You are my food, my drink, my music and my song.
You are my warmth, my shelter, my passion and my rest.
You are my world.

And I am yours.
Your friend, your lover and your soul mate.

So let the whole world hear and know
that I love you.
And I vow that my love will bring you joy.

Jonathan Blake
England

The Exchange of Rings/Symbols

In the turning of the earth and the cycle of the seasons, in the dance of sun, moon and stars, on the great wheel of life which knows of no end nor even its beginning; so the circle of love encompasses all, promises all, gives birth to all and protects all.

Heavenly Father, by your blessing, let these rings be to *N* and *N* a symbol of unending love and faithfulness, to remind them of the vow and covenant which they have made this day; through Jesus Christ our Lord. Amen.

Whenever you hold this ring know that I shall always come home to you, and my heart will be brimming over with love for you.

I give you this ring as a sign that I have chosen you above all others to share life's journey.
May we be encircled by each other's love all the days of our lives.

I give you this ring: because I love you, because I always want to be with you, because I place my life in your hands, because I will hold you for ever.

Jonathan Blake
England

The Sharing of Wine Ceremony

You have shared together the fruits of love and your times together have been blessed.
Drink now this rich wine, fruit of the earth, symbol of life, of creation, of passion and of love.

The couple sip wine from the same silver vessel.

May the power of love as strong wine ever flow within your veins and may the taste of the grape ever remind you of this moment when your mouths, as your lives, were burning with the joy of each other.

Jonathan Blake
England

The Sharing of Honey Ceremony

You have tasted the sweetness of love, intense and profound. Refresh each other now with the touch of honey upon your lips.

The partners in turn collect a tiny amount of honey with a silver spoon from a silver vessel and give it to each other.

May the touch of your lips as your lives be delicate and sweet and as a thousand bees upon a thousand flowers have gathered this rich nectar may the exercise of your love be as constant and as colourful all your days.

Jonathan Blake
England

Thoughts and Prayers

How we long for your happiness.
Treasure one another as life's greatest gift.
Cherish the days you share,
The warm moments of your waking and sleeping,
The grind and marvel of your years side by side.
The intoxicating liquor of love with its pain and its passion,
its loving and its hating.
Cherish all this.
It is but for a tiny moment
upon life's ever turning wheel.

*****

Walk peacefully.
Dance joyously.
Love passionately.
Kiss tenderly.
Live fully and so may it only be.

*****

God the Holy Trinity, make you strong in faith and love, defend you on every side, and guide you in truth and peace; and the blessing of the all loving God, the Father, the Son and the Holy Spirit, be with you and those whom you love and remain with you always. Amen.

*****

A symphony of words draws to its end. The last strains of love's orchestra fill the air. Love is all around us and so it should be on this most profound of days. The wedding feast bids us welcome. Fine food and wine will carry us away to yet more happy hours and so let us with radiant smiles and happiest hearts greet N and N.

Jonathan Blake
England

Our Wedding Ceremony

A Family Ritual (as each entry is read, family members light a candle, then pass the candle to a member of the opposite family)

Spouse One: Many in our community reach this time in their lives when they wish to memorialise their commitments to one another through ceremony and ritual. Unfortunately, not all of us are able to do so in their places of worship.

Spouse Two: Nor are all of our sisters and brothers able to do so with the support of, and in the presence of, their families of origin. We feel blessed that our families are with us today.

Spouse One: However, the presence of our families is more than a blessing, and means much more to us than fulfilling an obligation or a symbolic gesture of acceptance. As we express our love before you today, with our families bearing witness, we do so with an even greater sense of commitment, not only to each other, but to our families, as well.

Spouse Two: Our love will not subsist and thrive by itself. In order to grow, it must be shared and visible for all to see. We are tempered by and have learned how to love by the models exemplified by our families. Our union today is also a tribute to them, and we wish to contribute back to them, with a pledge to participate in their well-being, as well as our own.

Spouse One: The lighting of this circle of candles today represents the circle of love that our families have woven around us throughout the years.

Spouse Two: We now become a part of that circle, and promise to continue to extend our deep love and commitment to one another beyond our own home and into the hearts and lives of our families.

Both: We shall always treasure their presence on this special day. We are truly blessed and we feel deeply loved.

Joe McMurray and Eric Cole
USA

Order of Prayer for Recognising a Change of Gender

Hymn

Optional Sentence From One of the Following:

O Lord, how manifold are your works! In wisdom you have made them all. (Psalm 104:24)

Your hands have made and fashioned me;
give me understanding that I may learn your commandments.
(Psalm 119:73)

The Lord your God has blessed you in all the works of your hands; he knows your going through this great wilderness; you have lacked nothing. (Deuteronomy 2:8)

In the Lord, woman is not independent of man, nor man of woman. All things are from God. (1 Corinthians 11:11)

My house shall be called a house of prayer for all peoples. (Isaiah 56:7)

Minister: The grace of our Lord Jesus Christ, the love of God, and the communion of the Holy Spirit be with you all.

All: And also with you.

Introduction

We live in a world of infinite variety and beauty. Blessed be God! Whatever our background and culture God calls us to be lovers and from birth to death we struggle to love Him and each other. He places us on a pilgrimage and protects us as we travel. Blessed be God!

To some of us this will involve a long search for a true sexual identity; and at a particular time in a particular place a change of gender will be an outward and visible sign of a new life beginning under God. After prayer, thought and the support of family and friends a decision is made. Medical and surgical skills aid the process so the gender of reality brings a new life.

This service is an opportunity to ask God's blessing on N's new adventure. Anxieties, pain and suffering are not denied but taken up into the heart of the vulnerable God whose Son through his Spirit joins us on our journey and is with us now.

Our commitment today is that N will never be alone. In hope we witness his/her new beginning and surround him/her with our love.

The Questions

Minister: You have come here to receive strength and courage. We know that long ago you began to weigh and ponder all this and that you are fully determined by the grace of God to give yourself to a new life as a man/woman.
Do you ask God's forgiveness for the sins and shortcomings of the past?

N: I do.

Minister: Do you ask for God's blessing?

N: I do.

Minister: Will you trust in God and in His power to help?

N: I will.

Minister: Will you give yourself anew as a man/woman to the
              service of God and others?

N: I will.

Minister: Because you cannot bear the weight of this alone will
              you reach out to others for help?

N: I will.

Minister: Will you strive to fashion your own life and that of your
              household according to the way of Christ?

N: I will.

Minister: Almighty God who has given you the will to undertake
              all these things give you the strength to perform them,
              that He may complete the work already begun in you.
              We ask this through Jesus Christ our Lord.
              Amen.

              Eternal God,
              your wisdom is present in all your creation
              and your Spirit overshadows your work of love,
              recreate us in the likeness of Christ
              that we may have courage in our discipleship
              and serve your purpose in the world
              through Jesus Christ our Lord.
              Amen.

              Or:

              Almighty and everlasting God,
              you are always more ready to hear than we to pray
              and give more than either we desire or deserve;

pour down upon us the abundance of your mercy,
forgiving us those things of which our conscience is
afraid
and giving us those good things
which we are not worthy to ask
save through the merits and mediation
of Jesus Christ our Lord.
Amen.

Possible Readings:

Proverbs 3:13–26	Mark 7:25–30	Acts 10:9–15 (30–5)
Isaiah 12	Luke 8:42b–48	Romans 14:10–19
Zephaniah 3:14–end	John 4:7–15	Galatians 4:21–31
Ecclesiastes 3:1–8	John 15:1–11	Philippians 1:3–11
Psalms 20; 63:1–9; 116; 121; 123; 139:1–18		Colossians 3:12–17

A song or songs may be sung between readings or a favourite piece of music may be played.

Hymn *possibly preceded by a Creed or an Affirmation of Faith*

Minister: Dear Friends
This day is important for N as s/he comes to lay before God the new identity that s/he has assumed. The duality of gender is a given of creation with which every society and individual has to struggle and within which we are all called to serve God and our neighbour. The step that N is taking has been reached after careful thought and prayer. It requires courage and means that s/he is learning new ways of relating towards himself/herself, society and God.
Will you support him/her in the journey ahead and reflect to him/her the love and faithfulness of God?

All: **With the help of God, we will.**

The person may come forward and stand with a group of supporters before the congregation.

Prayer of Blessing and Dedication

This prayer may be shared with/by friends and supporters as indicated or led by the minister alone. Friends may lay hands on his/her head.

Minister: Blessed be God who calls us to life in Christ,
and gives us freedom as the sons and daughters of God.
Blessed be God for ever.

Voice A: Blessed be God who has made humanity male and female,
and calls us to embrace the mystery of gender.
Blessed be God for ever.

Voice B: Blessed be God who declares all people clean,
and excludes no one from the temple of the new creation.
Blessed be God for ever.

Minister: May the name of the God of Jacob protect you
and go before you in all your ways.
The Lord give you his blessing.

Voice A: May God grant you your heart's desire
and fulfil all your plans.
The Lord give you his blessing.

Voice B: May God give you a place among his people
and security among those who love you.
The Lord give you his blessing.

Minister: May God grant you holiness in your calling,
faith to follow his way,
and a life fruitful in his service.
The Lord give you his blessing.

Minister: May Christ rule in your life;
May heaven be open to your prayer;
May the Spirit lead you to the city of light
The Lord give you his blessing.
Amen.

It may be appropriate at this point for the person to place a symbol of their past identity on the altar and take from it a symbol for the future.

The service continues with the Lord's Prayer and other prayers. Also with the Eucharist where desired.

The Blessing

Malcolm Johnson
England

Blessing the Four Elements

Let us bless the four elements of the universe – fire, air, water and earth – for they have called home to the world our friend N *(name of person coming out)*.

(Four blessers, in turn, bless four elements.)

Blesser of Fire: South

(The blesser walks to the centre-south and lights a candle on the altar.)

> Source of Fire,
> O Searing Flame,
> Fill N's heart and all our hearts with a spark of passion.
> Empower us and every lesbian, gay and bisexual person
> with courage
> To emerge from cocoons of hibernation and isolation.
> Release our imaginations from their hiding places.
> Guiding Light,
> Fire of Justice,
> One Who Brings Us Home.
> Amen. Blessed be. Let it be so.

Blesser of Air: East

(The blesser walks to the centre-east and plays the chimes on the altar.)

> Source of Air,
> O Whispering Wind,
> Fill N's lungs and all our lungs with the breath of
> healing.
> Blow away the staleness.
> Bring freshness into our lives.
> Gentle Breeze,
> Rustling Sound,
> One Who Brings Us Home.
> Amen. Blessed be. Let it be so.

Blesser of Water: West

(The blesser walks to the centre-west, pours water into the bowl, and sprinkles participants with the evergreen branch.)

Source of Water,
Ever-bubbling spring,
Fill *N*'s being and all our beings with emotions that flow
freely.
Wash away the hurts and pains of all oppressed people.
Quench our thirst for spiritual and sexual connection.
Ocean Womb,
Wellspring of Life,
One Who Brings Us Home.
Amen. Blessed be. Let it be so.

Blesser of Earth: North

(The blesser walks to the centre-north and places a basket of bread on the altar.)

Source of Earth,
Mother of Our Being,
Fill *N*'s body and all our bodies with courage for loving
one another.
Enlighten us with dreams, visions and inner wisdom.
Sacred Ground,
Fertile Soil,
One Who Brings Us Home.
Amen. Blessed be. Let it be so.

Reading: Invisible for Too Long

For a very long time I have wanted to reach out to you in solidarity, to
work with you to transform injustice . . .
    . . . But I have been invisible for too long.

Response: Come out, come out, wherever you are!

I work next to you in so many places. I am the doctor who comforted
your dying mother. I am the teacher of your nine-year-old daughter. I
am the therapist who helped you free yourself . . .
    . . . But I have been invisible for too long.

Response: Come out, come out, wherever you are!

I stand beside you in so many places. I am the minister who marched
next to you as we advocated for a woman's right to choose. I am the

nun by your side at the women's shelter where you volunteer. I am the social worker at the mental health centre who works with your sister.
. . . But I have been invisible for too long.

Response: Come out, come out, wherever you are!

I am your invisible sister, your invisible brother. I have been invisible for too long. I yearn to be known for who I am. As you come out, you give me courage.
. . . I yearn to be visible.

Response: Come out, come out, wherever you are!

Honouring the Person Who is Coming Out

Thank you, N, for trusting us enough to share your life with us. We respect you. We honour you. We support and affirm you. And, we would like to honour you with a few mementoes.

N, this candle symbolises your passion for truth. When you burn it, and every candle, re-ignite this spark. (Give her the candle)

N, these chimes symbolize the unique melody that is yours. When you play them, remember your powerful story. (Give her the chimes)

N, this water pitcher symbolizes the deep well that you are. When you pour water from it, feel your pains and hurts wash away. (Give her the water pitcher)

N, this basket of bread symbolizes the nourishment that you are to us and to others you meet. When you use this basket, visualise the many ways you fill others with your love. (Give her the basket)

Litany of Thanksgiving

Gracious and Loving Wisdom Sophia, we praise you for creating N a lesbian. We praise you for creating us, your lesbian, gay, bisexual, transgendered, queer and heterosexual people.

For bringing us out of our closets and into full life,

Response: We praise you.

For embracing us with your love and care . . .

For giving us a company of friends and a family of choice . . .

For teaching us that our sexuality is a gift for the community . . .

For strengthening us to cope with misunderstanding, fear, and hatred . . .

For helping us break through the heterosexism and homohatred in ourselves, our families and friends, our culture and society, our churches and synagogues . . .

For enlightening us with dreams of holy impatience . . .

Gracious and Loving Wisdom Sophia, we praise you for creating N a lesbian. We praise you for creating us your people.

Words of Reflection for a Commitment Ceremony: 'What's Love Got to Do with It?'

Good day to all of you, and warm wishes to you, N and N, on this festive occasion. On behalf of all of us gathered, let me thank you two for inviting us to share in the goodness of your love. Thank you especially for giving us this opportunity not only to support you in your commitments to one another, but also for the chance to meet people from many facets of your lives, and in so doing to be enriched by what I think of as your love seeking community. That is what makes this day different from every other day. You have decided to mark time in a new way from this day forward, dividing your lives into the time before you proclaimed your love and the time after, in what I, speaking for all of us gathered, hope will be many happy, healthy years.

Thank you for inviting me to express a few thoughts on this special occasion, thoughts which, borrowing boldly from Tina Turner, I have focused around a central question for all of us, 'What's Love Got to Do With It?' In all the hoopla of the parties this weekend, and especially in all of the debate which surrounds same-sex marriages this political season, I worry that love may be moved off centre stage just when it deserves a solo. Or, that in overusing the word we might miss its power completely.

Getting married is a gutsy thing to do today. Standing before the people you most want to think well of you and promising to keep at this relationship through thick and thin is risky business, human frailty being what it is. I admire you as I catalogue just how frail I am, indeed how frail most of us are, in this regard. But love insists.

In your case, commitment is made even more difficult by loving at a time when the President of the United States doesn't believe in such things for women like us, and can't seem to keep his prejudices to himself. I know you don't need his approval, but it is hard for some people to understand what we're about here today when the President doesn't get it and is ready to sign our rights away before we receive them. Between that attitude and the outcry of the Religious Right, it is amazing that you and other lesbian/gay/bisexual and transgendered friends have the courage to trust your love, live it out, and more so in this climate, to entrust it to the rest of us. Good for you!

Your efforts are thwarted too by so-called Christian churches, the churches of which you are both a part whose doors are all but closed to you today. History alone will judge those churches that disgrace themselves by offering blessings to animals for the feast of St. Francis but withhold their sacraments from same sex couples who seek nothing more than to call attention, religious attention, to their love as heterosexual people have done for millennia. I know you don't need institutional approval, but it is important that you know that the People of God are with you today in the persons of your family and friends, despite the recalcitrance of the kyriarchies. Given such behaviours, it is a wonder that you want to celebrate your love in the context of a religious community. But you do, and so we are here from a range of backgrounds to offer you our religious support.

Your love and your choice to celebrate it in this way is even controversial in the larger community of lesbian/gay people. No less a theological expert than comedienne Kate Clinton speaks of events like today as cases of 'mad vow disease.' There may be days down the road when you will think she was right – I must have been made to do it – but I think that something far more powerful is at play here for which we who are privileged to participate as witnesses can only express our gratitude. That something is love. The answer to Tina Turner's question, 'What's love got to do with it?' is everything.

Love is what brought you together for reasons you'll never fully understand and no one has a right to expect you to explain. Love is why you bother to work out the little things like whose turn it is to do the dishes, and the big things, like whether and when to choose children. Love is the excuse for giving each other extra time in a day when there just isn't another minute. Love is the reason why you've decided to enter into one another's families when you each have a family of your own. There is no other good explanation for such things, and love will have to do, and it does just fine.

Love is not a political matter at base, nor only a private one. Rather, love is the very essence of ourselves in community which some, like you have found and touched and hope to deepen together. You have been lucky in love because many people long all their lives for what you have in such abundance today. Guard it, but above all enjoy it to the max. It may not happen again. Love is like that.

Given this very unique but quite abundant experience called love, it is no wonder that love is the name of God, of the divine, of Sophia. And Her nickname is love and His middle name is love, and its confirmation name is love because there is no other better way to describe what is so palpable this important day when you put us in touch with something so precious. The insights of Alice Walker and Ruth that we have just heard, these sacred texts by two other loving, justice-seeking women, the music, prayers and vow sharing that make up this ceremony are vivid testimony to the presence of the divine in all things, and above all, in love. Likewise, our sharing of bread and wine reminds us that love is always very concrete, and that it has consequences that shape the world. It is for this that we can only be grateful for love, just grateful.

Thank you for standing before us today, giving love two beautiful faces, so that we may see it in ourselves, in one another and in our God forever. That's what love has to do with it, all of it. Amen. Blessed Be. Alleluia.

Rite of Partnership
(from A Ceremony of Union and Commitment)

We read in the book of Ecclesiastes that 'for everything there is a season, and a time for every matter under Heaven.' We as a community are here to witness the vows of N and N. N and N come forward to speak your promises to one another.

Vows of N and N

N *and* N *face each other, join hands, and repeat in turn:*

I take you N to be my partner // and I promise you these things: // I will be faithful to you and honest with you // I will respect you, trust you // help you, listen to you, // and care for you.

I will share my life with you // in plenty and in want, // in sickness and in health, // I will support you and encourage you // to share your gifts with family and friends and with the larger community to which we belong.

Family Vows

Would the families please come forward and form a circle around N and N. The vows N and N have made affect not just each of them but everyone around them. It is a union not just of two individuals but of two families and two communities. We ask now if N and N's families will promise to come together as one and support N and N as they build a life together. We also ask N and N to commit to their families to continue to grow in love and support their families as they build their lives.

To the families: Will you support, celebrate and witness N and N's relationship? Will you forgive and ask for forgiveness when there is hurt and misunderstanding? Will you strive with them as they strive to live together in mutuality and love, as they work toward making their dreams a reality?

Response: **We will.**

To N and N: N and N will you support and celebrate with your families who have loved you, cared for you and let you go? Will you forgive and ask for forgiveness when there is hurt and misunderstanding? Will you strive for deeper understanding, love and mutuality with your families?

Response: **We will.**

Community Vows

All gathered here, you have come from diverse parts of N and N's lives. You are friends from childhood, college, work, church, but you all have in common your relationship with each of them. You have been brought together today as one community and are asked to witness, support and celebrate the commitment N and N have made.

To the community:

> This community of N and N, will you support, celebrate and witness N and N's relationship? Will you forgive and ask for forgiveness when there is hurt and misunderstanding? Will you strive with them as they strive to live together in mutuality and love, as they work toward making their dreams a reality?

Response: **We will.**

N and N: N and N, this is your community which over the years has grown and will continue to evolve throughout your lives. Do you promise to support and celebrate with your community? Will you forgive and ask forgiveness when there is hurt and misunderstanding? Will you be a source of love and strength to them?

Response: **We will.**

Exchange the Rings

In partnership ceremonies, the giving and receiving of rings is not simply a perfunctory act; not simply the giving of a piece of jewellery. Rather, rings are a visible sign of the sealing of a promise, an announcement that can be seen for all the days and years to come.

N and N, rings are made of precious substances and symbolise the treasure that your relationship holds. Fashioned to be worn as a circle, they are a sign of love that has no beginning and no ending but is a continuous, strengthening tie. N and N as you give and receive rings may you be attentive to the bond of love that is ever deepening between you.

The couple exchange rings and say in turn:

N, I give you this ring as a sign of my love for you, // as a symbol of the communities to which we belong, // and as a reminder of the vows and promises we have made here today.

Pronouncement of Union

Said by all, in unison:

We speak for the circle, for the Spirit of love in each heart gathered around us, seen and unseen. With the power of love invested in us, we pronounce you joined together as partners in life, love, and spiritual integrity.

Blessing the Bread *from* A Ceremony of Union and Commitment

(One partner blesses the bread.)

Come, extend your hands toward the bread and wine.

Blessed are you, Gracious and Loving Holy One for this Eucharistic love feast. We take, bless, break and eat this bread in thanksgiving for the love we have known, in thanksgiving for the love we have received, in thanksgiving for the love we have given and will give. May our love increase.

Blessing the Wine *from* A Ceremony of Union and Commitment
(The other partner blesses the wine.)

Blessed are you, Holy One of Joy, for creating this fruit of the vine. Young wine reminds us of new love; aged wine, growing richer and fuller, symbolises long-lasting love. We give thanks for this fruit of the vine and recall the lasting love of beloved partners and dear friends. May our love increase.

Closing Blessing *from* A Ceremony of Union and Commitment

Let us ask the God of Love, Wisdom Sophia, to bless and keep N and N in Her care. I invite each of us to respond 'Blessed Be' to the following blessing.

N and N, may your lives together be joyful and content, and may your love be as bright as the stars, as warm as the sun, as accepting as the ocean, and as enduring as the mountains.

Response: Blessed Be.

May you respect, have patience with, and delight in your cultural, spiritual, and personal differences.

Response: Blessed Be.

May you remember that your love, like planet Earth, when nurtured, fertilised, and watered can withstand the most treacherous storms. May you let the roots of your relationship be planted into the solid ground of love so that in the dry season you may drink deeply from its source.

Response: Blessed Be.

May your heart hear more than words ... listening to each other's silences and exploring each other's processes. May you have the courage to not always agree but always understand.

Response: Blessed Be.

May your love for each other pull you beyond yourselves into the hearts and lives of all those calling for justice, dignity and love.

Response: Blessed Be.

May you be blessed with wisdom to find the path upon which you both may walk, and with clear vision to keep sight of the grace which surrounds you.

Response: Blessed Be.

May you continue to make your love clearly and truly a reflection of the infinite love which embraces us all.

Response: Blessed Be.

And may you, N and N, be blessed in the name of the Holy One, Wisdom Sophia, who loves us into being, the Beloved who is the way of love, and the Spirit whose burning love sets us free. Amen. Blessed Be. Let It Be So.

Sending Forth *from* A Ceremony of Union and Commitment

With this blessing, this part of our celebration is concluded. Let us go forth in the name of the God of Love, filled with the power of love revealed through N and N.
May we each treasure love this day.

May we give thanks for those we have loved and for those who have loved us.
May love increase so that violence and injustice may cease.
Amen. Blessed Be. Let It Be So.

Diann Neu and Mary E. Hunt
USA

A Rainbow People

In the marvellous production of Tony Harrison's Mystery Plays at the Cottesloe Theatre, London, God was seen at the top of a large iron mast creating the world. As he called out the names of the sea, land, plants and creatures, so strips of coloured material with outlines of these new forms unfurled from him and were held out for all to see. When all the strips were complete, a band struck up and the mast and materials were transformed into a Maypole. Holding the cloths, men and women danced around, under the loving grin of their creator, weaving in and out and displaying the dark shades and bright flashes in a riotous pattern of movement. On the two nights I saw this performance the audience unselfconsciously stood up and began to jig around and clap their hands, trying to find their own place in the extraordinary event. On the stage level people even began to join in the dance with the actors and we saw tired after-work businessmen in suits, children excited at still being up and seeing their parents make a fool of themselves, giggling women from the office, the whole spectrum of a London audience – gay, straight, elderly, young, rich and unemployed – all finding a place, straightening their postures for the music and hoping the dance would go on into the night. It was a true liturgy for the human spirit and as we bopped around and clapped, the actor playing God slowly outstretched his arms over us all in blessing, willing us to carry on but as his arms remained there, we also saw the form of a cross. His love that night, we knew, was both celebration and anguish. The music played on.

Mark Oakley
England

Select Bibliography

Alison, James, *faith beyond resentment: fragments catholic and gay*, Darton Longman & Todd, 2001

Duncan, Geoffrey, *Seeing Christ in Others*, The Canterbury Press, new enlarged edition, 2002

Wisdom is Calling, The Canterbury Press, 1999

A World of Blessing, The Canterbury Press, 2000

Dare to Dream, Fount, 1995

Shine on, Star of Bethlehem, The Canterbury Press, 2001

Gabriel, Thelma, *Yours With Pride*

Glaser, Chris, *Uncommon Calling: A Gay Christian's Struggle to Serve the Church*

Coming Out to God: Prayers for Lesbians and Gay Men, Their Families and Friends

The Word Is Out: Daily Reflections on the Bible for Lesbians and Gay Men

Coming Out as Sacrament

Reformation of the Heart: Seasonal Meditations by a Gay Christian, Westminster/John Knox Press, Louisville/London/Leiden

Come Home! Reclaiming Spirituality and Community as Gay Men and Lesbians, Chi Rho Press, Gaithersburg, Maryland, USA

Heskins, Jeffrey, *Unheard Voices*, Darton Longman & Todd, 2001

Hopper, George S. E., *Reluctant Journey: A Pilgrimage of Faith from Homophobia to Christian Love*, 1997, PO Box 5846, Basildon SS15 4GS

John, Jeffrey, *Permanent, Faithful, Stable*, Darton Longman & Todd, 1993, 2000

Lesbian and Gay Christian Movement, *Christian Homophobia*, 2001

Nugent, Robert and Gramick, Jeannine, *Building Bridges: Gay and Lesbian Reality and the Catholic Church*, Twenty-Third Publications, 1995

Schaper, Donna E., *Alone but Not Lonely*, Twenty-Third Publications, 1999

Stuart, Elizabeth, *Religion is a Queer Thing*, The Pilgrim Press, 1997

Turney, Kelly, *Shaping Sanctuary – Proclaiming God's Grace in an Inclusive Church*, published in co-operation with the Welcoming Church Movement, Reconciling Church Programme, 2000

Acknowledgements

Introduction
Blessing, The © Geoffrey Duncan
My Creed – My Beatitude © Geoffrey Duncan

Who Am I?
Am I Alone? © Richard Watson
As Children of God, from *Shaping Sanctuary: Proclaiming God's Grace in an Inclusive Church*, edited by Kelly Turney, Copyright © 2000 by Reconciling Church Programme.
Because a Woman … © Rosie Miles
Blessing the Thorn in the Flesh © Norm S. D. Esdon
Body Meets …, The © Janet Lees
Christianity, Love and Gay Sex: A Practitioner's View © Christopher Bagley
Coming Out (1) © Suzi B.
Coming Out (2) © Sigrid Rutishauser-James
Coming Out Poem, A © Jan Berry
Force of Nature © Louise Green
God Release Me By Your Power, Andrew Pratt © Stainer and Bell Ltd
God Who Meets Us © W. L. Wallace
Homosexual Declaration © The 10% Club, Hong Kong
I'm A Lesbian © Suzi B.
I Am © Liz Styan
I Am A Loveable, Creative Person © W. L. Wallace
I Have Been Broken © David Coleman and Zam Walker
I Thank You For Those Things Which Are Yet Possible © Janet Schaffran and Pat Kozak from *More Than Words*
In A World Of In-Between © Norm S. D. Esdon
It Is Not A Crime © Rosie Miles
Jesus Rose and Went Out to a Lonely Place, reproduced from *Coming Out to God: Prayers for Lesbians and Gay Men, Their Families and Friends* © 1991 Chris Glaser. Used by permission of Westminster/John Knox Press.
Leah's Story © Jill Thornton and Clare McBeath
Let Me Be Me, reprinted with permission from *Alone but Not Lonely* by Donna E. Schaper. Copyright © 1999. Published by Twenty-Third Publications, Mystic, CT 06355 USA.
Life From Your Love © Michael Reiss
My Body © Rabeta
Proof © Rosie Miles
Reflection © Ken DeLisle

Silence and Reflection © Kate McIlhagga, first published in *Encompassing Presence, The Prayer Handbook 1993*, United Reformed Church.

Single Woman's Manifesto, A © Nicola Slee

Solo Voice © Peter Colwell

Thanks For Gay Men © George M. Wilson from *More Light Prayers* January 1991.*

To Know Myself, reprinted with permission from *Alone But Not Lonely* by Donna E. Schaper. Copyright © 1999. Published by Twenty-Third Publications, Mystic, CT 06355 USA.

To Reflect On … © W. L. Wallace

Walking God © Richard Watson

We Are … © Reprinted with the permission of The United Church of Christ Coalition for Lesbian, Gay, Bisexual and Transgender Concerns.

When Israel Camped In Sinai © Larry Berthier and the Universal Fellowship of Metropolitan Community Churches, USA.

Where Do I Fit, What Is My Place? Andrew Pratt © Stainer and Bell Ltd

Who Am I? © Sian Wallis

With Confidence We Stand Before You © Richard Watson

Woman Caught in Sexuality, The © Suzi B.

Wrestling the Unnamed to a Blessing © Norm S. D. Esdon

Creating Love: Sustaining Love

After a While You Learn – source unknown

Alien Messiah © Duncan L. Tuck

All-Loving God, The © Tony Gryzmala from *More Light Update*, November–December 1998*

Alternative, The © R. S. from *Sustaining Stories*, Methodist Lesbian and Gay Caucus

An Inclusive Church © Eugene G. Turner from *Rainbow Prayers – More Light Update*, January 1994*

An Inclusive Community © Duncan L. Tuck

Aspects of Our Worship © Duncan L. Tuck

Blessing of Diversity, The, Paul Louie © *Rainbow Prayers – More Light Update*, January 1994*

Celebrate Values, reproduced from *Coming Out to God: Prayers for Lesbians and Gay Men, Their Families and Friends* © 1991 Chris Glaser. Used by permission of Westminster/John Knox Press.

Coming For Many © Duncan L. Tuck

Consider Your Call, reproduced from *Coming Out to God: Prayers for Lesbians and Gay Men, Their Families and Friends* © 1991 Chris Glaser. Used by permission of Westminster/John Knox Press.

Courage to Love © Julie M. Hulme

Deliverance, reproduced from *Coming Out to God: Prayers for Lesbians and Gay Men, Their Families and Friends* © 1991 Chris Glaser. Used by permission of Westminster/John Knox Press.

Discernment © W. L. Wallace

Easter Liberation © Jan Berry

Family of God, The © Duncan L. Tuck

Family Prayer During Coming Out Process, Jennifer Pope, from *Shaping Sanctuary: Proclaiming God's Grace in an Inclusive Church*, edited by Kelly Turney, Copyright © 2000 by Reconciling Church Programme.

Father's Prayer of Thanks, A, Merrill M. Follansbee, from *Shaping Sanctuary: Proclaiming God's Grace in an Inclusive Church*, edited by Kelly Turney, Copyright © 2000 by Reconciling Church Programme.

Flowers for My Wife © Geoffrey Herbert

For A Young Man and His Mothers © Betty Lynn Schwab

Gay Christians and the Church © George S. E. Hopper from his book *Reluctant Journey*, PO Box 5846, Basildon, SS15 4GS UK, www.reluctantjourney.co.uk

Hamilton Conversation, A © George Bourne

He Was Waited On By Angels © David Coleman

He Went On His Way © Geoff King

Here's A Church © Helen Garton, from *Sustaining Stories*, Methodist Lesbian and Gay Caucus

His Deepest Nature © *More Light Prayers*, January 1991*

Housewarming, A © Elizabeth Stuart

I Thought of You © Michael Reiss

I Will Not Leave You © Debbie Hodge

Jesus Said © Suzi B.

Just Now and Then © Helene McLeod

Let Me Be © Jean Mortimer

Love of Family and Friends, The © Christine Holt

Lover of Us All, reproduced from *Coming Out to God: Prayers for Lesbians and Gay Men, Their Families and Friends* © 1991 Chris Glaser. Used by permission of Westminster/John Knox Press.

Love One Another, reproduced from *Coming Out to God: Prayers for Lesbians and Gay Men, Their Families and Friends* © 1991 Chris Glaser. Used by permission of Westminster/John Knox Press.

Mamzer Jesus © Robert Nugent

Marriage © Omar Nahas

Meditation on the Stories of David and Jonathan and Ruth and Naomi, A © Joe McMurray and Eric Cole

New People Came This Time © Geoffrey Herbert

New Piece of Wood, A © Betty Lynn Schwab

Not Freak You Out ... © Betty Lynn Schwab

Number the Stars, reproduced from *Coming Out to God: Prayers for Lesbians and Gay Men, Their Families and Friends* © 1991 Chris Glaser. Used by permission of Westminster/John Knox Press.

Poisoned Chalice © Janet Lees

Prayer for Women © Rosie Miles

Prayer for the Church's Children Coming into an Awareness of Their Sexuality, reproduced from *Coming Out to God: Prayers for Lesbians and Gay Men, Their Families and Friends* © 1991 Chris Glaser. Used by permission of Westminster/John Knox Press.

Prayer of Confession © Gary Gotham and Clare McBeath

Prayer Round the Tree © St James's Church, Piccadilly, London

Reflection on Thomas © Ken DeLisle

Regarding Making A Public Witness © Allen V. Harris

Ros and Liz Housewarming Celebration © Liz Bodycote

Samaritan, A © Rosalie Sugrue

Silence in the Suburbs © Jean Mortimer

So Here We Are © Rosie Miles

So Many Kinds of Awesome Love © Nicola Slee

Song of Welcome, A © Stephen Jay from *Sustaining Stories*, Methodist Lesbian
and Gay Caucus

Strengthen Me To Act, reprinted with permission from *Alone but Not Lonely* by
Donna E. Schaper. Copyright © 1999. Published by Twenty-Third
Publications, Mystic, CT 06355 USA

Tauranga Story, The © George Bourne

To See Christ © Chris Glaser from *More Light Prayer Book*, January 1988*

To Seek with Open Minds, reproduced from *Coming Out to God: Prayers for
Lesbians and Gay Men, Their Families and Friends* © 1991 Chris Glaser. Used
by permission of Westminster/John Knox Press.

Tread Lightly © Alix Brown

True Parent © Duncan L. Tuck

We Praise You God For You Have Made, Andrew Pratt © Stainer and Bell Ltd

Wife of My Lover, The © Omar Nahas

Women and Men © Rosie Miles

You and Me © Omar Nahas

You are My Beloved Child; With You I Am Well Pleased, reproduced from
*Coming Out to God: Prayers for Lesbians and Gay Men, Their Families and
Friends* © 1991 Chris Glaser. Used by permission of Westminster/John
Knox Press.

Yours, With Pride © Thelma Gabriel from her book *Yours, With Pride*

Breaking the Barriers

Be A New Creation © This copyright material is taken from *A New Zealand
Prayer Book – He Karakia Mihinare o Aotearoa* and is used with permission.

Birthing A Revolution, reproduced from *Coming Out to God: Prayers for
Lesbians and Gay Men, Their Families and Friends* © 1991 Chris Glaser. Used
by permission of Westminster/John Knox Press.

Blessing for a Lesbian, Gay or Heterosexual Relationship, A © Peter Colwell

Breaking the Barriers of Prejudice Against Lesbian and Gay People © Alan
Sheard

Call to Justice, A © Colleen Darraugh

Captivity © Naomi Young

Chavrusa © Art Addington

Confusion © Marjorie Dobson

Dancing on the Edge © Alix Brown

De Profundis © Peter Colwell

Demands of Love and the Intimacy of Justice © Dale Rominger

Disturbing Comforter, The © W. L. Wallace

Form of Confession, A © Richard Watson

Glad to Be Gay © Jean Mortimer

Go Out Into the World © John Cornwall

God of Night © Sarah Ingle

God, You Are the God of Hulda © Dumbarton U. M. C. Used with permission. Also published in *Shaping Sanctuary: Proclaiming God's Grace in an Inclusive Church*, edited by Kelly Turney, Copyright © 2000 by Reconciling Church Programme.

Growing Up Gay and at School: The Stories of Two Survivors © Ian Rivers

I Am Swinging at the End of My Tether, reprinted with permission from *Psalms for Times of Trouble* by John Carmody. Copyright © Published by Twenty-Third Publications, Mystic, CT 06355 USA, www.twentythirdpublications.com

I Have Heard Your Cries © Jean Mortimer

In Honour of Rev. Dr Martin Luther King, Jr. © Colleen Darraugh

Keep Our Minds Open © Marjorie Dobson

Life From Your Love © Michael Reiss

Litany of Compassion and Consolation in Times of Particular Difficulty, A © Christopher Wardale

Litany of Healing © Diann Neu from 'Like Drops of Water', *Waterwheel* Vol. 4 No. 1**

Matter of Human Rights, A © Drew Payne

Meditations for Starters © W. L. Wallace

Newspapers Say it All, The © Jean Mayland

Open the Box © Sarah Ingle

Openness and Sharing © Jeffrey John from *Permanent, Faithful, Stable*, published by Darton Longman & Todd. Used with permission.

Oracle for YHWH's Rainbow People © Diane Gilliam-Weeks

Our Gay Youth in Our Church, reproduced from *Coming Out to God: Prayers for Lesbians and Gay Men, Their Families and Friends* © 1991 Chris Glaser. Used by permission of Westminster/John Knox Press.

Outsiders © Jean Mortimer

Prayer for Lesbians and Gay Men in Latin America, A © Tom Hanks from *Rainbow Prayers – More Light Update*, January 1994

Prayer for Straight Men Who Are in the Closet, A © George M. Wilson from *Rainbow Prayers – More Light Update*, January 1994*

Prayer for the Spirit © Jana Opocenska from *Rainbow Prayers – More Light Update*, January 1994*

Prayer of Confession © Betty Lynn Schwab

Prevention of Anti-Gay Violence Starts in Your Congregation, Timothy Brown. Reprinted with permission of the United Church of Christ Coalition for Lesbian, Gay, Bisexual and Transgender Concerns. © WAVES November 1998.

Rights of Passage © Jean Mortimer

Scripture is a Conversation © Kim Fabricius

Shame © Liz Styan

Silence of Jesus, The © Michael Halls. Permission sought.

Someone's Sexual Orientation © Alina Rastam from *In God's Image* Vol. 20 No. 2 (June 2001). Used with permission.

Statement of Solidarity on Religious Intolerance and Sexual Diversity © International Gay and Lesbian Human Rights Commission USA

Stranger Within Thy Gates, The © Kate Compston

Them © David Coleman

This Day Is Ours, from *Shaping Sanctuary: Proclaiming God's Grace in an Inclusive Church*, edited by Kelly Turney, Copyright © 2000 by Reconciling Church Programme.

Time to Speak, The © Norm S. D. Esdon

To A Gay Christian © Jenny Dann

To Mercy, Dead of AIDS at Twenty-One © Anne Richards

Vast Varieties of Humankind, The © W. L. Wallace

Violence and the Gay Question © James Alison from *faith beyond resentment*. Used with permission.

Waiting for Full Acceptance by the Church © Sarah Ingle

We Patiently Wait © Naomi Young

We Wait in Praise and Freedom, Andrew Pratt © Stainer and Bell Ltd

Welcome to the Rainbow World © Colin Gibson

What Would Happen? © W. L. Wallace

What's In A Word? © Naomi Young

Wisdom, reproduced from *Coming Out to God: Prayers for Lesbians and Gay Men, Their Families and Friends* © 1991 Chris Glaser. Used by permission of Westminster/John Knox Press.

Who Will Stop the Cart? © Colin Gibson

Wise and Loving God © Marjorie Dobson

Words With Mother, Winnie Ma © *In God's Image*. Used with permission.

Spirituality and Sexuality

Basic Human Characteristic, A © Hope S. Antone from *In God's Image* Vol. 20 No. 2 (June 2001). Used with permission.

Charis © Nicola Slee

Cherish © Rosie Miles

Could Jesus Have Been Gay? © Michael Kelly. Spokesperson for The Rainbow Sash Movement http://users.bigpond.net.au/gbaird-SONGRISE/rsm

Creation © Marcie N. Wexler from *More Light Update* January 1992*

Extravagant Love © Margaret Donald

Factor in Salvation History, A © Ann Wansbrough from *In God's Image*, Vol. 20 No. 2 (June 2001). Used with permission.

Grounded Angel © Naomi Young

In Church © Rosie Miles

Intrinsically Sexual © Ng Chin-pang, from *In God's Image*, Vol. 20 No. 2 (June 2001). Used with permission.

Is There a Gay Men's Spirituality? © Bill Kirkpatrick

Love Poem to God, A Suzi B.

Lovemaking © Clifford Frasier, from *More Light Update*, January 1992*

Making Love with You © Nicola Slee

Our Senses, reproduced from *Coming Out to God: Prayers for Lesbians and Gay Men, Their Families and Friends* 1991 Chris Glaser. Used by permission of Westminster/John Knox Press.
Prayers Inspired by the Works of Derek Jarman © Steve Carr
Rainbow Steeple © Colin Gibson
Renewed Vision, A, reproduced from *Coming Out to God: Prayers for Lesbians and Gay Men, Their Families and Friends* © 1991 Chris Glaser. Used by permission of Westminster/John Knox Press.
Rich Tapestry of Creation, The © John Austin Baker
Sexuality © Janet Lees
Sexuality and Spirituality © Bill Kirkpatrick
Spirituality of Friendship, The © Bill Kirkpatrick
Thou-She, Thou-He © Mary Robins
To Enhance Our Delight © W. L. Wallace
To Offer Our Inner Wealth © W. L. Wallace
To Reflect Upon ... © W. L. Wallace
What Would I say to Christ? © Hector Cumming
Zacchaeus © Suzi B.

Listening: Learning with Liturgy

An Adaptation © Helen Garton from *Sustaining Stories*, Methodist Lesbian and Gay Caucus
Bad Verse Prayer © David Coleman
Blessing for A Pride Parade © Justin Tanis
Celebrate a New Day Dawning, reprinted with permission from *Praying with Christ-Sophia* by Jann Aldredge-Clanton. Copyright © published by Twenty-Third Publications, Mystic CT 06355 USA. www.twentythirdpublications.com
Coincidental God © Marjorie Dobson
Collect, A © Richard Watson
Companions Let Us Pray Together © David Clark and Witi Ihimaera
Desert, The © Roman Catholic Caucus, Lesbian and Gay Christian Movement
Dialogue Together, reproduced from *Coming Out to God: Prayers for Lesbians and Gay Men, Their Families and Friends* © 1991 Chris Glaser. Used by permission of Westminster/John Knox Press.
Divine Feminine, The Mary Robins
Embrace Every Layer of My Being © Julie M. Hulme
Gay Psalm, A © Sigrid Rutishauser-James
God of Our Fathers © Kate Compston
Good Friday Blessing, A © Norm S. D. Esdon
Ground of Being © Peter Colwell
I Hold A Memory Within My Heart, Anonymous
I Sing the Spirit's Life Within You © Colin Gibson
Litany, A © Richard Watson
Litany of Blessing, A © Steve Marlowe and Terri Echelbarger
Litany of the Eternal Word © Ken DeLisle
Liturgy to Celebrate a Saint's Day, A © Elizabeth Stuart

Love is a Miracle © Colin Gibson

Love of God, The © Liz Styan

Maker of Love © Mary Robins

Neti, Neti (Not This, Not That) © Harvey Gillman

O God, Who Conceived Me © Sigrid Rutishauser-James

Our Gifts, reproduced from *Coming Out to God: Prayers for Lesbians and Gay Men, Their Families and Friends* © 1991 Chris Glaser. Used by permission of Westminster/John Knox Press.

Praise My Soul, the One Who Gives Life © Sigrid Rutishauser-James

Prayer for Our Bodies, A © Colleen Darraugh

Prayer of Adoration, A © Gary Gotham and Clare McBeath

Prayer of Affirmation, A © Anna Cory

Prayer of Approach (1), A © Rosalie Sugrue

Prayer of Approach (2), A © Lis Mullen and Clare McBeath

Prayer of Confession, A © Kate McIlhagga

Prayer of Forgiveness, A © Rosalie Sugrue

Prayer of Intercession at the Beginning of a Year, A © Rosalie Sugrue

Pride – Call to Worship (1) © Justin Tanis

Pride – Call to Worship (2) © Justin Tanis

Pride – Call to Worship (3) © Justin Tanis

Pride – Call to Worship (4) © Justin Tanis

Psalm of HIV Lament © Jeannine Gramick

Series of Pride Litanies based on the Psalms, A © Justin Tanis

Sharing Pain and Peace © Richard Watson

Statement of Faith © Ken Delisle

Thanksgiving, A © Richard Watson

Through Touching and Loving Our Faithfulness Shows, Andrew Pratt © Stainer and Bell Ltd

To Be … © Ted Dodd

To Love More and More © Susan S. Nimmo, from *Rainbow Prayers – More Light Update*, January 1994*

We are God's Choice People © Edward Moran

We are Part of the Church © Ann B. Day, from *Shaping Sanctuary: Proclaiming God's Grace in an Inclusive Church*, edited by Kelly Turney, Copyright © 2000 by Reconciling Church Programme.

We Are So Slow © Roman Catholic Caucus, Lesbian and Gay Christian Movement

We Are the Body of Christ © Ann B. Day from *Shaping Sanctuary: Proclaiming God's Grace in an Inclusive Church*, edited by Kelly Turney, Copyright © 2000 by Reconciling Church Programme.

We Believe in a Sacred Power © Susan Kramer from *More Light Update*, 1992*

Wise and Wonderful Creator of Infinite Variety, reprinted with permission from *Praying with Christ-Sophia* by Jann Aldredge-Clanton. Copyright © published by Twenty-Third Publications, Mystic CT 06355 USA. www.twentythirdpublications.com

You Are Love © Michael Reiss

Eucharist
And Now We Remember One Who Gave Up Power © Andy Braunston
Candle Prayer, A © St James's Church, Piccadilly, London
Invitation to Communion (1) © Peter Colwell
Invitation to Communion (2) © Janet Lees
Living in the Spirit © John Simmonds (The Lord's Prayer paraphrase © *Your Will Be Done*, Christian Conference of Asia)
Mother and Father of Us All © St James's Church, Piccadilly, London
Post Communion Prayer, A © St James's Church, Piccadilly, London
Preface for the Thanksgiving Prayer © Christopher Wardale
Remember Me © Jean Mortimer
Ritual of Welcome, The © Elizabeth Stuart
Service for Eucharist, A © Judith E McKinlay
To Celebrate Communion © Anne Sardeson
We Give You Thanks for Your Call © Andy Braunston

Celebrate! Rejoice!
An Act of Confirmation and Commitment © Jan Berry
Blessings from the Netherlands © The Remonstrant Fraternity
Blessing of a Relationship © Neil Dawson
Blessing the Four Elements © Diann Neu and Mary E. Hunt**
Celebration of Coming Out, A © Elizabeth Stuart
Celebration of Love, A © W. L. Wallace
Covenant Commitment to the Single Life, A © Nicola Slee
Covenant to Celebrate Diversity, reprinted with permission from *Praying with Christ-Sophia* by Jann Aldredge-Clanton. Copyright © published by Twenty-Third Publications, Mystic CT 06355 USA. www.twentythirdpublications.com
Exchange of Rings/Symbols, The © Jonathan Blake***
Hymn for the Blessing of a Relationship © Karen Hutt and Clare McBeath
Like a Star, source unknown
Litany for a Same Self Couple Celebrating © Christopher Wardle
Liturgy for Coming Out, A © Elizabeth Stuart
Open Road to the Open Table © Kate Compston
Order of Prayer for Recognising a Change of Gender © Malcolm Johnson
Our Flesh © W. L. Wallace
Our Wedding Ceremony © Joe McMurray and Eric Cole
Prayers for a Couple © Lesbian and Gay Christian Movement
Promise, A © Hazel Barkham
Rainbow People, A © Mark Oakley
Selection of Vows, A © Jonathan Blake***
Service of Affirmation and Blessing, A © Jeffrey Heskins
Service of Commitment for a Same-Sex or Common Law Relationship © Margot Michaelis and Cornelia Kenke
Sharing of Honey Ceremony, The © Jonathan Blake***
Sharing of Wine Ceremony, The © Jonathan Blake***
Thoughts and Prayers © Jonathan Blake***

We Embrace © Andy Ulman (GABLE) from *Shaping Sanctuary: Proclaiming God's Grace in an Inclusive Church*, edited by Kelly Turney, Copyright © 2000 by Reconciling Church Programme.
Your Body © W. L. Wallace

* *More Light Update*, PO Box 38 New Brunswick NJ 08903–0038 USA
** Diann L. Neu, Co-Director of Water, The Women's Alliance for Theology, Ethics and Ritual, 8035 13th Street, Silver Spring, MD 20910 USA, www.hers.com/water; dneu@hers.com
*** Bishop Jonathan Blake, Whispering Trees, 273 Beechings Way, Gillingham, Kent ME8 7BP. Tel. 01634 262920
bishop@jonathanblake.freeserve.co.uk
www.bishopjonathanblake.com

Every effort to trace copyright holders has been made, and the author and publishers would welcome details of any omissions to be included in future reprints.

Readers wishing to reproduce any of the material in this anthology should write to Geoffrey Duncan c/o Darton, Longman and Todd, 1 Spencer Court, 140-142 Wandsworth High Street, London SW18 4JJ.

Index of Authors

Index of Titles by Chapter

Breaking the Barriers

Index of Titles